HAMLYN JUNIOR STORY LIBRARY

EXCITING STORIES FOR GIRLS

She could see the flickering flame of a candle, casting huge, distorted shadows.

HAMLYN JUNIOR STORY LIBRARY

EXCITING STORIES FOR GIRLS

by well-known authors

*Selected
and edited by
PETER ROLLS*

HAMLYN

London · New York · Sydney · Toronto

First Published 1975
Published by The Hamlyn Publishing Group Limited
London · New York · Sydney · Toronto
Astronaut House, Feltham, Middlesex, England

ISBN 0 600 39521 9
Printed in Czechoslovakia

Contents

GYPSY'S WARNING

by Judith M. Berrisford

Jill was indignant when her cousin said that her pony, Gypsy, was too wild for her to ride. But when the mare attacked a man at the horse show, it seemed at first that he must be right. Gypsy, however, had her own reasons for making the attack.

"Steady on, Jill!" Charles warned as he rode his grey, Shadow, out of the way of his cousin's shying pony. Then he added anxiously: "Don't you think Gypsy may be too wild for you to handle?"

Jill Madison shook her head and wished that Gypsy hadn't done her shying trick. Charles was her favourite cousin, two years older than herself, and an absolute wizard with horses and ponies. She had been longing to impress him.

"Gypsy shied at that tar patch," she said, "She shies at anything dark. She's done it ever since she fell into a bog. Dark patches remind her of half-drowning in black mud. If only she'd forget!"

They rode on uneventfully for a few yards.

"Hey, look out!" Charles' voice again rose in alarm, as Gypsy eyed a large pool of oil outside the local garage. " 'Ware riot?"

Gypsy reared-up with a terrified snort.

Jill leaned forward and patted the mare's neck.

"Steady, Gypsy!"she soothed.

Gypsy began to go in circles.

Jill tried hard to calm her, while Charles got down from Shadow and reached up to take Gypsy's head. Between them they got her past the oil and into a side street, out of the way of the traffic.

"One thing's sure," said Charles emphatically. "You'll never do much good with Gypsy while she's like that. Better admit it and let me school her for you."

"I'll do no such thing!" Jill retorted. "Gypsy will prove her worth yet."

"I certainly hope so," Charles said, doubtfully, and then added anxiously, because she was his favourite cousin, too, "for your sake, Jill!"

I did want Gypsy to do well, so that Charles would like her!

That thought kept on going through Jill's brain as she lay in bed that night.

Oh, it was too bad that Gypsy had let her down! But she wasn't going to disown her. She'd be loyal to Gypsy – whatever she did. Jill drifted off to sleep.

Suddenly she awoke. Downstairs she could hear the television set. Her parents and Charles must be still looking in, so it wasn't the noise of their coming upstairs which had awakened her. She listened for a minute. The programme sounded like a thriller. She could hear gunshots from the TV set. Then there was a sound like a window opening. Was it real? Or was that also on the TV? She shivered. Then Gypsy squealed, high and shrill.

Jill jumped out of bed and ran to the window which overlooked the paddock. Surely Mummy and Daddy and Charles must have heard the noise. Yes, they were running to the back door. In the halflight Jill saw Gypsy cantering down the field, mane and tail streaming. In front of her ran a man.

"A prowler!" Jill shouted. "There he goes!"

"After him!" Charles urged his uncle.

Together Jill and her mother inspected the bedrooms. Jill opened the door of Charles' room and gasped. So the prowler *had* been in the house. Everything was upside down; drawers had been ransacked, and in the open wardrobe doorway lay Charles' riding jacket, half off its hanger. On the bed lay the deed box in which he kept the money he was saving for the motorscooter he meant to buy when he was seventeen. It was open – and empty!

She went to break the news to her cousin as she heard him hurry back upstairs.

"The burglar dodged into Vixen Spinney and got clean away!"

Charles groaned. His lips were grim as he gazed at the empty box. "The wretch must have climbed through here and crept along the branch of the apple tree."

"And landed on poor Gypsy," said Jill. "She always dozes under that tree."

"Well, good for Gypsy," sighed Charles. "She certainly gave the burglar a scare."

"Now don't touch anything, anybody," Jill's father was saying. "I'm going to telephone for the police."

But the police could not trace the burglar, either from finger-prints, their records or their investigations.

Some of Charles' clothes were missing. He wrote them off as a total loss, along with the money he had saved for the motor-scooter. Gradually the burglary faded into the past. Charles entered Shadow for the under-sixteen jumping at a local Show, and Jill entered, too, hoping to show Charles that Gypsy was good at something.

At last the day came. The show was crowded. People, and waiting ponies and cattle, thronged the ground.

"There! Nothing to get in a flap about, Gypsy," Jill told her pony, as they looked at the course. "You've cleared much bigger jumps than these at home."

They had not too long to wait. The under-sixteen jumping took place at eleven o'clock. Charles – number fifteen – was second in the ring. There was something to be said for schooling, Jill thought, as she watched Shadow, perfectly balanced, complete a faultless round which earned him a round of applause.

Three competitors later, Jill's number was called, and she cantered Gypsy into the ring and up to the first fence. Gypsy tackled it easily, jumping with the untaught freedom of the natural jumper she was. Good, thought Jill. Suddenly, in mid-air, Gypsy seemed to pause, corkscrewed, and threw up her head. Jill saw a dark patch of tan on the landing side of the jump.

Gypsy extended her leap, in a desperate effort to avoid the dark patch. She landed oddly, on her hind legs.

The saddle seemed to come up with a bang against Jill's spine. But there was no time to feel pain: Gypsy was away at a gallop, fleeing from that dark patch of tan. Fighting for control, Jill put her at the next jump. Gypsy tossed her head, tried to run out and then stopped.

Jill quaked. What would Gypsy do next? With bared teeth the pony was now advancing towards a man in the crowd.

"Gypsy!" Jill tugged at the reins.

Then she stared at the man in utter surprise. He was wearing the tan-coloured, horseshoe-patterned tie that she had given Charles for his birthday a few months earlier.

"No!" moaned the man, covering his face with his hands as Gypsy lunged at him. "Take her away . . . she's hunting me down, just like she tried to in the paddock that night."

"Jill!" Mr Madison came running across the ring. "What's happening?"

"I think she's caught our burglar," Jill explained breathlessly. "Gypsy recognized him. Apparently she hasn't forgiven him for the fright he gave her when he landed on her back that night."

"What's going on here?" demanded a policeman.

"Call off that mare . . . she'll do for me, I know she will," wailed the cornered thief. He glared at Charles who had just come up. "We're both out of luck, mate. I blued that money I took, weeks ago – and none of your clothes would fit me!"

As the policeman led the thief away, Jill rode Gypsy back on to the course for a third attempt. But it was no use. Gypsy would not jump another of the fences.

"Number twenty-nine is eliminated." said a voice through the loudspeaker. "Number thirty-two into the ring, please."

Trying hard not to show her disappointment, Jill rode Gypsy out of the jumping ring. The mare might be a super burglar-warning-thief-catcher, but she was, as yet, no good as a show-jumper.

"Well done, Gypsy," Charles said. "I mean for remembering the burglar."

"Maybe she's got *too* good a memory," Jill said. "If only she'd forget that mishap in the bog!"

Just then, over the loudspeaker came the announcement: "The last competitor had eight faults. Competitor number fifteen is the winner."

"You've won!" Jill said breathlessly. "I *am* glad! Now you'll be able to use the prize money for your new scooter."

"Yes. I'll put it safely in the bank this time," Charles declared, mounting Shadow to ride him into the ring to receive his rosette. "I only wish Gypsy had won something, too."

"Oh, Charles! She will next year," Jill said happily. "With all the schooling you're going to give her!"

A RACE AGAINST TIME

As soon as Jill Hathaway saw Sunnymead Stables she loved the place but she did not know that there was a plot to deprive her of her inheritance. It was Beauty, the horse, who saved the situation and Sunnymead Stables.

'There it is! There's Sunnymead Stables!" Jill Hathaway drew an excited breath as she gazed down the moorland lane towards the little white-walled cottage, one end ablaze with virginia creeper–and the stableyard beyond, with its low outbuildings–and the gnarled old apple tree that shaded the tiny lawn in front.

Jill had been at boarding school on the Continent, and it was more than a year since she had last seen Sunnymead Cottage, though she had often spent summer holidays there in her earlier schooldays.

Now had come the news that Uncle Ambrose had died and left the cottage and adjoining stables to Jill, whose guardian he had been.

The train had brought her to Burley Junction, the bus had carried her to the crossroads by the water tower–and here she was, striding towards the white gateway of Sunnymead Cottage.

"Uncle wanted me to carry on here," she mused. "I haven't had much experience, I know–but I love horses."

She quickened her pace, listening eagerly for the familiar clop-clop of hoofs.

Surely, on a fine afternoon like this, there would be something doing. Riders coming in or going out–or maybe old Tom Chubb, the groom, giving a nervous beginner a few hints on how to mount.

But all was silent–strangely silent–as Jill reached the cottage gate.

"Well, miss! What's your business?"

A pair of sharp eyes regarded her from beneath a cloth cap as a short, wiry man barred her path.

"Well–er–I've just come in to look round," Jill replied softly, looking beyond him to the stables. "You see, I'm Jill Hathaway – Mr. Ambrose Hathaway's niece."

"You're welcome, I'm sure," he said bleakly. "I'm Luke Riggs, and I've been in charge here since Mr. Hathaway died."

"I'm just wondering," Jill smiled, "where the horses are?"

"Oh, they're out," he answered hastily. "All of them–that is, all except Beauty, your uncle's own chestnut he wanted you to have. But now I guess you'll want to be settling in at the cottage, miss. I'll fetch the keys and open it up."

He hurried away. Jill hardly saw him go. Brown eyes shining, she put down her bag and wandered along the line of horse boxes.

"Everything's just as I remember it," she whispered. "The pump and the watertrough, the old weather-vane over the harness-room, the horses' names printed over their stalls–Boxer, Brownie, Snowball, Twilight."

As she walked slowly along the line of stalls, she noted one odd thing. In each stall, normally, hung a halter. But now–

"They're all missing," Jill told herself. "That's queer, because if the horses are being ridden they certainly wouldn't want halters–ah! There's Beauty!"

A whinny reached her ears. A glossy, reddish-gold head emerged over the lower half of the last stable door.

Beauty–the chestnut–her own horse now! Strength and fire and spirit were in every line of him. She ran to him.

It was then that she glimpsed the open door of the harness-room.

And the harness was all hanging there-head-bands, saddles, everything. Which meant, that the horses couldn't be out on a ride.

"Luke Riggs led me to believe that they were," Jill told herself.

Where was Luke? That wiry, thin-faced man seemed to have vanished completely, without fulfilling his purpose of opening up the cottage. But Jill had a duplicate key of the front door.

She let herself in.

A brief tinkle from the telephone in the parlour caught her ear, and she picked up the receiver. A voice sounded over the wire.

"Mr. Flashman? Is that Mr. Flashman?"

It was Luke Riggs speaking!

In a moment Jill realised what was happening. This telephone had an extension in the little office at the back of the stables, where the booking was usually done. Luke Riggs was talking on that extension–talking to a Mr. Flashman.

Jill's brain clicked. Surely Flashman was the owner of the big stables and riding school in Moorstone–a showy, sumptuous establishment beside which Sunnymead Stables looked very small indeed.

"Mr. Flashman! Thought I'd better let you know–that girl's here! She's arrived sooner than we thought. Eh, what's that? No, she doesn't guess. And, as you say, everything will be signed and settled with the lawyer by four o'clock and it'll be too late for her to do anything about it then."

She heard the extension receiver put down. Luke Riggs had finished his brief talk with the owner of the rival stables.

What did it mean? Why had he been warning Mr. Flashman that she–Jill–had arrived? What was it that was going to be signed and settled with the lawyer by four o'clock that afternoon?

"There's something fishy!" Jill's eyes flashed. "I'll tackle Luke–now!"

She fairly raced for the back door. But the bolt was stiff; it was a few moments before she could pull it back.

As she sprang out into the open she saw a small car turning into the lane. At the wheel sat Luke Riggs.

What was happening? Where could she get at the truth?

Northwards lay a patch of spruce, and a thatched roof peeped through the trees.

"Tom Chubb's cottage! I'll ask Tom. He'll know!"

Even as Jill turned away, a shrill whinny came to her ears–and halted her.

It was Beauty, who seemed restless. She had an odd, almost panic-stricken feeling that he might be spirited away like the other horses.

"I'll take Beauty with me!" she decided.

She saddled and bridled Beauty, thrilling at the fire and spirit of him in spite of her anxiety. He let her lead him away.

And ten minutes later–

"Eee! By all that's wonderful, if it isn't Miss Jill!"

There was the old groom at his cottage door, apple-cheeked and rosy.

"Tom! I want to know what's happened!" she burst out. "Why did they send you away? Where are the horses?"

Tom blinked at her, scratching his head.

"Horses? Why, 'twas understood you weren't going to carry on, Miss Jill," he answered. "Struck me kind of a heap, it did, because somehow I'd reckoned that you would. But seemed you weren't! And so, of course, all the horses–except Beauty–would certainly have to be sold."

A rumour that she wasn't going to carry on at Sunnymead stables–and the horses being sold! And suddenly, to her memory, darted those words of Luke Riggs' which she had overheard on the telephone: ". . . everything will be signed and settled with the lawyer by four o' clock . . ."

The blood flamed in her cheeks.

"Tom, I must get in touch with my uncle's solicitor. What's his telephone number–you are still on the phone?"

Tom Chubb nodded. Jill found the solicitor's number in the directory and dialled it. But there was no reply. A few minutes later she tried again, with the same lack of result.

"I'm just wasting time!" Jill exclaimed. "I must see Mr. Bentley–before four o'clock!"

"You couldn't do it, Miss Jill–not by four!" Tom told her. "There's no bus for another hour–"

"I don't need a bus, Tom. I've got–Beauty!"

Jill raced outside, swung herself into the saddle, and headed the chestnut towards the moor.

She heard old Tom's almost despairing shout.

"You've forgotten, Miss Jill! Wreckers' Rift! You've –forgotten–the–Rift–"

The groom's voice died away behind her. But she hadn't forgotten the Rift. Very clearly did she remember that twisting chasm which snaked across the moor, at the bottom of which at high tide the water loamed and thundered.

"Beauty! You'll jump it!" she whispered.

There it was in front. A dark line zig-zagging across the moor. Wreckers' Rift! One false step here and they would crash to their doom a hundred feet below.

"You'll do it, Beauty! You'll do it!"

She felt a wonderful confidence in the horse. She put him straight at that perilous jump as if it had been a three-foot hurdle in the home paddock.

Her blood chilled as she glimpsed white foam and dark rocks down there in the shadowy depths. And then–

"We're over! Oh, Beauty–you wonder!"

He had taken it with never a check or falter. She glanced at her wrist-watch.

"Twenty to four. Oh, Beauty–there's a chance!"

A startled rabbit leapt away from Beauty's flying hoofs as they flashed onwards.

Later, in Mr. Bentley's office, which was on the upper floor of his private house in West Road, three people were gathered.

One was the white–haired lawyer himself, bending over his desk as he rustled a little pile of papers. Near the window sat the other two occupants–Mr. Eric Flashman, the burly owner of the large riding stables in Moorstone, and his son Ray, who was a sleek, dark-haired young fellow of eighteen.

The clock on the mantelpiece gave the time as eight minutes to four.

"At four o'clock, gentlemen, the time limit which I gave Miss Jill Hathaway expires," the solicitor stated in his precise, dry tone. "Her uncle stated in his will that she was to be given the opportunity of carrying on the stables, if she so desired. I wrote to her to that effect."

He coughed behind his hand, while the Flashmans fidgeted.

"I told her that if I had not heard from her by four o'clock today," Mr. Bentley continued, "I would take it that she wished me to dispose of the horses and riding business, with the exception of the horse Beauty, which her uncle expressly wished her to have. Well, gentlemen, I understand that you are prepared to purchase the horses."

Mr. Flashman nodded.

"We're busy folk, sir," he said. "If we could get the papers signed right away–"

"At four o'clock, Mr. Flashman–ah, it's time!"

"MR. BENTLEY!–STOP! DON'T SIGN ANYTHING!–STOP!"

Mr. Bentley glanced up in amazement. The Flashmans whirled round. And there, at the window, clung Jill!

Approaching the building, she had heard the voices through the window. So completely had she won Beauty's confidence that he was standing like a statue while she perched on his saddle.

A moment later she had climbed through the window.

"I'm Jill Hathaway, Mr. Bentley. I don't know what's been happening, but I want my horses!"

So flurried was the lawyer that his pince-nez, unheeded, flew off his nose and dangled by their cord.

"Your horses? But, my dear young lady–my letter–"

I didn't get a letter, Mr. Bentley. Only the first brief note telling me uncle was dead."

Gradually the truth dawned on Jill. The lawyer had sent his letter to Sunnymead Stables, to be forwarded to her; and though she couldn't prove anything, she felt sure that Luke Riggs had destroyed it, to give his friends–the Flashmans–a chance to buy up the establishment.

The scheme had failed.

Sunnymead Stables were safe–for Jill! She had legal authority now to retrieve the horses, which early that morning had been led away to Belvedere Riding School, owned by Mr. Flashman and his son.

"And Mr. Flashman"– squarely Jill faced that baffled rival and his son– "will you tell your friend, Luke Riggs, that he won't be wanted at Sunnymead Stables any more? Tom Chubb's all the help I need. And we'll collect my horses as soon as we can!"

The sun was dipping as a string of horses moved, that evening, towards a white cottage on the moors.

Jill, mounted on Beauty, was leading them. Old Tom Chubb rode beside her.

"All's well that ends well, Tom," she said softly. "I know it won't be easy for me to make a success of the stables, but'gosh!–I'll try!"

A LODGER CALLED TINA

by Joan Aiken

When Tina, the donkey, saved the mayor of the town from danger, it brought her a new home and new friends.

It all began quite suddenly on the last day of our summer holiday. We'd shared a bungalow at Carlion Sands with the Hamiltons – there are six children in their family and with Sally and me it was enough for lots of beach games. We used to pool our pocket money and hire one of the beach donkeys by the day, which was marvellous fun. We always asked for Tina. She's so gentle and sweet-tempered that you can do anything with her. She's as good at rounders as I am, which admittedly, isn't saying much.

Well then, on the last day, when we were saying good-bye to Mr. Trevann and Tina, he suddenly said, out of the blue: "You've made such friends with Tina, how about having her for the winter? It's the end of the season, and I'm stabling the donkeys next week."

We all looked at each other and I said: "How much would it cost?"

"It'd be free; in fact, I'd pay you her board."

"We'd have to ask," Lynn Hamilton said. And we all rushed off to ask our mothers.

"What'll we do – take her in turns?" I panted as we ran.

"Oh, they're sure to say no", Lynn called back over her shoulder.

Mrs. Hamilton did say no. You could see her point – they have a flat in Plymouth, there'd really be no place for a donkey. But Sally and I begged so hard that our Mum said: "Well – I suppose it wouldn't make much extra work. But only if Mr Trevann will pay for her board. She could go in the old cowshed. You children must look after her."

"Oh *yes!*" we said earnestly. "We can feed her before school and groom her when we get back."

Daddy was more doubtful when he came with the Landrover to take us home. "Oh, I've no objection to *having* her," he said, "but what happens in April when she has to go back? You know as well as I do–broken hearts."

"No," I said firmly, "because we'll remember all the time that she's just a lodger, not a – a permanency, so it'll be all right."

"You can really be sensible about it?"

We promised we would.

"Well, I suppose it'll be good for you to learn to look after her. You're to do it all yourselves, mind!"

So a couple of days after we got home, Mr. Trevann came along with a horse-box and unloaded beautiful Tina into our yard. We haven't really got a farm, just a smallholding with some pigs and hens, and Daddy grows anemones for the early market.

We'd cleaned out the cowshed and made it really comfortable.

"Good–bye, Tina," he said. "You be a good girl and I'll be back on April 20th. Let me know if you can't manage her," he told us, "or if you get fed up, and I'll find her another home."

"We shan't get fed up," I said.

We felt wonderful. Instead of being all flat and miserable because the holidays were over, we were busy with Tina. We brushed and brushed and brushed her, day after day – it meant a bath each time for us, too, because we got absolutely smothered in sand and donkey-dust – until in the end Tina looked like a model donkey. Her nice grey coat was velvet-soft and her ears were like silk and she thoroughly appreciated all the attention she was getting. We cleaned her tack, and we set up a bending-course on the lawn – it's only rough grass, not proper lawn, so Daddy soon gave up objecting. When it was fine Tina lived out in the orchard – we had to move Mum's clothes line after the time when Tina ate two teacloths, but she couldn't be expected to know that washing is not donkey-food.

Well, of course, you can guess what happened. By Christmas, Tina was absolutely one of the family – Daddy gave her carrots, Mum knitted her two red earcaps, and Sally and I clubbed together for a basket of apples – and by March, the thought of April 20th weighed like a lump of lead in my heart. And I know it did in Sally's too. I went into the shed one day and found her sitting on the hayrack with her arms round Tina's neck.

"How much does a donkey cost?" I said.

Sally said: "I thought of that. And I asked Daddy, and he said: 'It's no use, love. She'd cost at least twenty pounds, and I just can't afford to spend that on a pet!' "

"But she's *useful,*" I pointed out. "We go shopping with her."

We did, too. It was a horrible, rainy spring, pouring every day till the road to the village was flooded four feet deep, and the only way from our farm was by the high path over the moor. We rigged up panniers on Tina's saddle and she was very obliging about carrying potatoes and paraffin and chicken-food. We couldn't play outside in such weather, so we kept Tina company in the shed by doing our homework lying on the bales of hay and playing cat's-cradle with the twine from the binder. This turned out to be a lucky habit as you'll hear.

But all the time April 20th was coming closer.

Then one soaking Saturday I was coming home over the moor with some groceries. Mum was in bed with a cold and Sally was looking after her. I had on my duffle coat, and I'd put a groundsheet over Tina, but even so we were drenched.

Halfway home, near the old china clay workings, I thought I heard a shout. I wasn't sure, but Tina pricked up her long ears and looked curious, so I went to see. Then I saw a car parked by a rock, but the shouting seemed to come out of the ground.

"Anybody about?" I called.

"Help!" the shout came again. "I'm down here."

I guessed whoever it was must be down an old shaft, so I went carefully. It was as well I did. Suddenly I saw it – a deep hole, like a big well, about twenty feet deep. There was a man at the bottom.

"Don't come too near," he called. "The sides are rotten – that's how I fell in. A bit of ground gave way under me."

It was Mr Pentecost, the Mayor. He was up to his knees in thick blue clay.

"Hallo, Sue," he said, recognizing me. "Is your father with you? If not, could you go for help quickly, like a good girl? I'm sinking in."

I saw that. I could see, too, that there was another big piece of the edge that was likely to come away and fall on him at any minute. If it did, it might bury him completely. I was pretty scared, especially as the ground under me seemed to quake.

"I'd better not wait to get help," I said. "I'd better pull you out now."

"My dear, you couldn't. I weigh fourteen stone."

"I've got my donkey here, she can help."

He looked more hopeful. "I have a rope here – if I can throw an end up . . ."

But when he tried, it brought down another bit of of the edge.

"Wait," I said. "I've a ball of twine in my jeans pocket." This was the twine with which I had played cats-cradle. I let down one end. He carefully tied his rope to it, and I pulled till I had the rope. Then I wriggled back – I'd been lying on my tummy – and passed the rope round Tina's chest, padding it with the groundsheet.

"Come on now, Tina – *pull!*" I said, and urged her away from the hole. "Pull, Tina! Put your back into it!" She got the idea and pulled like mad.

I couldn't see what was happening in the hole. I pulled, Tina pulled – for a minute I began to despair and be terrified that we'd just bring down another avalanche into the hole. Then there was a sort of slithering plopping sound and the rope gave – Tina and I shot forward. Then I picked myself up and looked back. There was Mr. Pentecost, mud to the eyebrows but okay.

"That was a near thing," he said, rubbing some more mud on to his forehead. "Your father told me those workings were dangerous and I came up to inspect them. He was right! I thought I was done for that time. And so I might have been, if it wasn't for you and that wonderful donkey of yours."

"She's not really my donkey," I said. "I only wish she was."

"She's your donkey from this day on," said Mr. Pentecost, "if I have any say in the matter. Now we'd better both get home and have a bath."

I plodded home. It was two miles to go, still raining torrents, and I was blue-black muddy all over, but I didn't mind. The worry about April 20th was gone for good.

NOREEN, AIR HOSTESS

by Heather Granger

Noreen Farraday loved being an air hostess with the International Air Corporation and was delighted when one of her special passengers was a baby. Little did she realise, though, that the baby would involve her in some very exciting moments in the Middle East.

"Well, here we are, young Barry. I hope you're going to enjoy your flight with us!"

Noreen Farraday, hostess with the International Air Corporation, smiled at the youngest passenger on the flight from India to London. And little Barry Whitecross chuckled back at her. He couldn't speak. Little Barry was only six months old–the first baby to be given into Noreen's charge. She was looking forward to taking care of him during the flight–for he was alone. His mother was ill, and his father was forced to stay in India.

"Now let's make you comfortable before the other passengers arrive," Noreen said to the gurgling baby.

She carried him into the main body of the aircraft, a lively bundle in his white shawl. Here, as was the custom, she slung a small hammock from the overhead rack. On aircraft of the International Air Corporation, babies were always carried in this way. It saved them being bumped about should the aircraft strike bad weather.

"Like it?" laughed Noreen, as she placed little Barry in the hammock, and gave it a push that sent it swinging. Barry gurgled and waved his arms. It seemed he did!

Then on board came Mr. Lacey, an older steward who was travelling with Noreen on this flight from Karachi Airport to London.

"Ah, the baby's arrived, I see!" he said. "Good! The other passengers are just coming along. Better get ready to meet them. I've got their papers here."

"Oh, good!" said Noreen, as he held up a sheaf of papers. One thing that had been troubling her was that Barry's nurse, when she had handed him over, had not handed over his papers as well. The nurse had said she had left them with someone. If Mr. Lacey had all the passengers' papers, Noreen's worry was removed. She and Mr. Lacey took up positions at the top of the aircraft steps, to greet the passengers and show them to their seats.

By now Noreen could judge what a passenger would be like on the flight, and she heaved a sigh of relief as her passengers came on board. There were no young people amongst them, but they all seemed kindly, and had a friendly smile for herself and Mr. Lacey. But then, the last to come aboard–five minutes only before take-off–was a man well past middle age. A man with grey hair, a tense and worried expression, and a breathless manner. He carried a large briefcase in his hands.

"Ha!" he said. "Just made it. I'm B. H. Grant–you'll find two seats booked in my name. I don't want anybody next to me, because I've work to do on the journey–urgent, important work. I specified that when I booked. Also–I must be in London on time. You can guarantee we'll arrive on schedule?"

Noreen nodded. Mr. Lacey had told her about this passenger. And she fancied she knew his type. He was one of the "nervy" sort–a man who lived, slept, ate and drank with work and had no mind for anything else.

"Good! Good! Very well!" He sat down, looking quite reassured. "Don't think I'm fussy," he added–unconscious of the fact that Noreen had already formed that impression of him! "But I have to be at a conference two hours after we're due to reach London. I daren't be late. I'm chairman of the company, you see. We've got a big deal going through, and only I can sign the necessary agreement. If we don't clinch it, we're sunk. That's why it's so important there should be no hitch."

"Y-yes," Noreen agreed; she thought she understood.

She went along the gangway to lend a hand to passengers who were fumbling with their safety belts. Then she took her own seat, under where little Barry's hammock swung, and strapped herself in. The aircraft taxied to the end of the air-strip— they were off. Wheels raced faster and faster over the ground–until suddenly all sense of movement stopped and they were climbing, the earth falling away beneath them. A sudden mist–that meant they were among the clouds. For a short space it seemed that dense, white cottonwool seemed to envelop the windows, as the plane climbed through the clouds. Then it had flattened out with the white fleece forming a seemingly frozen sea on either side of them.

Noreen wondered how Barry was enjoying it all. She looked towards Mr. Grant, who was immersed in sheafs of papers and feverishly scribbling.

"I wonder he finds it all worth it," she thought. "Looks to me as though he's just wearing himself out."

She went along to the flight deck to get particulars about their flight from the second officer for her broadcast over the Public Address System. Having given the announcement, she hurried on to Barry, swinging in his hammock. Little Barry was sleeping soundly, though there was a waxiness about his face that had not been there when she had taken him from the arms of his nurse. Noreen frowned a little critically. He certainly didn't look so bright and well now.

"He'll probably be all right when he's had his food," she told herself.

She turned away to get the bottle, to warm it and fill it and put it in the hot cupboard above the grill until it was exactly the right temperature. At that moment Mr. Lacey, the steward, came along.

"Just want to check with you. Noreen." he said. "About the baby. You received him from his nurse, didn't you?"

"That's right," Noreen said. "Why?"

"Well, have you got his papers?"

"Why, no!" Noreen gave a sudden start. "Haven't you got them? I thought you had. You have the papers of the others on the flight."

Mr. Lacey stared at her, and then sharply bit his lip. "I haven't got the baby's papers. They must have gone astray!"

There was a moment's silence. Noreen could see difficulties ahead. There were so many formalities accompanying the flight of a passenger from one country to another – if that passenger were without papers it could be awkward.

"I–I'm terribly sorry—" she stammered. "The nurse said she left the papers with someone, and I'm afraid—"

Mr. Lacey gave her a reassuring smile, and patted her shoulder.

"Oh, don't you worry, Noreen. It's just one of those things. You just keep your eyes on young Barry. I'll see if I can sort it all out—"

He went off, shaking his head in a way which told Noreen that he'd never be able to sort it out until–perhaps–they broke journey in Rome. She should have asked him at first if he had young Barry's papers, she told herself guiltily. But she had taken it for granted that Mr. Lacey would have them. "Oh, dear! Things never seem to go smoothly for long!" she told herself with a sigh. But it wasn't really more than a minor upset–and she still had Barry to care for. She took his bottle from the hot cupboard and went back to him. She lifted him out of his hammock, and this woke him. He opened his eyes and gave her a rather wan little smile. But when she put the bottle to his lips he shook his head, pushed it away with a little hand and closed his eyes again.

"Barry, please," Noreen coaxed. "Nice milk—"

But Baby Barry did not open his eyes. Noreen, gazing at him, felt her heart jump wildly. That waxy pallor of his face had gone, but in its place was creeping an unhealthy flush. His lips also had a faint blue tinge. He seemed to be very still in her arms. She put a hand to his heart. It was beating wildly. She rose in agitation, Barry in her arms. Then, horrifyingly, the truth flashed upon her.

"He–he must have some sort of heart trouble," she told herself. "He's having an attack now!"

It was obvious little Barry needed a doctor or medical care. She knew by the passenger list there was no doctor on board. The baby's lips now seemed more blue; he was still motionless, and Noreen wondered what on earth she could do. Frantically thinking, she had an idea.

"We could get help in Bahrein," she told herself. "That's the nearest airfield. But we're not scheduled to stop at Bahrein–"

Then, after more fierce thought–

"We'll *have* to stop," Noreen decided firmly. "Barry mustn't suffer just for a time schedule. I'll go and speak to the captain."

With Barry in her arms, she hurried up the aisle. Entering the Flight Deck, she at once went over to the captain. He was not at the controls, for the aircraft was flying on the automatic pilot–a mechanical system which kept it at the right route without human aid.

"Captain–I had to come. It's the baby!" Noreen jerked.

Rapidly she explained, while he stared at Baby Barry. He jumped when she outlined her plan.

"You want us to land at Bahrein—"

"I know it's unscheduled, but I can't see what else we can do. The baby's ill!" Noreen gulped.

He stared again at Barry, frowning.

"Are you sure he's as ill as you think? You've never taken care of a baby before. Are you sure it isn't just some minor upset?"

"I'm sure!" Noreen cried, in distress. "He's so flushed, and blue! And so still."

The captain hesitated only a moment longer. "All right," he said. "I've never done anything like this before–and you'd better be right or there'll be a heck of a lot of trouble. But I'll radio ahead and ask Bahrein to receive us. Warn the passengers. Joe, go with her," he added to his first officer, "to answer any questions."

While he called Bahrein, Noreen went back to the microphone in the main cabin, followed by the first officer. Still with the baby in her arms, she made her announcement.

"Ladies and gentlemen, may I please have your attention. I am sorry to say that the flight must be interrupted, because there is a baby on board who is very ill, and must have attention as soon as possible. The journey, therefore, will be broken at Bahrein, where it is hoped we will be able to find a doctor. After that we shall go on to Rome."

As she finished, she caught the sympathetic and anxious murmurs from the passengers. With a word from the first officer, she went back down the aisle to where Barry's hammock swung. Her intention was to make the sick baby as comfortable as possible in his hammock until they got to Bahrein. But as she reached the seats occupied by Mr. Grant:

"Miss Farraday!" he cried.

His eyes were ablaze; his face was white with anger.

"What is this? What is this?" he spluttered. "You are breaking the journey at Bahrein? We already break it at Rome, don't we?"

"I am sorry," Noreen said quietly. "But it is for the baby—"

He flashed a look at Barry. It was very obvious that he had paid little attention to the Public Address announcement, except those parts that immediately concerned himself.

"What's wrong with the baby?" he snapped.

The first officer broke in quietly:

"Miss Farraday is not sure. She thinks he is very ill—"

"Thinks?" His nervous anger rose to the surface. "Don't you *know*, girl?" he snapped at Noreen.

"Well–no!" Noreen admitted, feeling an inward tremor as she realised the fact. "But I'm certain he is ill. He looks odd—"

"Looks odd?" Mr. Grant turned red. "Is that all you're going on? You're going to stop a plane-load of people, strand them right in the middle of nowhere, because you think a baby is ill?"

Noreen herself turned red. She could understand that it was important he should get to his conference; but she was equally sure young Barry needed urgent help.

"I'm sorry," she said. "But I've asked the captain to make the stop at Bahrein, and he's agreed. I'm sure it's the right thing to do."

"*You're* sure! A young girl like you!" he turned in scorn to the first officer. "Can you trust her judgment? Listen. A vast sum of money hangs on my getting to that conference. How long do we stop at Bahrein?"

"It depends on how long it takes to find a doctor—" the first officer began uneasily.

"That's not good enough!" Mr. Grant barked. "We MUST arrive in London on schedule! This whole situation is intolerable!" He hammered one hand in the other. "I refuse to be held up because of what some incompetent girl thinks! I demand that we go on. Your airline is under contract to deliver me to London at the stated time–and if you don't I'll make so much trouble for you that none of you will ever fly again!"

"You–you can't mean it. Mr. Grant! You can't mean you'll try to have us dismissed if we don't get to London in time – when you know we've got to make an unscheduled stop because little Barry is ill?"

Wide-eyed, Noreen Farraday gazed at the angry businessman who confronted her in the main cabin of the aircraft. In her arms, still and hardly breathing, his cheeks and lips faintly tinged with blue, lay six-month's-old Barry Whitecross. But Mr. Grant's gaze only flicked in Barry's direction before turning back to Noreen and the first officer, who stood behind her.

"We've only your word for it that the baby is ill, Miss Farraday," he retorted coldly.

"But look at him –" Noreen begged. "I think he's had some sort of heart attack."

"You think! I grant you he doesn't look well . . . but how do you know it isn't a passing thing? You don't know that he's seriously ill, do you? What do his papers say about him? Do they mention any heart trouble?"

Noreen caught her lower lip between her teeth. Those papers! They might have helped.

"I – I'm afraid the papers have been mislaid" she murmured.

"I know! So you're just guessing. Well, I DEMAND that we fly on!" cried Mr. Grant. "I demand that your proposal to stop at Bahrein is abandoned. I have to get to London on time–or I stand to lose a lot of money in my business deal. I refuse to be held up because of what a young stewardess thinks."

"I'm sorry, sir!" the first officer said finally. "The captain has made his decision, and will stand by it. We land at Bahrein to find medical aid for the baby."

"Very well!" Mr. Grant sat down heavily in his seat. "On your own heads be it. If you find out, after all this delay, that the baby only has a stomach ache, or something . . . I'll see you lose your jobs!"

He picked up his papers, and glared at them. This was his last word. Shakily Noreen went along the aisle to the place where hung the hammock in which Baby Barry was carried. The first officer followed her.

"Well, I don't know—" he said uneasily. "I hope to goodness you're right. Noreen–for our sakes. On the other hand, for the baby's sake, I can't help hoping you're wrong!"

"I know what you mean," Noreen said quietly. "I'm just hoping we find a doctor quickly for Barry, when we get to Bahrein. So that we know one way or the other about him–and can get on to London and arrive on time. But I'm sure–I'm sure there's something seriously wrong!"

She placed the baby in his hammock as she spoke. He lay there, silently. She felt his heart. It was still beating unusually fast. Shaking his head, the first officer went back to the flight deck, and Noreen–after making sure there was nothing more she could do yet for Baby Barry–went along to the galley. Mr. Lacey, the elderly steward who was travelling with her, was there. He gazed at her sympathetically.

"Don't let Grant upset you too much, Noreen," he said softly. "Here, help me with the lunch trays. That'll take your mind off things a bit."

"Thank you," Noreen whispered.

How wonderfully kind everyone was – except the disagreeable Mr. Grant. She busied herself in the galley, laying out the lunch dishes, and arranging the trays. The steward himself did the waiting. But all the time her mind was on Baby Barry, and the problem which he presented. Was he, as she feared, very seriously ill? It certainly seemed to her that he had had some sort of heart attack. But what if she were wrong? Oh, yes, she would be glad for Baby Barry's sake–but if she did not find out quickly, not only she but the rest of the aircrew might lose their jobs!

The meals were all served and eaten at last. Then she washed up and stored the lunch things away. After that, with anxious heart, she went back to little Barry. All through lunch she had been keeping an eye on him. He had not stirred, his appearance had not changed. She was adjusting his shawl when Mr. Grant came along. He had worked all through lunch, refusing his meal. Now he had his watch in his hand. He still looked grim; but also worried.

"I've talked to your captain," he said. "Apparently he's determined to take your word about this child's condition and land at Bahrein. Do you think you'll be able to find a doctor quickly?"

"I–I'm not sure," Noreen said quietly.

"You'd better," he said warningly. "If I don't get to London in time to pull off this business deal of mine—"

Noreen could not help it. The sight of little Barry, still frighteningly limp and silent . . . Mr. Grant's apparent concern only for his business . . . roused in her a sharp anger she could not control.

"How *can you?*" she quivered. "Oh, how can you stand there and just talk–talk about BUSINESS when a baby's life might be at stake! Don't you realise–don't you care about anyone else . . ." Then her voice trailed away as she realised what she had said.

But to her surprise, Mr. Grant did not blaze back in anger. Instead he winced.

"You're being rather harsh, Miss Farraday—" he said uncertainly.

"I'm sorry—" Noreen stammered. "It's just . . . if you had a little son who was ill, perhaps—"

She stumbled to a stop, even more startled now by the look on his face. He was pale; the corners of his mouth quivering, and he held on to a seat to steady himself.

"No, I have never had a son," he said tautly. "But I once had a daughter—"

There was something in the way he said it that stilled Noreen's anger. He was not, she realised, as hard as he appeared to be. Or he was hard now, because something had made him so.

"I'm sorry," she said again. "I—" And then, daringly: "Did you–did you lose your daughter?"

But in an instant his lips had tightened again. "Not in the way you mean, I think!" he said curtly. "She ran away to get married–to some man whose name she refused to give. I never even met him, and I never saw my daughter again from the day they got married!"

He turned abruptly back to his seat, leaving Noreen staring after him. It was strange–but suddenly she felt almost a twinge of pity for Mr. Grant. Then came Mr. Lacey's voice, over the Public Address system:

"Ladies and gentlemen, your attention, please! We are now approaching Bahrein. Please adjust your safety belts for the landing."

There was a rustle, a stir. Noreen moved along the aisle, to give any help she could. But this time no help was required, so she went back to her seat below Barry's hammock, and strapped herself in. The aircraft, gliding down through the clouds, suddenly gave them a lop-sided view of the Bahrein archipelago, dominated by its crater-like hill of Jebel Dukan and dotted with palm trees around oases of blue water.

The pilot began to throttle back, and they straightened out for the landing.

"Thank goodness!" Noreen breathed. "Now, perhaps, we'll soon know about Barry."

Down, down they went. Down to run smoothly along the landing-strip. The aircraft came to a stop. The doors opened. Throwing off her safety–belt, Noreen rose and took the limp baby from his hammock. With little Barry in her arms, she was the first to step out. But on her heels was Mr. Grant.

"Now, be quick!" he snapped warningly.

Noreen just gave him one glance. How she could ever have felt sorry for him, even for an instant, she did not know.

She hurried across to where a group of airport officials waited. They had been warned by radio to expect her, and had a car waiting to rush her to the airport doctor. Then they were at the airport hospital, and a young doctor was bending over little Barry, making an examination. But, after several minutes, he shook his head.

"I don't know. I really don't know," he said. "Barry's heart and colour point to something being wrong, but how serious it is . . . I'm only a general practitioner," he explained to Noreen. "This is a job for a specialist."

"Is there one–here in Bahrein?" asked Noreen anxiously.

He drew a deep breath. "As it happens, you're lucky. There is. James Jennison, the heart specialist, is in Bahrein at the moment. Not professionally–on holiday, you understand. But he's a grand man! He'll look at the baby for you. I'll give you a note for him. The airport car will take you there."

While Noreen waited, he scribbled a note and handed it to her. Then she was rushed out to the car. Mr Jenninson could not be warned of her coming, because his house was not on the phone. Desperately Noreen hoped he would be in–for her sake, as well as Barry's. The car sped away from the airport on to a sand-covered road. She was dimly conscious of palms and blue water–nothing else. Her main thoughts were for little Barry, whose racing heart she could feel as she clutched him to her. The bluey tint of his cheeks and lips seemed to have deepened.

It was only a short distance really, but to Noreen it seemed miles. At last they entered the town–to find it a place of gaiety and carnival. Crowds filled the streets, which were decorated with flags, pennants, balloons and grotesque model figures raised on poles.

"Today is Festival of the Five Islands," her driver told her. "Today much rejoicing in Bahrein. Big procession in one hour."

"Oh?" Noreen said, not really taking it in just now. "How long before we reach Mr. Jennison's villa?"

"Five–six minutes," the driver promised.

They sped off downhill until the greeny-blue waters of the sea rippled into view. Outside a trim bougainvillea-covered villa, they halted.

"This the place, missy," the driver informed her.

"Thank you!" Noreen threw at him as she climbed out.

Carrying little Barry, she hurried down the path and rang the door bell. An English manservant answered her.

"Mr. Jennison?" he said in dismay, when she explained her mission. "I'm sorry, miss, but Mr. Jennison is out. I'm not expecting him back for an hour. He and his wife are touring the town, photographing the decorations for the festival. You can wait here for him, of course."

There was nothing for it but to wait. In a sumptuously furnished sitting-room, Noreen perched herself on a chair, Barry in her arms. But she could not rest. Time and again she rose to walk about the room, her anxiety refusing to let her keep still. It was an hour and a half before the door opened again. In came a tall man, with iron-grey hair and a keen face. No need to ask who he was. This was obviously Mr. Jennison.

"I'm sorry you were kept waiting, my dear," he said, and came at once to take Barry from her. "Now, what's the trouble . . ."

He read the note the airport doctor had written, then began to examine Barry. As he did so, his kindly smile faded. His face became tense. When he looked up, Noreen's heart jumped at his expression.

"I'm sorry, my dear! It's bad news," he said quietly. "The baby's in a bad way–a very bad way indeed."

Noreen drew a deep, trembling breath. She had been right. She had her answer now to Mr. Grant. Her request to have the plane stopped here was justified! But the thought gave her no pleasure. Little Barry was seriously ill.

"Can you do anything?" she asked the famous heart specialist. "Can you help him in any way?"

He dropped a hand quickly on her shoulder, and smiled again briefly.

"He can be helped, my dear–but I can't do much here. I can give him an injection which will keep him going for the next twelve hours. But he must be got to a heart clinic in London before the twelve hours are up. I'll give you the address. Ask there for Mr. Greaves. If anyone can do anything for this baby, he can. Meantime–is your aircraft full?"

"No–no not completely," Noreen said, wide-eyed.

"Then I'll send someone to the local hospital, to tell them to have a nurse and oxygen equipment waiting for you when you get back to the airport. The nurse will travel on your flight, helping you to look after the baby. While you're travelling, I'll send a radio message to Mr. Greaves, telling him to expect you. Now–the injection."

Gently he gathered the still form of little Barry into his arms and carried him away. Noreen sat down again, her own heart bumping. Though she had only had little Barry in her charge a short while, she had grown to love him. It was dreadful to think he was so ill . . . in fact, might not recover if they did not get to London on time.

Oddly, at that moment, the thought of Mr. Grant came to her again. He had wanted to get to London on time, and she–for Barry's sake–had delayed the flight. Now she had to carry the news back that the flight MUST get in on time–for Barry's sake! How strangely things worked out.

Five minutes later, with Barry again in her arms, she raced back to the waiting car.

"The airport!" she cried. "Quickly! The baby is sick and must be got to London as soon as possible."

"Missy, I race!" the driver promised quickly.

The car shot off–away from the sea, up the climbing streets. Noreen was making feverish calculations as they went. Twelve hours to get Barry to the clinic in London . . . no, only eleven and a half now. It could be done–but only just!

The car sped on. Now they were on the outer districts of the town, and her hopes began to rise. But suddenly— they braked swiftly; with squealing tyres they pulled to a halt.

"Missy, I am sorry!" the driver panted. "We no get by."

And Noreen, gazing ahead with new despair, saw that he was right. For in front of them, stretching from pavement to pavement, was a line of camels. Beyond that, moving amid cheering crowds, was a procession of carts, cars, oxen, mules, and dancing youths and girls that stretched as far as the eye could see. The road was completely blocked!

"Oh, no! We can't get held up here!" Noreen thought, in frantic dismay.

From her seat in the airport car, she stared at the road ahead–at the carnival procession that seemed to be taking up every inch of space. In her arms, limp and weak, lay little Barry Whitecross, the six-months-old baby given into her charge.

"Surely there's some way to get through!" she cried, to the airport driver in charge of the car.

"Missy, I sorry," the driver said helplessly. "We not move–not perhaps for one hour."

Clutching Barry tightly to her, Noreen rose quickly. Ahead the crowds thronging round the carnival procession of camels, horses, oxen and cars were cheering, singing and dancing. It was a happy day for them, but for Noreen— Then she caught in her breath. A little way ahead she had spotted something–something so British as to be almost out of place in this procession. It was a red fire engine. Behind it was a dray on which was a large model of an airliner, some blue-uniformed figures grouped around it. This, apparently, was the International Air Corporation's–her airline – entry in the procession. In an instant she had a desperate idea.

"Follow when you can!" she cried to her astonished driver–and opening the car door, she jumped down into the road.

"Missy—" the driver cried out.

But Noreen was already running forward, hugging the baby as she did so. She passed through the lines of camels. With laughter still on all sides, she zigzagged her way through the dancers until she reached the fire engine. Two of the airport's firemen–driver and captain–sat in the front. Half a dozen others were clinging to the outside rails of the engine. So slow-moving was the procession that, though Noreen had Barry in her arms, she was able to leap on to the step.

"Oh, please— please—" she cried. "Help me! I must get through.

The road was completely blocked!

The baby's ill, and he's got to be flown to England–as soon as possible."

She swayed unsteadily as the engine lurched. The captain bent forward, and flung a steadying arm round her.

"Gosh! One of the I. A. C. stewardesses!" he cried. "Are you serious, miss?"

"Oh, yes! Yes! Please get me through!" Noreen panted; and then had another inspiration. "Please–get the bell going! Clear a way!"

The captain did not hesitate a moment longer. Her air of frantic urgency convinced him. He flung open the door of the driver's cabin and helped her inside. In a few agitated sentences, Noreen blurted out her story, while the singing and dancing went on all around her. But even before she finished the captain was signalling to the driver.

"O. K., boy! Sound the bell. Hold on, miss. We'll get you through."

Suddenly, deafeningly, the great brass bell above them clanged. The horses in front of them snorted, prancing to one side. The fire engine jerked forward. Dancers dodged out of the way. The engine began to move faster. Clang, clang, clang! Urgent, commanding, the bell rang out. In a short while a clear way was opened up. Deafened by the din that seemed to vibrate right through her, Noreen flinched; and even little Barry opened his eyes wonderingly. But–they were making speed! Noreen's heart leapt with hope. Clang, clang, clang! People stared from the wayside, plainly amazed. Faster, faster the engine moved, its bell still beating out its urgent warning. And then, at last, they had reached the head of the procession. The driver put his foot down and, at full speed, they raced along a palm-fringed road. Houses and oases whipped past; desert and more palms . . . until at last the airport loomed ahead. With a squealing of brakes the fire engine pulled up in front of the main building.

"Thank you! Thank you!" Noreen just gasped those words–then dashed across the airfield to where her own aircraft waited.

And there, waiting alongside it with the crew and other passengers, was Mr. Grant, the businessman who had caused her so much trouble on the flight. He was pale and coldly angry. As he had told Noreen often enough, since they left Karachi, it was vital to him that the aircraft arrived in London on time. If it didn't, he would miss out on an important business deal–and probably lose a great sum of money.

He barred her way now.

"Well, miss? And what's the verdict?" he demanded unpleasantly. "After holding us up–and probably ruining my business deal–you found out that baby wasn't seriously ill after all? You took too much on yourself, young lady."

But Noreen was calm now. She faced this man who had threatened to have her, and her crew, dismissed if they were late arriving. Her voice was as icy as his own.

"I think not, Mr. Grant," she said. "I've been to see a specialist–and baby Barry is seriously ill. We have to get him to London as quickly as possible, for an operation. Which should please you," she was unable to resist adding. "For now we MUST be in London on time, despite our delay here."

He started, flushing. From the other passengers came murmurs–murmurs of sympathy for little Barry, and scorn for this man who had tried to stop them landing to get treament for the baby.

"I–I—" Mr. Grant seemed to swallow hard. "He really was ill—?"

"As I said, Mr. Grant. The specialist has given him an injection he needed, but the effects will only last for about eleven hours–by which time he must be in London." The sound of a lighter bell, ringing out across the airfield, made her turn. "Here's an ambulance–it's probably bringing the nurse and the oxygen equipment for the baby. They will come with us on the flight now."

Then she turned and hurried past him as the pilot came running down the steps of the aircraft. She answered his questions by panting out again the full story of what had happened–and, as she did so, the ambulance came to a stop beside the airliner, and officials came running from the airport buildings to confirm her news. Mr. Jennison, the specialist, had phoned them. The nurse–a pretty young Persian girl–stepped down from the ambulance and began supervising the loading of the oxygen equipment. Suddenly all was bustle around the aircraft; but Mr. Grant, stepping back among the other passengers, was silent now. No one spoke to him. No one had any time for him. And he, perhaps, realising just what might have happened if they had not landed here, and flown on as he had demanded, had nothing to say for himself. Perhaps he was ashamed.

"We will only use the oxygen if necessary," the nurse told her. "And I am sure you could do with my help, to care for the baby."

They carried baby Barry on board, making him comfortable in a portable cot that could also be converted into an oxygen tent if necessary. Ten minutes later the aircraft was filling up again. A quarter of an hour after that–with ten hours to get Barry to the surgeon–they were off.

It was an anxious journey for Noreen. Though the nurse was there to help her with Barry, her fears for the baby did not lessen. For the first part of the flight, however, he slept more or less peacefully. But then, while they were over the mainland heading for a landing in Rome, the flight became bumpy. As he had done before, he refused to eat, and later was sick. The only thing he would take was some boiled water from a spoon. His bottle he persistently pushed away.

"I fear he is very ill," the nurse murmured. "We must hope we get to the Clinic in London, where he must have his operation, in time."

With all her heart Noreen hoped that, too. In Rome they made only the minimum fuelling stop–then took off again for London. But the weather was worsening now, and they encountered a head wind which slowed them down. Noreen was worriedly walking up the aisle attending to the wants of the passengers, when Mr. Grant stopped her. He had his watch in his hand.

"I think we'll be on time, Mr. Grant. We're doing our best," she said coldly.

Again that flush rose in his cheeks and he really did look ashamed.

"You won't forgive me for not wanting to stop at Bahrein, will you, Miss Farraday," he said quietly. "As a matter of fact, I–I wasn't thinking of my business conference this time. I was thinking of the baby—"

Noreen was startled. But she knew, by his tone, that he was sincere.

"I'm sorry," she apologised quickly.

"Don't be. I deserved your scorn," he said, equally quickly. "And–and I've been thinking of what you said before we landed in Bahrein. If that baby had been my own daughter–I know she's grown up now, and ran away to get married. But if she WERE a baby again–THAT baby–I would have hated the man who refused to let anyone fetch help for her."

Noreen said nothing. There was nothing to say.

"My conference means a lot to me," he muttered. "But even if I miss it . . . it'll be worth it to know I didn't stop the baby receiving treatment—"

"I don't think you will miss the conference, Mr. Grant," Noreen said softly. "As I said, we've got to be in on time, for the baby's sake."

But she left him feeling more sypathetic. Was it the fact that his daughter had run away to get married that had made him the hard-headed businessman he so often seemed? If he had been hurt–badly–by his daughter's action–he would want to become absorbed in his work, to forget. The aircraft droned on. Now little Barry was very quiet again. The blue tinge Noreen had seen earlier was returning to his lips and cheeks. The effects of the injection given him by the specialist were wearing off.

Every minute that ticked on was like an hour to Noreen. In the time she had had Barry in her charge, she had grown to love the baby. Nothing must happen to him now–nothing."

And then, at last, when they began to run in to the English airport, she knew by a glance at her watch that the aircraft was on time. They had made up for their delay. They would get baby Barry to the Clinic in under the time the specialist had mentioned.

But–another fear came to haunt her. What of the operation? Would Barry come through THAT safely?

They were down at last, taxi-ing along the runway. An ambulance came racing out to meet them, radioed for by the pilot. And, as Noreen came down the steps, followed by the nurse carrying little Barry in her arms, an anxious-looking grey-haired woman stepped out of the ambulance.

"They told me at the airport this was for little Barry," the woman panted. "I'm his grandmother. I was to meet him here. How is he? He has a heart ailment, you know. He was coming to London for treatment–"

"I didn't know. His papers were mislaid," Noreen said, with a swift little smile. "But since we found out he was ill, we've done everything we could for him, Mrs.–Mrs.—"

"Whitecross!" whispered the woman, who had eyes only for the baby. "They said he must be got to the Clinic at once. Oh, hurry—"

But even as she and the nurse stepped into the ambulance and Noreen made to follow, a Customs officer came hurrying up.

"I won't delay you. It's just a question of the baby's papers!" he exclaimed to Noreen. "Miss Farraday, they were mislaid at Karachi, as you know. They were delivered to the wrong aircraft, which arrived an hour ago." He held out a sheet of papers. "We have all the baby's case history here, among other things. Barry Bartholomew Wayne Whitecross–that's his name, isn't it?"

"WHAT!" There came an exclamation from behind them.

Noreen whirled. Descending the aircraft steps was Mr. Grant. His face was white and startled.

"Barry Bartholomew Wayne—" he blurted. "Here, let me see—"

And, before the surprised officer could stop him–while Noreen, the nurse and Barry's grandmother stared–he snatched the papers from the other man's hand.

"Barry Bartholomew Wayne—" he read feverishly. "Father–George John Whitecross. Mother–Patricia Eleanor Whitecross, née Grant–oh, great Scott, what did I nearly do?" he ended in horror.

All at once he seemed to crumple before their eyes. Haggard, he gazed and gazed at baby Barry's papers. Though he had caused her so much trouble, Noreen again felt a stab of pity for him.

Then Mrs. Whitecross tugged at her arm.

"I don't know what's the matter—" she whispered distractedly. "But we must–MUST–get Barry to the Clinic. It's very kind of a stranger to be so concerned, of course—"

"But he isn't a stranger!" Noreen burst out.

And suddenly she knew. Grant had been the name of Barry's mother before she married–and Grant was this man's name. Barry must be the baby of Mr. Grant's daughter and the man she had run away to marry . . . the man whose name Mr. Grant had never known.

"Mr. Grant–Mr. Grant—" she whispered. "Is–is Barry really your grandson?"

He lifted his haggard face to look at her.

"You know? I didn't–until I heard his full name. Bartholomew Wayne . . . they are *my* Christian names. And Whitecross–of course—"

He looked at Mrs. Whitecross, who was staring at him, wide-eyed.

"Don't you remember me now, Mrs. Whitecross? Your husband and I–we were once great business rivals! We hated each other. No wonder Pat ran away to get married, and never told me her husband's name. She was afraid I'd try to stop the marriage in some way, if I learnt she was marrying the son of my bitter rival—"

He stopped, shaking his head. Mrs. Whitecross put a hand on his arm.

"We knew, of course–but we could forgive. Pat was afraid you never would–and she would have hated to see your anger, so she just disappeared from your life. She's ill now, but it's nothing serious. She'll be back in England soon, to be with Barry if—"

"If he recovers from his operation!" Mr. Grant said, with a deep breath. "And he might not have reached here! I–I would have sacrificed him for a business meeting—"

"Never mind that now," the nurse put in briskly. "The baby must be got to the Clinic. You will come, too, Mr. Grant—"

"At once!" he said.

It was then Noreen remembered his business conference. But he had forgotten it–and she knew that even if she reminded him, he would not go to that conference now. He was thinking only of Barry–as they all were. So Noreen rode with Barry's two grandparents and the nurse to the Clinic. It was a silent ride, and she could feel the tension growing all the way. For time and again the nurse bent anxiously over Barry; and Barry's little lips and cheeks seemed to grow more blue. Then they reached the Clinic, which had been alerted for their arrival. The baby was taken at once to Mr. Greaves, the famous heart surgeon. Noreen and the others waited outside, while he examined little Barry. When he came out, his face was grave.

"I'll pull no punches," he said quietly. "The baby is very ill."

"But you'll operate?" Mrs. Whitecross and Mr. Grant gasped together.

"I shall," he said, with a brief smile. "But it will mean a long wait for you–several hours."

They waited. It was a long, anxious wait. Occasionally Mrs. Whitecross and Mr. Grant conversed in whispers with each other, and with Noreen. They all shared the same anxiety. Would Barry be all right?

It was five hours later that the door opened, and Mr. Greaves came in. Anxiously they all jumped up. And then they saw he was smilling.

"The operation was a complete success," he told them. "I can see no reason why Barry should not make a complete recovery. Will you please come to see him tomorrow?"

"Oh, thank you! Thank you!" Mrs. Whitecross cried.

Mr. Grant echoed her, and then turned with glowing eyes to Noreen.

"And it's thanks to you, Miss Farraday, that Barry ever got here at all!" he exclaimed. "If you hadn't taken him to the specialist in Bahrein, who gave him that injection to keep him going—"

Mrs. Whitecross slipped an arm round Noreen's shoulders.

"He's right, my dear. And, look–it's very late now," she said softly. "It's a little thing, I know, after all you've done . . . but would you come to my house to dinner now? You, too, Mr. Grant," she added quietly.

Mr. Grant looked rather confused.

"I–I've booked up at an hotel—" he murmured. "And I'm not so sure if your husband would welcome me, as I was once his rival—"

"If we have said hard things about you–that was long ago," smiled Mrs. Whitecross. "You're Pat's father, and we couldn't bear ill-will to anyone who is a relative of Pat's. We love her as if–as if she were our own daughter."

"Then let me go back to my hotel, just to see if there are any messages," murmured Mr. Grant. "And–you can cable Pat from there, and tell her everything. Particularly that Barry is all right."

They were so happy, Noreen thought. And she shared their happiness at that moment. All the clouds seemed to have passed.

And there was more good news to come.

When they had reached Mr. Grant's hotel–and the telegram had been sent off to his daughter in India–the receptionist reached into a pigeon-hole behind his desk.

"Now–there's a message for you, Mr. Grant," he said. "Will you take it?"

He handed over a slip of paper. Mr. Grant took it. He read what was on it, and then gave a gasp.

"Great Scott—"

Then he looked up.

"It's about the business conference, which I missed," he said quietly. "I was so worried about Barry, I didn't give it another thought–and thank goodness I didn't. I meant to sign a contract at that conference. If I had, instead of gaining my firm a great deal of money, I would have lost it!"

"Oh—" Noreen breathed.

After all that had happened–after all Mr. Grant's urgency to get to his conference–this was heaping coals of fire on his head with a vengeance. But when they went to the Clinic next day, little Barry was already well enough to greet them with a wide smile. Mr. Grant had stayed the night with the Whitecrosses; and now he told Noreen that, as soon as the baby was well again, he would himself be going back to India to stay with his daughter.

"I hope–when I go back with Barry to Pat–you'll be hostess on our aircraft again, Miss Farraday," Mr. Grant smiled.

But Noreen had a new briefing by the airline. Owing to shortage of staff, she had been posted to one the "domestic" lines of her company–and would be hostess on one of the smaller aircraft which travelled between London and the Channel Islands.

"Quite a change from the mysterious East," she smiled, as she told Mr. Grant. "But I know I'm going to enjoy it."

THE SECRET OF MUNDY ROCK

Who was the strange visitor to the Lobster Pot Hotel who said he was a bird-watcher? When Elizabeth Gregory noticed lights flashing from his window like the dots and dashes of the Morse code, she decided to investigate.

"Welcome to the Lobster Pot Hotel," said Elizabeth brightly, as a rather portly gentleman carrying three enormous suitcases pushed his way through the hotel door.

"Good morning," said the man. "I'm Mr. John Smithson. I've booked a room here for a few days."

"Oh, yes," replied Elizabeth. "My name's Elizabeth Gregory. My mother told me you were expected. We've given you a room overlooking the harbour as the hotel isn't very full at the moment. Port Trewis is a quiet little place until the summer rush."

Mr. Smithson signed the hotel register and Elizabeth helped him up the stairs with one of the suitcases. "Golly, these cases are heavy," she remarked, as she showed him into the bedroom.

Mr. Smithson glanced coldly at her. "As a matter of fact, I'm an ornithologist, a bird watcher you know," he said, "and I like to carry my reference books around with me."

"Oh, I expect that you've come to study the birds on Mundy Rock," said Elizabeth, throwing the bedroom window open wide. She pointed, "See, you've a wonderful view of the rock from here."

"Yes, that's it, Mundy Rock," said Mr. Smithson, hurrying to the window.

The little Cornish bay sparkled in the bright spring sunshine, and about a mile offshore was the bird sanctuary, a small rocky island inhabited only by birds.

"I suppose you've heard that the swallow-tailed kite has been seen there," said Elizabeth.

"Er – kite?" replied the visitor vaguely. "Oh, really?"

Elizabeth looked at him in surprise, but the man was busy gazing out to sea through his binoculars. Later, after telling her mother of Mr. Smithson's arrival, Elizabeth ran down to the beach to find her friend Bill Davies. He was busy painting one of his dinghies in readiness for the summer tourist trade.

"I say, Bill," she said, perching on the keel of the boat, "what would you think of an ornithologist who didn't seem to know about the swallowtailed kite?"

Bill stopped his painting and looked up. "Well, it's a very rare bird, you know. It's only been seen in the British Isles twice."

"Yes, that's what I mean," replied Elizabeth excitedly. "Most naturalists would give anything for a glimpse of the bird, but this chap Smithson, who is staying at the hotel, didn't seem even faintly interested when I told him. Besides, I noticed the initials E. C. on one of his suitcases and–"

Bill laughingly interrupted her. "The trouble is, Liz, that Port Trewis is too quiet for your vivid imagination. Come on, let's try and catch some mackerel."

The sea was calm and blue as they rowed out of the bay. Suddenly Elizabeth glanced towards the shore and gave a cry. A mirror flashed in the window of the Lobster Pot Hotel, the sun reflecting the signal over the water.

"That message is being flashed from Mr. Smithson's room," Elizabeth whispered. "I wonder what he's up to."

The question was answered almost immediately. A powerful motor-boat sped round the point and headed towards shore. Its wake rocked the little rowing boat and the two men at the wheel grinned as Bill and Elizabeth gripped the sides of the boat to steady themselves.

"Idiots!" said Bill. "They nearly overturned us."

They watched the motor-boat slow down and edge up to the quay. They saw a figure waiting. The person jumped into the boat and it turned and sped out towards Mundy Rock.

Back at the hotel again, Elizabeth's curiosity about the new arrival got the better of her. She decided to take the pass key that was kept in the office and see if Mr. Smithson had done any unpacking. The room was exactly as it had been that morning. The cases, still locked, were standing at the foot of the bed. But there was a difference. Only two suitcases stood there. The third one was missing.

A quick glance through the bedroom window told her that the motor-boat, with Mr. Smithson on board, was heading for shore again, so she locked the door behind her and hurried downstairs to replace the pass key. From then on Elizabeth was busy helping her mother with the lunches, waiting at the tables and then washing up the dishes. There was no time to worry about the mysterious naturalist.

It was tea-time before Elizabeth saw him again. "Did you have any luck at Mundy Rock this morning?" she enquired. "Your friends in the fast motor-boat nearly overturned us in the bay."

Mr. Smithson eyed her shiftily. "Oh, yes, a very successful trip," he replied. "Saw quite a few of those birds you mentioned this morning, swallow-tailed kites."

Elizabeth choked back her astonished laughter. To see one of these rare birds would have been extremely lucky, but Mr. Smithson was obviously telling a stupid lie. It was plain that he was not a naturalist as he claimed. What was he then, and why did he show such an interest in the bird sanctuary? Elizabeth meant to find out.

That evening Bill drove Elizabeth over to Hewiston Police Station. The sergeant listened to her description of Mr. Smithson and he seemed just as puzzled as they, but he promised to visit the Lobster Pot Hotel the next day.

But Elizabeth and Bill were in for another surprise. When they returned to the hotel, Mr. Smithson had checked out. He had explained to Mrs. Gregory that an urgent call from London had forced him to postpone his holiday and that he would have to return later in the year.

"Well, it looks as if the bird's flown, Liz, and before you solved the mystery," said Bill.

But Elizabeth had an idea. "Meet me on the quay tomorrow morning. I want you to take me to Mundy Rock," she said.

The early morning mist still lay over the sea as they approached the rock. They secured the boat to a sharp piece of rock and scrambled up the sides of the sanctuary.

"This is where Smithson landed," said Elizabeth. "You can see the muddy boot-marks on the rocks." They followed the footprints to the seaward side of the rock, stepping carefully to avoid nests and young birds.

"Look, Bill!" shouted Elizabeth. "Help me roll away this rock. There's a cave behind here." With a mighty heave the rock rolled down to the sea and there were the three suitcases that belonged to Mr. Smithson. The initials E. C. were still plainly visible on one of them.

"We'll take these straight to the police station, Liz," said Bill.

The police station at Hewiston was a buzz of activity. The whole county was searching for a gang who had broken into Hewiston Manor while it was unoccupied and stolen a large quantity of valuable Georgian silver. Elizabeth guessed what was inside the suitcases before the sergeant broke open the locks. From her description, the County Police and the coastguards had high hopes of catching the thieves.

"I suppose Mr. Smithson thought he would store the stolen silver on Mundy Rock till the hue and cry died down," Elizabeth said.

"Yes," said the sergeant, "but he reckoned without your sharp eyes and ears didn't he, Miss? By the way, I think there's a handsome reward offered for this silver . . ."

A PENNY FOR A PONY

by Cecily Danby

Kathryn had always wanted a pony of her own and hoped she would win one in a competition so she was very disappointed when she received only a consolation prize. One day, though, she was helping a horse which had been lamed and her kindness had quite a surprising result.

Kathryn stood at her bedroom window watching for the postman. She was twelve, now that her birthday had come at last, and there would be cards for her, and perhaps a parcel from Gran. There would be a letter, too! Oh, that letter *must* come today. It *must*, it *must!* Kathryn curled her hands into tight little fists. She could hardly bear to wait for that letter, for it would tell her she had won first prize in a big competition. It would tell her she had won – a pony! She was wearing her favourite clothes in honour of her birthday – and that letter. Of course, the jodhpurs were tight for her now, and the green polo-sweater had been washed and washed.

It was three months since she had sent her entry for the pony competition. She had answered all the Quiz questions on how to groom a pony, how to saddle it, and how to care for it in stables. These were all things taught her by Daddy who had promised her a pony for her tenth birthday, but he had been killed in that horrible car crash, and there was no money after that. Not for ponies. She and her brother Peter still lived in the same house with Mummy, and went to the same schools. Gran had wanted them to go to her, in London, but they couldn't bear to be away from the Cotswolds. Here was the garden which Daddy had planned for them, and the brick stable he had designed, all ready for her pony. She was to call her pony *Emerald* because it was to be brought from Ireland. Peter had made a name-board for her, in poker-work. *Emerald,* it said, and at the back of the board, *Kathryn Delaney's Pony.* He was to be brown, the colour of milk chocolate, and maybe have four white ankle socks. Certainly he'd have big beautiful eyes with a bit of mischief in them. She would groom him quite hard, because ponies hated to be tickled, and she would exercise him every day . . .

Kathryn drew a sharp breath as the postman came ambling up the garden path just as if it were an ordinary day. He paused, and fumbled in his bag. Yes! A bulgy little packet that would not go through the letter box. There were letters in his hand, too. Kathryn's hands were cold and moist; she felt a little sick, and her feet were rooted to the ground. She waited, and it seemed as if the whole world stood still, waiting with her. Her eyes closed when she heard the knocking, and then Mummy's shoe-heels tapping down the hall.

"Kathryn!" Mummy called up the stairs. "Come for your birthday post, darling. There's a parcel from Gran–"

Kathryn flung away her fears and flew downstairs. "Mummy, Mummy has it come? My pony letter–has it come?"

It was there! A stiff business-like envelope with a newspaper's name on the back. Kathryn's fingers tore at the flap and a slip of paper fell from between the folds of the letter. Mummy picked up the slip of paper, while Kathryn read the briefly worded letter. At first she could not take in what it said. The letter had come, but she hadn't won. She hadn't won the pony. The letter said she had been awarded a consolation prize of five pounds.

"Look, darling," Mummy said, "this is a cheque. You've won five pounds! Isn't that splendid?"

Kathryn made no reply. It just couldn't be true. It must be a mistake. It wasn't five pounds she wanted. Peter tried his best to cheer her, and Mummy made a favourite omelette for breakfast. But she couldn't cheer up and she couldn't eat. She tried her best, because Mummy and Peter had got surprise presents for her. Peter, who was lame, and would never be able to ride a horse, had carved a beautiful pony for her, out of some pale brown wood. And Mummy had knitted her a sweater with horses' heads across the chest. Smiling at them both,

Kathryn slid from her seat and hugged them. Then she put her head on her arms, huddled in Daddy's armchair and sobbed bitterly.

"Kathryn, dear–" Mummy knelt very close and tried to comfort her. "I know what we will do! I will save every penny I can, and add it to your five pounds, and perhaps by the time you are fourteen we'll be able to buy a pony."

Kathryn sat up and wiped her face, sniffing a little. "No, Mummy," she sighed, "you can't do that. There'd be no little treats for you and Peter. No visits to Gran or anything–"

Scrambling to her feet, she smoothed the green sweater over her hips. "It's all right Mummy, honestly, I'm better now."

A watery smile flickered for a brave moment over Kathryn's face. Then she picked up the letter and the five pounds. "I think I'll go for a walk, Mummy. I've got a headache."

It was a gay spring morning with a tantalising breeze that frolicked the manes and tails of the string of horses that went cantering past. They were returning to Weatherby's, the famous stable and riding school. Kathryn watched them go; not so much in envy as in pure joy at their grace and beauty. Weatherby's! It was to have a new owner and manager today! It was a kind of birthday for the horses, too. She wondered if the old manager, John Walsh, had sold the puppies he wanted homes for. Peter had always wanted a puppy; a little dog who would share his slow and awkward ramblings in the wood; a little intelligent terrier dog that would understand he couldn't run like other boys. Kathryn took out the five-pound cheque. Could she spend it? Would it buy Peter a puppy; one of John Walsh's little terriers?

Mr. Walsh grinned all over his round red face. "Sure, Kathryn, my bonny. Sure it's enough to buy a puppy. I've one left; a little gem, he is, take it from me. He should just suit you."

Kathryn followed John Walsh across the yard, where the older pupils were mounting their horses, with Jackson coaching them. The yard had always given Kathryn a strange feeling of complete satisfaction. The fine horses tossing their heads and prancing a little, impatient to be off; the keen smell of harness and horse-flesh; the ring and jingle was music to her ears, filling her heart with an indefinable happiness. It was enough that the big beautiful creatures existed.

There was a joy deeper than disappointment, stronger than the sense of possession.

A white puppy cocked his little square head on one side and wagged his hind quarters. "There, see?" John Walsh laughed. "He's yours, lassie. Write your name on this bit of paper–that's the idea. Capital! Now he's really yours."

Half an hour later, Kathryn was about to leave the yard when a big black horse walked slowly and painfully into the yard. "Hey, you!" the rider called as she dismounted. "*Boy's* gone lame. Do something, quickly."

Kathryn hesitated a moment. What a stupid haughty girl! Couldn't she *see* what was wrong with her horse? The poor thing had a stone in the shoe, that was obvious. And the girl thought she was talking to a "stable-boy". Kathryn laughed and smoothed a hand over her hair. Then, placing the puppy carefully out of harm's reach, she walked up to the lame horse.

"Hurry, hurry!" called the impatient girl, who just stood there slapping her immaculate jodhpurs with a riding crop. "I can't wait all the morning!"

"Yes, miss," Kathryn laughed aloud. Really it was the limit. She must remember to tell Mummy and Peter about this. She gentled the nervous horse, speaking to it softly, as she passed slowly from its head to the hind legs. "Steady, *Boy,*" she coaxed, "steady."

Opening a small knife which was part of her "riding" equipment, she then lifted one of the hind legs, held it firmly between her own knees, and loosened the stone which was pressing so painfully. It was soon done, and the horse tossed its head in gratitude.

The rider remounted. "Here, you," she called, tossing a coin for Kathryn to catch. It was a penny! Kathryn turned it in her hands, too surprised to believe it was real.

"Not much of a tip, is it?"

Kathryn spun round to face a stranger, who held out a hand and smiled pleasantly. "I saw that pert young madam; she knows nothing about a horse, and less about manners. I know you're not employed here, because I'm Thomas Dawson, the new man."

"The . . . owner?" Kathryn breathed, in surprise, for she had heard much about the new owner. Wealthy and rather impulsive, he had

"Steady, Boy," she coaxed, "'steady."

a son who preferred fast cars to horses, and a young daughter who was afraid of them. John Walsh had told her.

"That's right. But never mind about me. Who taught you to handle a horse in the way you did? Weren't you afraid?" Mr. Dawson asked her.

"No! Of course not. I've always loved them too much to be afraid."

"Got a pony of your own, I suppose?"

A shadow dimmed the happiness in Kathryn's eyes. She shook her head. "Daddy taught me about a stone in the shoe, and John Walsh lets me help him sometimes."

She looked up into the quizzical blue eyes of the new owner. "I nearly had a pony," she told him. "I nearly had a pony–twice."

"And what happened?" Thomas Dawson asked. "Tell me about it."

The whole story tumbled into sympathetic ears. Kathryn was surprised at herself for she rarely mentioned her dream-horse, even to Peter. Now she told it all! About Daddy being killed; about *Emerald* and the nameboard with *Kathryn Delaney's Pony* burned into the wood; about the competition and the consolation prize. Thomas Dawson listened in silence. There was a curious expression on his face which Kathryn failed to understand. Her colour rose swiftly and she turned away.

"I'm talking too much," she said softly. "I'm sorry."

"I'm not," Thomas Dawson replied, and the smile came again to his eyes. He put an arm over her shoulders. "Come and have a look at my daughter's pony. Marilyn won't ride him because of his temper. He's called *Russet,* and he is rather lively. Spirited, you know."

Kathryn nodded. Her heart was suddenly beating high and fast in her throat, and as they crossed the yard together she somehow knew she was walking towards a dream. It couldn't possibly be happening to her! And yet–it was.

"There he is." Mr. Dawson drew her forward. In the half-light of the stable she could see him. A light brown pony, without white socks, but with more than a glint of mischief in his eyes.

"Bring him out!" Thomas Dawson urged. "Have a look at him. Do you think *you* could ride him now? He takes a good deal of handling you know."

Kathryn stroked the pony's neck and then laid her face on him, her eyes closed tightly because the tears were pressing through. He was beautiful and eager, and she loved him with all her heart. *"Russet!"* she whispered. *"Russet!"*

"I'd be much obliged if you'd ride him, Kathryn," Thomas Dawson said brusquely. "He's been neglected, waiting for that girl of mine to ride him. Maybe she will when she's older, meanwhile–poor *Russet.*"

Kathryn smiled into Thomas Dawson's eyes. She knew very well that he could sell the pony, easily, but he wasn't going to. It was to be *her* pony. She was to ride him, and care for him. He was to belong to her.

"Will you come to the yard and help me, Kathryn? Same as you've helped John Walsh? Splendid! I shall leave orders about that. Put you on the staff one day, and the pay-roll. Yes indeed, I mean it."

The tears slipped down Kathryn's face but she smiled through them as she tried to stammer out her thanks. Mr. Dawson would not listen.

"Take Peter his pup, Kathryn, and ask him to make a new name-board for Kathryn Delaney's Pony."

Kathryn ran home on feet that felt like wings. She had the white puppy in her arms, a penny in her pocket, and a heart full of unimaginable joy.

Thomas Dawson watched her go, compassion on his sober face. Poor child, that was the least he could do for her. She should have his daughter's pony, for it was his own son whose blind reckless driving had robbed Kathryn of her dream-horse–and of her father.

BARBARA'S STRANGE JOURNEY

by Carol Frontenac

In the Arctic wastes of North Canada, Barbara Massey was flown from her school to visit her sick father. Soon, he confided in her that he had hidden some precious rocks in a cave but when she tried to retrieve them she was ambushed by Indians.

Flying into the vast spaces of North Canada should have been an exciting adventure. When it was over, thought Barbara Massey, perhaps she would be able to think of it that way. For the moment, there was too much to remind her of the trouble lying ahead. Her brother must have been feeling much the same, for he was hunched gloomily in his seat. She wondered what the third passenger in this specially chartered machine was thinking. He was a surgeon; a brilliant man at dealing with bone injuries. When they reached the trading post where her father was lying injured, his strong hands would be busy. In the meantime, there was nothing to be done.

It seemed a long time since she had been roused from her bed in the school dormitory. After a swift meal there had been a car to the airport, where she found Jack waiting. She'd rushed eagerly to him, hoping he would know more than she did herself. But he'd shaken his head.

"Only that he's hurt and can't be moved. We're to go to him and a doctor's coming along with us."

It seemed so long ago – and yet it had only been a matter of hours. She wondered where they were now and strained forward to peer out of one of the cabin windows. But there was nothing to be seen, except a great sea of white cloud below them. She closed her eyes. She felt dreadfully tired. Suddenly, Jack was calling to her.

"Nearly there, Barbara!"

She jerked into wakefulness and looked out. Because they were gliding down, the landscape appeared tilted. For the most part it was a barren, greyish expanse. Snow lingered on some mountains and there were dark clusters of trees. Then she saw the small cabins, the coastline and the bleak waters of the bay beyond. The cabins! That would be the trading post. And in one of those cabins her father was lying. Perhaps her mother, attracted by the noise of the aircraft, was at the door, looking up . . . anxiously. In front of her the surgeon turned, his face mellowed by a smile.

"Soon be able to see what we can do for your father," he said cheerfully.

"You'll save him," she whispered. "I'm *sure* you will."

Twice, during past summers, Barbara and Jack had come to the trading post for their school holidays. It was so different from Montreal it fascinated them: the store itself, with its collected skins, and the fun of expeditions into wild and lonely country. This visit was different. Neither of them had much spirit for doing anything. The time dragged.

They learned the story of the accident. Their father, with two Indians, had crossed the barren country to a range of hills. Climbing to the highest point for the purpose of making a sketch map, he had fallen.

The Indians brought him home on a roughly-made stretcher, very slowly because the fall had injured his back. One of the Indians had since disappeared. The other, who was well-known to Barbara and Jack, was called "Stumpy".

It was Stumpy who told them the full story.

"But what was Dad doing there, anyway?" Jack wanted to know.

"I don't think we shall find out until Dad's well enough to talk," Barbara said.

Then the doctor came out of the cabin and smiled.

"Only a matter of time, now," he said confidently. "In a fortnight we'll have an air ambulance to get him to a hospital."

"He *will* be able to walk again?" Barbara asked eagerly.

"By the end of the summer, with any luck."

"That's wonderful! I knew you'd do it!"

Before, when they had seen their father, it had been only for a few minutes at a time and he could hardly speak to them. This time, though strain lines at his eyes and mouth showed the effort he was making, he began to talk as soon as they entered the room.

"I've a mission for you two," he said. "Barbara – you remember when I took you to the hills we called Desolation Range?"

"Gosh, yes, Dad! It was a grand trip."

Mr Massey went on: "Geology – the study of rocks – has always been my hobby. Some of the samples interested me. I found what I'd suspected might be there . . . pitchblende, in other words, radium."

Jack whistled. "Golly! That could mean a fortune, Dad!"

"Sure thing. I had the accident when I was drawing the sketch map to establish my claim. I hadn't told Stumpy and the other chap what I was after. So, when they brought me back, they didn't bring the rock samples. I must have those if I'm to make my claim."

"And we're to go for them!" Barbara cried. "That'll be exciting."

"You must have Stumpy with you! Barbara, you're the one who'll be able to find the specimens. Remember the small cave we found?"

"Yes. A tiny one. We used it as a store. It was wonderfully hidden."

"There's a skin bag. Inside it are the pieces of pitchblende, velvet–black in appearance with blue and silver veins."

Jack said: "We'll soon have them here for you."

"Just one thing, son. Look out for a trapper named Kedge."

His eyes fluttered, then closed. Barbara said: "You can leave the rest to us, Dad. We'll make a quick start."

They slipped quietly from the room, then hurried out of the cabin. Jack said excitedly: "I didn't tell Dad, but Red Nok – that other Indian – was seen a few days ago with Kedge the trapper. They were at the next trading post along the coast. Stumpy heard it from an Eskimo who brought in some silver fox pelts."

Barbara gasped: "You think . . . "

"I shouldn't be surprised if Kedge suspected what Dad was after. If so, he could get Red Nok to take him to the hills. Once he's there, if he finds the little cave you and Dad mentioned, we're done."

"We must be there first," said Barbara determinedly.

Long before they reached Desolation Range, Stumpy was grumbling about its being summer. It would be so much quicker, he said, with snow on the ground and being able to use dogs. Also, there would be fewer mosquitoes! They kept up a good pace and by late on the second day were feeling really pleased with themselves. It was then Stumpy made a discovery which cast them into gloom. He pointed to impressions in the thick carpet of caribou moss. "Two men and one limp a little. Red Nok, he limp."

They halted for a council of war. Owing to the great length of the summer day in the far North, they could reach the hills before the brief darkness set in. But the two men ahead must not see them and this meant it was impossible to overtake and get there first.

"Stumpy," Jack asked, "did Dad mark out any land – put cairns of stones?"

Stumpy nodded. "The other side of the hills. Not easy to find the cairns. Country very broken and rocky."

"Could Red Nok take Kedge to them?" Barbara asked.

"No. Red Nok very lazy. We had camp. He like stay there."

Jack said: "Seems to me that all Kedge could learn from Red Nok is where Dad camped and that he brought no samples of rock away. Kedge has plenty of searching to do."

"Of course," Barbara pointed out, "if he finds the right place, he doesn't need Dad's samples."

Jack agreed. "But that would take longer. Once he has some samples he can stake a claim and adjust the boundary lines later."

They adopted Barbara's plan. They would make for the far end of the hills and then sneak along to the cave, hoping to dodge Kedge and Red Nok.

"As soon as we get the samples we must be off as fast as we can go," Jack said.

They moved off early the next morning. Stumpy led the way, looking carefully for any signs of their enemies. At last, he went forward alone. He came back for them, his eyes glistening with excitement.

They crawled over rocks and peered from a ledge. A rocky valley was below them and from the far slope, behind some bushes, rose the lazy, curling smoke of a camp fire.

Jack whispered: "At least he doesn't suspect we're near. Where's your cave, Barb? Any idea?"

"I think it's on the same hill, but more to the right." Barbara paused. "I know! We'll leave our stuff here. Stumpy can take me down some of the way, until I'm sure of the direction, then he can come back. I'll sneak across and if there's any trouble you can cover me." She pointed to Stumpy's rifle and Jack's shotgun.

Barbara crept between boulders, gradually making her way up the slope. She knew now that she was near the cave, for there were several familiar landmarks. And at last there was the narrow cleft of the entrance right before her. She was scared as she raced across an open stretch to the cave. Her hands shook as she felt inside it, but her fingers closed on the leather pouch. She pulled it out, peered into it to make sure the samples were safe, then straightened up, ready to scamper back. Then she gasped in alarm. A rifle shot tore through the silence. Another . . . and another. She dared not go down the slope, where she would be exposed to fire. She'd have to climb further up and try to find out what was happening.

The firing still went on as she crawled up and up the rugged surface, making her way round gradually. And at last, peeping from behind a boulder, she was able to see puffs of smoke from the rock ledge across the valley. Immediately below her there was a movement in the bushes, then a shot. Another, a little to her right but still below her. And looking at the trees, which were much nearer, she saw the smoke rising from the enemies' camp fire. She was close to their camp and they were between her and her friends. She began to think, feverishly.

From the ledge, Jack fired again. There was still no sign of his sister. He could tell what was happening. Kedge and Red Nok were working down their slope, hoping to climb this one and close in.

Suddenly, from the heart of the trees opposite, there was a terrific crash, like an army going into action. A great column of smoke went up. The red-shirted figure leaped from cover and went tearing back to the trees. He was followed by another man, who was smaller and dragged one leg.

Jack turned to Stumpy. "What's happened?"

Stumpy shook his head. "It's a big fire," he said.

They waited, wondering. And then, with a feeling of joy, Jack saw

Barbara racing down the hill-slope. Both he and Stumpy made their way over the boulders to meet her.

From the far side, neither Kedge nor Red Nok reappeared.

Then Barbara was safely back with them, gasping for breath, holding tightly to the small leather sack. "We can . . . get going now. Come on, quickly."

"But what happened?" Jack demanded.

"I was near their camp. Trapped. I went . . . to it. Threw everything I could . . . on the fire . . . including a box . . . of cartridges."

Stumpy laughed. "They not follow us, I think," he said gleefully. "They short of ammunition now. We collect gear and go – but not hurry too much. No need."

SUE STUART, JUNIOR REPORTER

by Harold Whitehead

Susan Stuart knew that she was extremely lucky to be taken on by the Evening Star as a junior reporter especially as she had only just left school. But her very first assignment exposed her to great danger and only a trick was able to save her. However, she proved to the editor that she knew how to find a "story".

"If you could spare me just a few minutes, Mr O'Neill." The big man was seated at the desk in the office on whose door, in letters six inches high, was a notice which said it was STRICTLY PRIVATE. He looked up suddenly, startled.

"What? How the . . ." He glared at the girl. She was slim and scarcely more than five feet in height, with a tip-tilted nose and laughing blue eyes. "How did *you* get in here? And who are you?"

"Susan Stuart, commonly known as 'Red'. I came in via the fire escape." She smiled at him sweetly.

"The fire . . . My dear girl, the fire escape finishes at the floor below this."

"I know!" Susan grinned. "It *was* a bit tricky – the last lap, up the drainpipe, I mean."

"Bless my soul!" Henry O'Neill, editor of the *Evening Star*, a local newspaper which catered for the towns of Devon and Cornwall, mopped his brow. This girl with the bright red hair was unusual, to say the least!

"Well – er – now that you're here, what do you want?"

"A job – as a reporter," Sue stated simply. "I'm leaving school this term. I've sent you lots of my stories, but they have come back so quickly that I'm sure you haven't even looked at them. I've tried to get interviews with you, but up to now I've never got beyond the gargoyle in the outer office."

"Oh, I see! *That's* all you want!" Henry O'Neill was heavily sarcastic.

"I write quite well and I'm pretty resourceful," she went on.

"I've noticed *that!*" The editor's fingers were drumming the table top. He had a great deal of work to do and he had to get rid of her. Secretly he admired her nerve, but – a job as a *reporter!* A slip of a schoolgirl! Suddenly, inspiration came to him.

"Have you heard about the 'Crabber's Cove Monster'?" he asked suddenly.

"I read about it in your paper last week," Sue replied.

O'Neill's lips twitched. "Right! Get me a *real* story about it. The explanation, mind you! No eye-witness accounts. Then we'll see. Good morning!"

"If I succeed, you'll promise to give me a job as a staff reporter?"

"Yes, yes, YES! Now, I'm busy. Goodbye!"

The door closed behind the startling young lady and Henry O'Neill indulged in a minute's silent laughter, his big frame shaking. *That* would keep her quiet . . . *and* disillusion her about reporting! For Henry O'Neill had no illusions about the three fishermen who alleged they had seen the 'monster' recently. Drunken old reprobates!

Sue Stuart arrived at Crabber's Cove at lunch time. Her Aunt Margaret had taken a cottage there for the summer, so she paid her a visit. Within half an hour of arriving, Sue had the full story of the monster. Her aunt supplied her with most of the details. It was all mixed up with the legend of 'Neptune's Walk', a pathway up the cliffs. The peculiar thing was that the pathway started about a quarter of the way up the cliffs and was inaccessible from the sea, except at very high tide. It finished at a hole, or cave, about twenty feet from the cliff top. Legend had it that Father Neptune himself used the walk when he wanted to emerge from his watery depths. Sue soon located Barty Bell, one of the fishermen who was supposed to have seen the monster recently. Twenty pence in his horny palm made him positively loquacious.

"'Orrible it were, miss!" he shuddered. "With big webbed feet . . . "

"Webbed feet?"

"Aye! An' a big snout on 'is face. It were dark, but I could see it all right. I didn't stay long, though, I can tell you. Flip, flop, flip, flop! Walkin' up Neptune's Walk." Barty shuddered again. "I wouldn't live in Doctor Barker's 'ouse for a hundred pounds a week!"

Sue was interested. "Does the doctor live near Neptune's Walk then ?" she enquired.

"Not the doctor 'imself. He *used* to live there, but the 'ouse is let to an artist bloke from London – a feller named Black. The 'ouse is right on top of the walk, as you might say – right at the edge of the cliff."

Ten minutes after talking to Barty Bell, Sue was on her way to the cliffs. Over her shoulder she carried a coil of light, but strong, rope. Sue was fond of climbing. She had done quite a bit with her father during her holidays. Not only that, she had also held the school gymnastic championship for her last two years at school.

It was dull and cloudy when she arrived at Neptune's Walk. Looking down from the cliff she could see the 'steps' quite clearly, although she could not see where they finished. They wound left and a jutting piece of rock hid them from view. Almost immediately above where they vanished stood the doctor's house, a big, old-fashioned mansion of a place, with grounds running almost to the cliff edge. Ten minutes later she had fixed the rope securely to a rock and had climbed down to the point where the walk turned left. It was ticklish work hugging the cliff face and rounding the jutting rock, but she made it safely and found herself on a kind of platform, about ten feet square. There was a big hole in the rock, like a small cave, immediately in front of her; and above, the vertical cliff face. She switched on her torch as she entered the cave. It was barely six feet high and by the beam of her torch she could see that it penetrated the rock to a depth of about ten feet. She walked forward on the rocky floor. She had almost reached the far end when a voice, almost in her ear, said: "Good afternoon! Welcome to my humble home!"

"Ohhhh!" Sue's exclamation was almost a shriek. She jerked her torch round suddenly and saw a large young man calmly sitting in an alcove in the rock. No wonder she hadn't seen him!

"Hush! You'll waken the baby!" he said.

"You – you gave me a fright," Sue said, half angrily. "What are you doing here, anyway?"

"I want to be alone!" said the man, in such a serious tone that Sue had to chuckle. "And you?" he asked.

"Me? Oh, I'm a confirmed cave dweller," she bantered back. "I thought this would make a nice, self-contained flat!"

There was something likeable about the flippant young man who, Sue decided, was not as young as she had first thought. About thirty, she guessed. She decided to tell him why she had come.

When she had finished, he was silent for a minute. Then: "I think you are on a wild goose chase, young lady," he said bluntly. "If I were you, I'd pack up and go home before you break your neck!"

"Thanks!" said Sue coldly. "But I think I'll stay just the same."

"Well, if you will insist on wasting your time! I must be going. Can I help you up the cliff?"

"I can manage, thank you," she replied coldly.

The man paused, then he said, more kindly, "Look, Miss – er –"

"Stuart," Sue supplied.

"Well, Miss Stuart, you take my tip. It's no job for a young girl like you, climbing up and down cliffs and poking into caves – looking for ghosts! Besides, it might be dangerous." He suddenly checked himself, as though he had said too much. "Sure you'll be O.K. getting back?"

"Quite, thank you. I'm used to climbing and I have a rope."

"Well, so long!" He smiled, a very boyish smile. "Take my tip, there's no ghost in Crabber's Cove!" And with that he clumped to the cave entrance and disappeared.

Sue pondered on his identity as she searched the cave. What had *he* come to the cave for? Why had he warned her that there might be danger, then suddenly closed up like an oyster? On her way back to her aunt's she paid a visit to the grocer's shop in the High Street. Her request made that worthy gentleman open his eyes wide. He looked at Sue as though she were a little 'queer'.

"In separate bags indeed!" he muttered as she walked out of the shop.

After tea she sat talking to Aunt Margaret, giving her all the news from home. And just after nine o'clock, when she told her aunt that she thought she would take a stroll and "not to be anxious if she were a little late back," her aunt was not at all surprised – even when she saw the 'equipment' she was taking with her. Nothing her 'stop–at–nothing' niece did surprised Aunt Margaret. All she said was, "All right, dear. But be careful." She had great faith in Sue's ability to look after herself.

It was just half past nine when Sue neared Neptune's Walk. It was completely dark now. She had with her a powerful pair of binoculars, which enabled objects to be seen at night. They had belonged to her father during his naval service.

When she arrived near the spot, she focussed the glasses. Suddenly she stiffened. About half way down the 'walk', *something* had moved. Could it be . . . She flung herself full length and stared hard. With a thrill of surprise, she saw it was the young man she had met in the cave and he, too, was using binoculars–staring out to sea. What was he looking at? Sue turned her own pair in the same direction. She soon made out the lights of a vessel, about two miles out but coming in fast towards the cove.

Suddenly the young man put his glasses back in the case. He started to climb back up the cliff and Sue had to admire his cat-like ability to climb without a rope. He must have been entirely without nerves. He reached the cliff top about two hundred yards from where Sue lay. He set off in the direction of the doctor's house and Sue lost sight of him.

Sue got up and walked towards the steps. She reached the point where she had lowered herself that afternoon and was debating whether to do it again, when to her ears came the sound of a powerful motor-boat engine. Once more she focussed her night glasses. The ship, whose dim outline she could now make out, was about three hundred yards from the cliffs. Suddenly the engines stopped. It turned, so that it was broadside on to the cliffs. She couldn't see it very clearly, but there seemed to be a great deal of activity aboard. Then, as suddenly as they had stopped, the engines started again and the boat headed out to sea. Sue kept her glasses trained on it. After a mile it stopped again and hove to. The next minute her heart leapt. What was that noise? Squelching footsteps. Flip, flop, flip, flop!

Barty Bell's story!

Sue's hands were trembling a little as she focussed the binoculars on Neptune's Walk. A possible explanation suddenly dawned on her. The figure was no *ghost* – he was a *frogman!* And close behind him came two more; obviously they had swum from the motor boat. Smugglers? She had to get in touch with the police at once. She scrambled to her feet and began to run in the direction of the main road – to find a telephone box. Then, suddenly, she remembered the doctor's house. That would be on the phone. She was panting as she rang the front door bell. A rather stout man, wearing a mackintosh, answered the door.

"Mr Black?" Sue asked.

"Yes."

Breathlessly, she told her story.

"Come in, my dear. Come in." Mr Black led her through the dark hall to a room. He opened the door, stepping on one side to let her enter. "The phone is in there."

Sue walked in – then suddenly halted in amazement. Seated in a chair, handcuffed but calmly smoking a cigarette, was the young man. Beside him, revolver in hand, was a short, thick-set, bull-necked man.

The girl jerked round, startled. Black had closed the door behind him and in his hand, too, there was a pistol.

"What . . . what is the meaning of this?" Sue realised that her voice sounded funny. Her throat had suddenly gone dry and there was a peculiar fluttering in her stomach.

"It means, my dear young lady, that you, like Captain Baylis here, have been poking your nose into other people's business. Very unfortunate – for both of you!" Black turned to the thick–set man. "Go and check the new consignment, Amos," he ordered calmly.

"And tell François that he will have two passengers on the trip back."

The bull-necked Amos nodded and shuffled out of the room.

"I believe you have already met Captain Baylis, Miss Stuart," went on the crook, as calmly and politely as if he were at a party. "Captain Baylis is a highly respected member of our intelligence service. At the moment he is working with Scotland Yard."

His voice lost a little of its suavity. "I have spent a great deal of

Sue walked in – then suddenly halted in amazement.

money building up my smuggling organisation. I have nearly half a million pounds worth of–"

"Cut the cackle, Black," snapped Baylis. "If I hadn't been so careless as to get knocked on the head by one of your thugs, I should have had you all under lock and key by now. What do you intend to do with Miss Stuart?"

The fleshy man's lips parted in a cold smile. "I'm afraid both you and Miss Stuart will have to be – er – disposed of at sea!"

It was the merciless way he said it, rather than the words, which made it sound so horrible.

Sue gasped. "You mean . . . you mean you're going to . . . to *kill* me? Oh!" She grasped the table suddenly. "I . . . think I'm . . . going . . . to faint."

Baylis jumped to his feet.

"Stay where you are, Baylis!" Black snapped. The revolver in his hand was steady as he stared unmoved as Sue swayed and slid to the floor. That 'faint' was the finest bit of acting Sue had ever done – but neither man suspected. The next second, however, Black realized the truth, for Sue's hand came up in a half circle. Something in a paper bag hit the smuggler flush in the face. He staggered back, temporarily blinded. The air was full of particles of pepper.

Baylis did not hesitate. Manacled as he was, he took a flying leap at the gangster and brought him down with a crash. Before Black could get up the secret service man brought his handcuffs down on his head with all his force. Black ceased to feel the pain and discomfort of his eyes! There came the sound of running footsteps in the passage outside. Baylis grabbed Black's gun and turned to face the new threat. But Sue was already behind the door. As it burst open and Amos entered, gun in hand, another paper bag flew through the air and burst in his face. He staggered back moaning, his hands at his streaming eyes. Baylis put Amos out of his misery with a nicely timed blow on the head with the butt of his revolver.

"Nice work, kid!" he chuckled delightedly. "Every time a bull's-eye! We must work fast now. Hurry and phone for the police."

The rest was easy.

It was exactly ten o'clock next morning. For the past five minutes an almost incredulous Henry O'Neill had listened to Sue's story. "And it's exclusive," she said. "Captain Baylis has promised not to let any other paper have it until I give him the word."

O'Neill quickly checked the details with the police by phone. As he replaced the receiver he turned to Sue. "Well – what are you waiting for?" he snapped. "Get that story typed."

"I have the job, then?"

"Of course." The editor hid a smile. "But don't stand there arguing! We've no time for idle chatter on the *Star*." But the twinkle in O'Neill's eyes belied his irritability.

"*Right,* sir!" Sue said joyously. "Oh, by the way, my expense account." She thrust a single sheet of paper into the editor's hands.

She was at the door when O'Neill shouted: "Here, what's this? Four ounces of *pepper*?"

"Self defence!" Sue yelled back as she slammed the door.

And back in his office Henry O'Neill chuckled delightedly: "Pepper! *Pepper*! At the price it is today! Red Stuart, eh? Red Pepper!"

THE FANCY DRESS PARTY

Jean Meredith and her friend, Mary, were very upset when their fancy dresses failed to arrive in time for their party. But doing a good turn to an old lady led them to make a very interesting discovery.

"Oh, dear, Mary! What are we going to do now that our fancy dresses haven't arrived?"

There was dismay and disappointment on Jean Meredith's pretty face as she and her friend watched the last train from London chug out of the tiny country station.

"It looks as though we shall have to go to the dance just as we are," said Mary sorrowfully.

Jean bit her lip to stem the tears which threatened to flood her eyes. She and Mary had so looked forward to wearing fancy dress at the carnival dance in Welford that night. They had ordered two dresses of seventeenth-century ladies-in-waiting from a large London store and they had been assured that they would arrive in time. Obviously something had gone wrong.

"Oh, well," she sighed, "it can't be helped. We know that the dresses had to be altered. Perhaps they took longer than expected and the parcels missed the train. Anyway, it won't stop us from going. Fancy dress is not compulsory."

They turned out of the quiet country station and it was then that they saw the grey-haired old lady struggling along the road with two heavy cases.

"Poor thing, she'll never be able to manage those by herself," murmured Jean sympathetically. "Let's give her a hand." The two girls ran after the old lady. "Can we help you, madam?" Mary asked politely, as they overtook her.

"That's very kind of you, my dears." The old lady put down her cases gratefully. "I really can't think what has detained my young nephew. He knew I was arriving on the last train with these cases and he promised to be here with the car."

"Perhaps it has broken down," said Jean. "Have you far to go?"

"To Green Bank, and it's very kind of you to help me. I should never have managed them by myself. Are you sure they are not too heavy for you?" She glanced anxiously from one to the other, as they began to struggle along with the cases in the direction of the rambling old manor known as Green Bank.

"Yes, we're all right, really we are," smiled Jean, but she was already beginning to feel puffed because the road led uphill.

"I really can't think what can have happened to Norman," fretted the old lady, who told them her name was Agatha Morton and that she had just been to London. "He's usually so punctual." Her face paled. "I do hope he hasn't met with an accident in that old car of his."

Jean tried to comfort her. "Oh, I shouldn't think so, Mrs. Morton. He may have had a puncture, or perhaps he's run out of petrol. We shall probably meet him somewhere along the road."

But though they struggled on with the cases for nearly twenty minutes, there was still no sign of her nephew by the time they reached the manor.

Mrs. Morton started when she saw a light burning in the library. "Surely Norman can't have forgotten I was coming back home today."

"I don't expect he would do that," said Jean.

A few moments later the two girls had deposited the cases in the hall. "We'll be getting along now," smiled Jean.

"Certainly not. At least, not until you've had a nice cup of tea and some cream pastries!" beamed Mrs. Morton. "Norman? Norman! Where are you?" Her voice echoed hollowly in the large house, but there was no reply.

"He doesn't appear to be in," she frowned. "Perhaps you were right, Jean, and he has gone into the village to buy petrol. Never mind, I'm here, thanks to you both. Make yourselves comfortable in the library. It won't take me long to make a pot of tea."

"But really—" began Jean.

"I insist!" Mrs. Morton hurried off and the friends stared at each other.

"It's going to make us late for the dance," Mary murmured, glancing at the clock.

"Never mind," smiled Jean. "She's probably glad of our company." She frowned. "Funny about her nephew not turning up, Mary. Even if he did have to visit the village garage for petrol and missed the train, he should have arrived back home by now. Gosh, my arms still ache from the weight of that case."

"And mine, too." Mary's eyes twinkled. "It's given me an idea. We could go to the dance as railway porters. The station-master would lend us two jackets."

Jean sighed. "I suppose so. But it's not so romantic as being a couple of seventeenth-century ladies-in-waiting. I was so looking forward to dressing up and going to the – gosh!"She broke off with a little gasp, her eyes riveted on the faded oil-painting of a cavalier hanging on the wall over the fireplace.

"What's the matter?" asked Mary.

"The eyes in that picture— I'm sure they moved!"

"Nonsense!" replied Mary cheerfully. "You must be dreaming."

She blinked. "Why, Jean, you're right!" Her voice rose with excitement. "The eyes *are* moving!"

"Help! Help!"

Both girls jumped up, startled, as the faint cry sounded in the room. It seemed to come from nearby, but it was muffled as though someone were in a cupboard.

"Did you hear that?" gasped Mary.

"I certainly did! There it is again!"

They stared about them in perplexity. then a gleam sprang to Jean's eyes. "I've got it! Don't you see? There's someone behind that picture and they've been trying to attract our attention! It must be Norman!"

"But how did he get behind the picture?"

"It's probably a priest's hole," replied Jean. "You often find them in these old houses. Norman must have discovered a secret panel, gone exploring and become trapped. The trouble is, how do we find it?"

They looked at each other, then glanced again towards the eyes staring down at them from the picture. "Where's the secret panel?" mouthed Jean slowly.

Norman seemed not to understand or be able to hear her at first, but after she had repeated the question several times, his voice came faintly from the picture.

"Twist the sunflower on the mantel!"

"Right!" cried Jean, and she was trembling with excitement as she hurried over to the fireplace. "Ah, here's the flower. Now to turn it!"

She seized the wood carving and twisted it slowly. "He's right! The flower's moving, Mary!" She turned it completely round and held her breath. Next moment there came a low creaking sound and a section of the bookcase swung outwards.

"Look! There's a staircase here!" gasped Mary.

Even as she spoke a young man came hurrying down it and into the room. "Thank goodness you tumbled to where I was!" he said cheerfully. "I was beginning to think I was never going to taste one of Aunt Agatha's meat pies again!"

"Then you must be Norman!"

Before he could answer, Mrs. Morton came bustling in and she blinked. "Norman! So there you are. Where on earth have you been?" she asked. "If it hadn't been for these two young ladies helping me with my baggage I don't know what I should have done. What happened?"

"I started exploring the old house, Auntie," he explained. "I found a secret panel which led to a priest's hole. But it shut behind me."

"Well!" Mrs. Morton was flabbergasted. "I never knew *that* existed. But do sit down, girls. Tea is ready."

Soon they were all chatting happily and the girls learnt that the Manor had been left to Mrs. Morton and she had only recently decided to come there to live. Mrs. Morton said the girls were to come up and see her as often as they liked.

But presently Jean and Mary rose to go. "I hope you won't think us rude," said Jean. "But we must dash off now. We're going to the dance in Welford tonight."

"Oh, fancy dress, isn't it? I heard something about it. What are you going as?"

"Probably as railway porters," replied Jean ruefully, and she told the old lady what had happened.

"Oh, how disappointing for you," said Mrs. Morton sympathetically. "But you can still go in fancy dress."

"I don't quite understand," said Jean.

"Well," Mrs. Morton smiled. "I'm staging an amateur theatrical show in the village shortly, and in those two cases you carried are some of the costumes we are going to use! Would you like to wear two of those?"

"Would we!" exclaimed Jean and Mary together. And it turned out to be a wonderful evening, for Norman was their escort dressed as a laughing cavalier!

PEGGY WINS THROUGH

by Hilary Tempest

Peggy's favourite sport was being at the wheel of her father's powerful speedboat and she was anxious that he would let her race it for the Shellgrove Cup. After he had agreed, someone deliberately damaged the boat. Would the boat be repaired in time for the big race, Peggy wanted to know?

With every muscle in her lithe young body tensed to the limit, Peggy Crawford held her boat on a straight course. The tremendous effort needed to control the steering wheel, which seemed to have gone quite mad in her hands, left her almost empty with nervous exhaustion. The speeding cockle-shell which held her skidded less violently across the wavetops; the tremendous frightening clouds of stinging spray subsided. The superhuman struggle was won and she headed for the mark. A few inches from her back, Peggy heard the roar of the outboard engine rise to a new crescendo as she increased her vessel's speed. Laden with spray and spindrift, the racing wind snatched at her auburn hair and battered at her face.

"Golly, what a turn that was," she said to herself. "I'm sure I've never gone round a mark at that speed before!"

Out of the corner of her eye she spotted the blurred outline of a white yacht as she flashed past it. *Home,* she thought. *What a relief!*

The engine's note dropped rapidly as the planing hull fell slowly into the water and reduced its speed. Peggy relaxed gently, glad to be able to breathe freely once more, instead of being forced to fight for each breath against the gale caused by her speed. She eased her boat alongside the jetty, watched it come to a halt, then sat quite still for a moment's rest.

"Peggy, my girl, that was terrific!" The soft East-Anglian drawl drew her eyes upwards.

"Do you really think so, Jacko?" she cried excitedly.

To hear such praise from the dour mechanic was indeed a thrill. Jack Meredith had served her father well for many years and had an unsurpassed knowledge of cars, engines and boats. Peggy had developed the keenest interest in mechanical things ever since she had been a child and it was Jacko who had taken both her and her elder brother, Peter, under his wing, teaching them all they wanted to know with a quiet patience and an inexhaustible fund of good humour.

"Come on up out of there, Peggy. Don't sit there daydreaming too long." Jacko's friendly face smiled down at her as he bent down and offered her a white-overalled arm. "Up you come, lass."

"Do you really think it was as good as that, Jacko?" she asked, as she climbed out on to the jetty. "Does that mean that I've a chance of winning the Shellgrove Cup?"

"Steady on, lass," came the slow reply. "You've done well enough for a young'un, but there's many a long day between that and the Shellgrove!"

"You think I can't do it because I'm not a boy!" said Peggy dismally. "Oh! I wish I had been a boy, sometimes." She pouted as she took the hard crash-helmet from her head and let the mass of auburn curls fall about her ears.

"Steady on, Peggy!" There was a twinkle in the mechanic's eyes as he spoke. "You know as well as I that there's no reason why a lass shouldn't win the Cup. Indeed, one very nearly did these two years back. Remember Babs Whitehead?"

"Gosh, yes!" cut in Peggy excitedly. "She was terrific. It was jolly bad luck that she didn't win."

"That's true enough, Peggy." Jacko spoke quietly. "But remember that you're only just sixteen, love. You may be head girl at St Kits, but you're only a shaver at this game."

"Good heavens, Jacko," protested Peggy violently, "that's not so young. After all, Peter was only sixteen when he won the Cup just before the war."

"Yes, Peggy, I know all too well, but . . ." Jacko paused. "Remember that you've not yet got your Dad's permission to race. He may not mind you messing about in the boat, but he's no idea that it will go so fast and he'll have fifty fits when he hears all this talk about the Shellgrove Cup."

"But we've got to convince him, Jacko," broke in Peggy. "If I win the Cup it will really save his business, won't it?"

A shadow came over the pair as they sat gazing out over the sunlit expanse of the inland lake. In her protest, Peggy had brought up the subject which most worried both of them. Brilliant engineer though he was, Mr Crawford was no business man and had fallen on hard times indeed. Despite his desperate efforts, it was as obvious to his daughter as to his trusted mechanic that, unless something soon happened to change their fortunes, the garage must be sold and the business disposed of. And the true friends knew that such an event would break Mr Crawford's heart.

In the years of happiness before the War, Peggy had been too young to know much of what had gone on. From Jacko, more than from anyone else, she had learned that her brilliant father had invented a new outboard engine and had endeavoured to prove its superiority by fitting it to a racing hull and competing with it in the great speedboat races held every year upon their lake. More clearly, perhaps, than anything else, Peggy remembered her elder brother, Peter. It was Peter's dash and courage that had done so much to spur her father and Jacko to even greater efforts. She remembered his infectious smile and daredevil pluck and she recalled the tremendous excitement which had swept through them all when Peter had raced his father's boat to a brilliant victory.

But the War had followed immediately and their short-lived triumph became first anticlimax and then disaster. Torn from each other by evacuation and by duty, they had been forced to forget the thrill of speeding across glistening wavetops, of the shattering excitement of powerful engines, and to lay aside their great ambitions. The final blow had come when they received the news of Peter's death; when peace was almost in sight, he had flown to a gallant and glorious end.

Peggy's eyes dimmed with tears. As a child she had loved her big brother who had done so much to help her, to win her loyalty and affection. When she had grown up and gone away to school, she saw him as a smiling but serious young man in air-force blue. He became her idol, then, for his manly bravery and his affection for her warmed her right through.

"You're a fine pair, I must say, sitting here daydreaming." A rich deep voice broke in on Peggy's sadness and brought her to earth with a start.

"Good heavens, Daddy!" she cried. "Where on earth did you spring from?"

Mr Crawford laughed. "I've been watching the pair of you sitting there asleep for several minutes. What's troubling you both?"

Peggy looked intently at the tall, spare figure of her father. There was still something of a twinkle in Mr Crawford's eyes, but Peggy knew the worry that lay behind them.

"I was only thinking how lucky I am to have such a wise old man for a father." She grinned impishly. Her father's weather-beaten face creased into a smile.

"Jacko, be thankful that you've not a roguish girl like this as a daughter."

"Oh, I don't know, sir," came the reply. "She's not a bad girl really – as if you didn't know it. And she's quite an expert on speedboats."

Mr Crawford smiled indulgently at his daughter.

"Are you still playing about with that wretched old boat?" he asked. "That engine ought to be a mass of rust by now, considering how badly we had to neglect it all those years."

"It's a jolly good engine," protested Peggy. "I'm sure there's not a better one on the Broad."

"She's right, sir," added the mechanic. "There's nothing wrong with that engine now. That boat would win the Shellgrove Cup tomorrow if she were tried."

"Jacko!" exclaimed Peggy, aghast that her secret had been so precipitately revealed. There was a moment's surprised silence.

"What are you two up to?" asked Mr Crawford. He was stern now and his expression showed that the idea which was growing in his mind was one which did not please him.

"Daddy," broke in Peggy quickly, "wouldn't it be simply

wonderful if we could win the Shellgrove Cup again?"

"That's quite out of the question, Peggy," answered her father. "Just because Peter did it a long time ago, there's no reason to believe that we could ever do it again."

"But it would mean a tremendous amount to you if we could, wouldn't it?" persisted his daughter.

Mr Crawford was startled into rapid thought. Ideas and memories flashed swiftly across his mind. Winning the Shellgrove would certainly put the Crawford engine on the map, as it had begun to do before the War had intervened. The prize itself would undoubtedly help him over his immediate financial worries.

"Well," he said slowly, "I'm not denying that it would help a great deal to get us out of our difficulties, but it just isn't possible."

"We've a sporting chance, Mr Crawford," said Jacko quickly. "On a test lap this afternoon she put up as fast a time as last year's winner."

"And she went like a bird, Daddy," Peggy said excitedly. She was not slow to see her father's eyes light up with interest.

"Even so, Jacko," went on Mr Crawford, "that doesn't mean she'll take the Cup. You know how often you've said that you would never take part in another race. How on earth did you bring yourself to drive the boat so hard today?"

"I didn't, sir," Jacko spoke slowly. "Peggy did."

The silence was strained, tense and full of emotion. But Mr Crawford controlled his anger with an effort that was clearly visible to the two anxious watchers.

"Don't be angry with Jacko, Daddy," pleaded Peggy. "He didn't know that I was going to open her right up."

"It's no good, Peggy." Her father spoke quietly, but firmly. "I've told you that you were not to overdo it. Speedboat racing is a man's sport. I should hate you to have an accident."

"But, Daddy," protested the girl, "Babs Whitehead did very well two years ago and she wasn't so very much older than I am."

"She can do it, sir, if anybody can," said the mechanic. "She's got her brother's gift for it."

"And it would mean so very much to all of us, Daddy," went on Peggy, anxious to press home every advantage. "Think of what it would do for your engine. And it would help you with the business.

I know things aren't going too well."

"But, Peggy –"

"Can't you see how much it will mean, Daddy?"

Peggy refused to be stopped. "You would be able to devote your time to developing and making new engines, without having to worry about scraping a living from the garage. And Mr Morton wouldn't be able to buy you up and force you out of business. And . . ."

Peggy's words tripped over themselves as they poured out. Her face, flushed with excitement and pleading, was turned up to her father's. How could she make him see that she could win the Cup? How could she give him confidence in her and in his engine? She knew it was the only thing which could save him from ruin. If only she could make him agree.

She grasped her father's hands, gripping them fiercely between her own, her body tense with emotion, every nerve strained to its limit in willing her father's consent. Her voice vibrated with the intensity of the plea it carried.

"Please, Daddy – please –"

Mr Crawford looked down at the taut features of his daughter and his eyes softened. "Easy, Peggy," he said gently. "Don't get so worked up about it, there's a dear. After all, you know, this has been rather a surprise to me and I must give the matter serious thought."

"Does that mean you might change your mind, then?" asked Peggy.

"Seriously, old girl," her father spoke more as a friend, "I can't promise to say yes. But didn't you tell me you were expecting a couple of your school friends to arrive today?"

Peggy was suddenly shocked out of her pre-occupation.

"Good heavens, Daddy!" she exclaimed. "Pamela and Lesley! They'll be here at any moment and will find nobody at the station to meet them."

"Come on then, Peggy," said her father quickly. "There's a bus just coming down the hill. If we run along the quay, we shall catch it as it comes over the lock gates."

A quarter of an hour later the three girls were chattering excited greetings to each other as they met on the platform among a throng of holidaymakers. The two travellers seemed an ill-assorted pair in appearance. Pamela Markham was tall and slender with short golden hair that seemed to cling to her head; she was one of the most brilliant girls at St Kits, but her deep blue eyes and challenging look often belied the impression that she was a scholar. Lesley Browning, on the other hand, was short and inclined to be tubby. With her good humour and never-failing sense of fun, she was one of the most popular girls in the school. She was younger than her two companions, who shared a study during termtime, but had teamed up with them in the middle school, for it was then that they had first discovered a common interest – water. Lesley was a swimmer; Pamela had the artist's love for sailing yachts. Whilst the three could never agree about their respective views of which sport was superior, they found that the continual friendly arguments in which they had indulged over the years had made them the closest of friends.

After supper was finished, the three girls sat together on the lawn watching the summer sun reddening over the water.

"Well, Peggy," said Pamela, "what have you been up to since term ended?"

"Oh, nothing much," answered the redhead airily, "except that if I can get Daddy's permission I'm going to try to win the Shellgrove Cup."

"You're what?" exploded the two girls simultaneously. "You're kidding!"

"I'm not. I was never more serious in my life," retorted Peggy with an amused laugh at her friends' disbelief.

She went on to explain how she and Jack Meredith had secretly reassembled the engine and reconditioned the boat with which her brother had won the Cup so many years earlier. Her two friends had already heard much of Peter Crawford and of the Crawford engine; they knew that Peggy was passionately fond of speedboats and loved tinkering about with motors. But the idea of her entering for the famous Shellgrove Cup, one of the premier trophies of the sport was almost too much for them to grasp.

"Golly, Peggy!" laughed Lesley. "The Head always has called you a tomboy. What on earth she'll say when she finds out about this, I really don't know."

"One thing's certain," continued Pamela, her blue eyes alight with amusement. "She's sure to say something about not upholding the 'dignified tradition of the young ladies of St Kits'."

All three girls chuckled heartily.

"Well, girls, feeling tired after a long journey?" Mr Crawford joined them in the twilight. All was at peace now; nothing moved across the placid surface of the water at the end of the garden. Across the lake the dark marshes were already becoming one with the black water and the night sky.

"Do you think it will be a fine day, tomorrow, Mr Crawford?" asked Lesley. "If it looks nice we might all go for a swim."

"I think it will be a glorious day, Lesley." came the answer, "but remember that the water here can be quite chilly, even in midsummer. What was all the hilarity about, just before I came out?"

"We were just thinking of the Head," answered Pamela, "and thinking of the expression on her face when she finds out that Peggy has raced for the Shellgrove Cup."

Mr Crawford chuckled. "Remember that I've not given Peggy permission to race, yet," he said. "But, Peggy," he turned to his daughter, "Jacko thinks you can do it, so I want to see you do a trial spin in the morning."

"Daddy," cried Peggy excitedly, "what spiffing news! I'm sure I'll not let you down; I know we can do it!"

Peggy, Lesley and Pamela could hardly wait to finish breakfast before dashing down to the quayside. The morning had dawned bright and warm and now the smiling waters were iridescent in the brilliant sunlight. Pausing for a moment at the water's edge, they gazed out across the sparkling expanse of Broad, with its fringe of park and houses at the near end and a deep belt of wild reeds stretching away into the distance, as a natural border to the barely visible dyke which led to the main river.

"Golly, Peggy!" exclaimed Lesley enraptured. "It's really lovely, isn't it?"

"It's certainly breath-taking," said Pamela. "It must be very beautiful in the spring and autumn."

"It is," admitted Peggy. "Very beautiful. I think I love it most at the beginning and end of summer, although it's always just coming to its loveliest when school starts again."

The sound of a hammer ringing on metal brought them back to reality. From the shed at the end of the quay came the deep, unmelodious voice of Jacko, the warm Suffolk broque sounding strongly as he sang a traditional waterman's air.

"She'll be all ready to go in ten minutes, Peggy," he cried gaily as he saw the girls at the doorway.

Eagerly they pressed forward to watch his deft fingers making last-minute adjustments to the huge and powerful motor which would soon be driving Peggy over the water at speed. Once he had finished, the girls helped him launch the super-light racing shell and to attach the great engine firmly to its stern.

"Well," said Pamela, in wonder, "I thought I'd seen some outboard motors in my time, but this is far and away the biggest ever!"

"It is a big one, Miss Pamela," said Jacko with a grin, "but there are bigger. These racing engines are a good deal bigger and very much more powerful than the normal ones you see."

"That's true enough," broke in Peggy. "And it's ten times more powerful than it looks," she exaggerated in her enthusiasm.

"Ah!" said Jacko. "Mr Crawford's engine has got a lot of power. I reckon it's the best engine of its class in the world."

Pamela and Lesley sat on the quayside and watched the skilled mechanic filling the tanks and checking that all was well. Peggy went off into the shed to change into the tough slacks and leather jerkin which she would wear when racing. Round her chest she fastened the special life-jacket which would keep her afloat should she be flung into the water and finally tucked her auburn curls as far as they would go into the hard crash-helmet.

"Well, Peggy, are you all set?" It was Mr Crawford who spoke. He looked intently at his daughter, knowing full well the difficulties and dangers of the sport she could no more resist than her brother had been able to.

"Yes, Daddy," she answered. "Don't worry. I'll do one lap to warm up, one for timing and one to come in on. All right?"

She did not wait for more than a smile and a nod before she stuffed into her ears the plugs which would deaden the tremendous roar of the motor during the trip. She smiled gaily at her two friends as she watched them do the same; they would need them only until she had left the quayside. Swiftly Peggy slipped aboard her craft and checked over the controls and engine. As ever, Jacko had left everything perfect. She turned to the mechanic, her face calm and confident. As she gave the signal, the mechanic operated the starter and the great engine crashed into pulsating life. For a moment Peggy let the motor run, watching the frail craft strain at its warps and listening for the smoothness in the exhaust note which would tell her that all was well. She turned and nodded to the group on the quayside, a smile on her lips. At the signal, Jacko cast off the mooring line and the speedboat moved slowly out on to the lake. Once clear of the harbour, Peggy allowed her vessel to gather speed rapidly as she headed it out for the buoys which marked the course. Faster and faster she went as the racing hull lifted until it was skimming the surface of the water.

As she came near to the end of the first lap, Peggy waved to the group of watchers on the shore to tell them that all was well. Then she turned into the course and opened the throttle to its fullest extent. The speedboat sprang forward as the mighty engine gave a tremendous roar and settled slowly down to giving its maximum power. Peggy crouched low in the shallow cockpit, every muscle tensed against the biting, spray-laden wind that beat on her face like a solid wall of ice. Her eyes flickered from the instruments, which told her that all was well, to the yellow mark growing larger out of the water ahead, the mark around which she had to turn. She slackened the boat's headlong flight to give it more stability and put into the turning all that she had learned. The boat skidded wildly across the wavetops and the girl driver's heart missed a beat as she fought desperately for control. Then she was back on the straight and going even faster. Peggy felt conscious only of the tremendous excitement of this exhilarating motion and of the need to keep her boat tearing forward as fast as it would go.

The trial over, she slowed the fragile racing shell and brought it quietly alongside the quay once more. After the dynamic shattering roar of the exhaust, the sudden silence as the engine came to a stop was almost unbearable. Scarcely stopping to take the plugs from her ears Peggy leaped ashore, her eyes shining with hope and excitement.

"Well, Daddy?" she asked breathlessly, "how did I do?"

Mr Crawford looked quizzically at his daughter. "Fine, Peggy," he said. "You've just put up the fastest lap over that course that I've ever timed. I don't think Peter did much better when he broke the Shellgrove Cup lap-record!"

"Does that mean that you'll let me enter for the Cup?" asked Peggy, really excited now.

"I hardly think I can refuse you, dear," said her father softly, "but you must promise not to be rash."

The happy girl was deluged in the excited congratulations of her two friends and of the mechanic who had done so much to help her. All of them were now thoroughly convinced that she would win the Cup upon which her heart was set, although neither Pamela nor Lesley were really aware of just how much it would mean to the fast-falling fortunes of the Crawford family.

The whole party sat in the warm evening sunshine, the day's work over, still discussing Peggy's chances and her wonderful performance.

"I'll tell you one thing," said Jacko. "We weren't the only people interested in Peggy this morning. I saw another lass timing the laps and she looked mighty annoyed when you had finished."

"Golly!" said Lesley. "Any idea who she was? You sounded as if she were a stranger to you."

"That she was," answered the mechanic. "She was a stranger, all right, but I'm convinced I've seen her photo somewhere. If only I could place her."

"Wait a moment," said Pamela thoughtfully. "Now you mention it, I vaguely remember noticing her myself. Do you know, Lesley, I believe it was that woman we spoke to in the train."

"She was a foreigner," answered Lesley, "cos you spoke to her in French. She wanted to know if she had to change to get here, didn't she?"

"Yes." Pamela was thoughtful. "But she wasn't French. I should say she was probably Italian. Weren't the initials on that case of hers C.d.P.?"

"Camilla del Ponta!" broke in Peggy in a high pitch of excitement.

"That's the girl," followed Jacko. "I remember now! The trickiest speedboat driver in Europe, they say, and one of the fastest!"

"And not among the nicest to know, either," announced Peggy. "Some people say that she'll stop at nothing to ensure that she wins."

"You'd better watch her like a hawk when the race begins," was the advice of Mr Crawford. "Better get in all the practice you can."

As the day of the race grew nearer, it became evident that Peggy's chances of winning the Shellgrove Cup were really good. Indeed, many of the old hands who saw her practising were convinced that she would win. It was obvious that her most serious rival was the raven-haired young Italian and despite the efforts of Peggy and her friends, the foreigner had remained rather a bitter sullen stranger.

"A very early run this morning, I think," said Peggy, "and then finish. The Cup race is tomorrow and the Broad will be horribly crowded soon."

Even Mr Crawford made no secret of his excitement, whilst Pamela and Lesley were almost beside themselves that their school friend should be such a favourite. It was with cheer in their hearts that they dashed into the quayside shed once more.

"Come on, Jacko," cried the three girls together. "Get her out and let's get started."

The mechanic turned, his face a picture of misery and hatred. His voice broke as he spoke. "Peggy," he said slowly, "look!" In his hands he held two rods of gleaming metal.

"That's Daddy's special propeller-shaft metal, isn't it?" said Peggy, sensing that something was amiss.

"That is the propeller shaft. There was only that one," came the bitter reply, "and we haven't a spare."

Peggy was nearly in tears. "But, Jacko, it couldn't possibly break. It would mean I'd be out of the Cup. Oh, no! Daddy's work wouldn't let me down like that!"

The three girls had never seen such a look of violence on the mechanic's face.

"It didn't break," he said. "It's been deliberately sawn in two!"

"But who on earth could have done such a terrible thing?" Pamela asked.

Neither she nor Peggy noticed Lesley slip quietly away. Chins sunk deep in cupped hands, the two sat at the water's edge, gazing glumly out across the sparkling waves which glistened in the warm sunshine. Despite their misery, they could not stop their eyes from lifting to follow the breakneck progress of the white speedboat which skimmed across the waters at a tremendous pace.

"Camilla del Ponta!" said Peggy absently. "She's certain to win the Cup now."

"She certainly is going fast," said Pamela, interested in the Italian girl's brilliant technique despite herself. "I must say that she looks happier this morning than at any time since she came."

Suddenly the blonde girl sat upright and faced her companion.

"Peggy," she asked quickly, "you don't think she could have cut your shaft? I saw her crowd jabbering together in great excitement when I passed their shed this morning. Now I come to think about it, I'm sure they were talking about you and laughing. I'll bet one of them did it!" she ended vehemently.

"Never mind, Pam," Peggy answered without enthusiasm. "It's done now and can't be undone. Even if we could get the special material, we could never make a new shaft in time."

Yet even as they watched, the white speedboat came in. From it stepped the swarthy girl, her attractive face contorted into a malevolent smile of triumph. Seeing Peggy and Pamela, she walked over to them and gave both a look of sympathy. For a few moments she spoke to them in French, commiserating with her former rival, before departing to her shed.

Suddenly the air was rent by the pounding of feet and an excited cry. Running down the quyaside, her face flushed with excitement and exertion, came Lesley.

"Peggy! Pamela!" she cried. "Come here, quickly!"

Surprised at this sudden change in their normally placid friend, the two girls rose and went quickly to meet her.

"What on earth's the matter?" asked Pamela.

Lesley's breath came in gasps. "Peggy . . . get the bits of that shaft . . . quickly. When's the next train . . . to London?"

"But, Lesley," expostulated Peggy, "what's this all about? Calm down and tell us what's exciting you."

"Well, girls," came the quick answer, more coherent now that the plump girl had recovered her breath, "I've been on the phone to Daddy and he says he'll make us another shaft if we can get the drawings or pieces to him in time!"

"Oh, Lesley," cried Pamela, "what wonderful news!"

"But, Les," queried Peggy, her heart beating loudly, hardly daring to be convinced, "that shaft was made of a special alloy. How can your father make another?"

"Your dad spoke to mine," came the answer. "Mr Crawford found that Daddy had something which would do the trick – at least, for the race. Your dad gave mine the general idea of what is wanted and Daddy will get the works cracking on the job right away. All we've got to do is to get the details right!"

With a concerted whoop of joy, the three girls rushed back to Peggy's house, pausing only to collect the sabotaged shaft from the startled Jacko. Despite the efforts of her father and friends, Peggy refused to remain at home to rest for the race. She was determined to go with the precious job, to hold tightly to this slender chance of real hope as long as she could.

A glance at the time-table and a brief word from Mr Crawford assured the three friends that it would pay them to make the journey by rail, for there was a fast train within the halfhour and another which would get them back late the same night. They knew that the train journey would be quicker than the trip by car and that, in any case, if they failed to catch that last train back, they would not return in time to have the engine reassembled for the race. Soon they were speeding southward towards London, the great express racing across the flat marshlands of the East Anglian coast. The three girls sat together in the dining car, tucking into a very early lunch.

"Golly," said Lesley, "I'm really hungry now!" Her companions chuckled, as the remark really broke the tension of the last hours. Neither could recall the time when Lesley was not able to face up to a meal, no matter how awful or discouraging the situation in which she found herself placed.

"Well," said Pamela, "it's a good thing we came by train. We won't have to stop to eat."

"I don't think I could bear to stop anywhere to eat," commented Peggy. "I couldn't swallow food if it meant delaying us."

"Which is the best reason for our being here!" retorted Pamela, ever watchful of her anxious friend's needs. "Now you have no excuse for not having lunch."

Yet even as they approached London, the girls began to grow more anxious. Gradually they became conscious that the train was moving more slowly. They grew certain that it would be late in arriving. Peggy's heart sank slowly as she felt every precious minute slipping past, each one lessening her chances of getting back in time for the big race. All her thoughts were concentrated on willing the train to greater speed, for she knew that failure would mean ruin for her father. Only by winning the Shellgrove Cup and the huge prize that went with it could she do anything to save her father's business. Surely it could not be that, having once been cheated by some unknown agency, this heaven-sent miracle would fail her. It was with an anxious face that Lesley's father met the train at the terminus and drove them right across London to his factory. The train had been very late in arriving and he was ever growing more doubtful whether the new shaft could be made in time, although he did not show his anxiety to the girls.

As the afternoon wore on, the girls waited. They had wandered through the great factory and watched the gleaming machines for a while. The whole works were aware of Peggy's plight and each man toiled with all the skill and speed he could muster, so that she might have a perfect job in time. The girls had tea in the office, but as the evening grew and the shadows lengthened, Peggy grew paler with worry and fear. Time was rushing past and she felt the agony of despair as she became more and more convinced that she could not return in time. Time and again her two friends urged her to rest, but she could not. Her eyes grew hot and tired as she gazed ceaselessly at the clock, relentlessly ticking off the minutes.

Even as Lesley's father came rushing to the office with the new shaft, her heart told her that it was too late, that it was impossible to cross London in time to catch the train back.

"It's no good," she said slowly, her broken voice revealing all too clearly the depth of her misery. "We couldn't possibly catch the train!"

All eyes in the room turned towards the clock on the wall. Peggy had told the truth which they had not dared to admit to themselves; it was too late! The train would have gone almost before they had begun their journey across the city.

Swiftly, Lesley's father crossed to his desk and spoke into the telephone.

"Don't despair, Peggy." He turned to the heart-broken girl. "All is not yet lost. I've told my wife what's happening and I'll drive you all the way home. We may be a bit slower than the train, but I'm sure we'll get there in time."

Swiftly he led the three girls out into the car, ordering Pamela and Peggy into the comfortable rear seats. Dumbly, Peggy allowed her fair-haired friend to settle her down snugly under a couple of warm travelling rugs. Worn out with the long slow despair, she could not really believe that they would succeed. But the smooth, gentle swaying of the car as it raced out into the darkened countryside, quieted her overwrought nerves a little and the wheels softly drummed out their reassuring message. "Will I be in time? Will I be in time?" The question ran endlessly through her anguished brain. The cry grew for a while in intensity as fatigue caused her to lose grip on her selfcontrol, but slowly it settled into quiescence, became softer and less insistent, came less frequently and more drowsily as she fell exhausted into sleep.

"Come along, sleepyhead!"

Peggy opened her eyes and saw Pamela smiling down at her, proffering a cup of tea. She sat up slowly and looked around her sun-flooded bedroom. As she drank her tea, the events of the previous day came back to her.

"We're all to have some lunch and then – off to the boat," said Pamela.

"Is it as late as that?" queried Peggy, in some alarm.

"Don't worry yourself," came the reply. "It will be an early lunch and you'll be in plenty of time for this afternoon."

Soon the two girls joined Lesley and Mr Crawford at the table. Despite the growing excitement and tension, Peggy ate a huge meal, for she was aware of how little she had eaten since noon the previous day. She was overjoyed to hear her father's reassurance that everything would be ready in time for the big race. Jacko had been working on the precious Crawford engine since dawn.

"Incidentally, Peggy," he said, "I've told nobody about the shaft, but most of the people seem to know about it. Even the stewards came round this morning to see if you would be racing. How on earth they found out, I don't know."

"I've a pretty shrewd idea," cut in Lesley. "Those Italian mechanics have been telling several people that Peggy's shaft is broken. They've been boasting that Camilla del Ponta is certain to win now."

"But how did they know?" asked Mr Crawford. "Jacko hasn't said a word to anyone."

"They could only know all about it if they were responsible for doing the damage," Pamela told them, with an air of conviction.

"Well," said Peggy quietly, "since I doubt whether we can prove it now, it doesn't matter."

Lunch was soon over and it was a happy party that made its way towards the boathouse. The brilliant sunshine was reflected from a million tiny wavelets on the glistening expanse of water. Around the fringe of the Broad lay scores of white yachts at anchor, each one crowded with spectators and bedecked with flags. Thousands more, who had come to watch the famous race, thronged the great park and the specially erected stands. The more privileged spectators were already wandering about the harbour and quaysides, inspecting the boats which were soon to be competing for the famous trophy and chatting to their favourites among the drivers. The girls noticed that the Italian team was not without followers and that the sallow, dark-haired Camilla looked confident.

"You'll want to watch her every inch of the way, Peggy," said Jacko, who had now joined them. "She'll spare no effort to beat you by foul means if she can't do it by fair!"

"Jacko!" exclaimed Peggy, her excitement growing as she spun round to face the mechanic who was now garbed in spotless white overalls. "How's that engine?"

"Never fear, lass," came the quiet reassuring answer. "I've tickled the new shaft into place and she sings as sweetly as a bird."

Eagerly the three girls followed Mr Crawford and the mechanic into the shed for a last inspection of the great Crawford engine. Peggy's heart beat happily as she saw it, glistening and polished, all ready to spring into shattering action. Eagerly she helped her friends to carry to the water the scarlet racing shell in which she would soon be hurtling over the waves. Whilst the mechanic and Mr Crawford busied themselves with the great motor upon which so much faith was pinned, Peggy retired to the tiny room at the back of the boat-house.

As her two friends helped her to change into the slacks and leathers which she would wear during the race, Peggy felt a lump swell in her throat, for she was conscious of the debt she owed both of them. Without their help and encouragement she would not now be facing the greatest task of her life, the winning of the famous Shellgrove Cup. Out in the brilliant sunshine once more, the three girls realized from the swelling turbulent murmuring of the huge crowd that the tension was growing rapidly even among those who had come to watch.

Peggy looked at her wristwatch. Ten minutes to go!

"Scared?" The soft voice of her father at her elbow broke into the tumult of her thoughts. She nodded quietly. Her father knew the fear which grips every competitor a few moments before any great race.

"It will be all right once you get started," he said reassuringly.

Amid the excited well-wishing of her two friends, Peggy plugged her ears against the deafening roar of the engine, gave her father a long, warm hug and climbed aboard her speedboat. With every nerve tensed to concert pitch, she joined the mechanic in a careful last-minute check of the engine, adjusted the controls and gave the starting signal. The great Crawford engine at once crashed into life.

Conscious suddenly of the task which lay ahead, Peggy felt her heart sink. It seemed impossible that she could hold her own against these experienced competitors, let alone beat them.

Slowly the fragile-looking speedboat moved across the sunlit water towards the official starting line. As her craft cleared the general melée in the harbour and became visible to the many watchers, Peggy heard a great warm-hearted cheer rise from the crowd assembled to watch this epic race. Whatever her chances, she had been taken to their hearts! Rapidly the cheering grew, as boat after boat moved to take up its position for the start. Peggy glanced at her watch. Two minutes to go!

She looked around fearfully, seeing the grim goggled faces and tensely-held bodies of her competitors. Away to her right, the glistening white hull and dazzling green helmet showed where Camilla del Ponta lay. Peggy tried to steady the violent beating of her heart as she watched her rival for a moment. Her wrist flicked open the throttle lever with an automatic gesture as she saw the flash of the starter's gun. The craft leapt forward, snarling like some unleashed

Ten minutes to go!

terror of the primitive jungle, jerking her body first backwards then forwards as it accelerated.

Wildly Peggy's eyes sought the brilliant yellow of the distant buoy which marked the first turn. Her eyes narrowed to slits as she held her course and accelerated to avoid the closing in of her nearest competitor. All fear was now forgotten. There was no thrill left, only a dreadful cleaving of a huge parched tongue to the roof of a very dry mouth and a feeling of tension. She swung wide at the first mark, tucked closely behind the crashing spray of a black shape ahead, then raced down the next leg striving to coax more speed from the roaring engine so that she might overtake before the next turn. Spray flew off the water and beat like gravel on her face.

Desperately Peggy clung to the bucking wheel as the fragile shell danced and bounced around the mark. Even as she fought the incipient skid with all her strength, her attention was caught. Out of the corner of her eye she saw a flashing white shape almost on her tail, a flash of white topped by a brilliant spot of green! Camilla del Ponta!

Slowly the Italian girl drew closer, until the two boats drew level, racing neck and neck. Side by side the two girls raced, lap after lap, each trying desperately to outwit and outmanoeuvre the other. *Only three to go now!* Her thoughts raced ahead for a moment. The great-hearted Crawford engine had proved its worth, keeping her level with her more experienced rival. But the race had still to be won. Dimly she realized that she and Camilla had drawn out ahead of the fleet; the battle must be won by one or the other. Grimly each held on to her course, striving to delay the turning to the last moment, striving to force the other to make the fatal error.

The Italian girl was growing more anxious as her every trick was countered by the superior speed of her English rival. Neither girl was conscious now of the roaring of the crowd, or even of the other competitors. Nothing mattered save the tremendous duel they fought. Suddenly Peggy screamed! Camilla del Ponta was not slowing down for the turn into the last lap, but was creeping ahead, close – terribly close – beside Peggy. In a flash the Italian's intention became clear. She was going to risk everything on a sharp turn close to Peggy in the hope that the wave caused by her sudden change of course would roll Peggy's boat right over!

Desperately the English girl slowed, hoping that Camilla would get far enough ahead to turn without doing the damage she intended. *Better to be second than to be rolled over,* thought Peggy. *At this speed it might be fatal!* Conscious that she had drawn ahead, the Italian girl looked back. Her ruse had succeeded and she laughed. But the strain of twisting her body, already almost exhausted by the gruelling race, poved too much. As she lurched in an endeavour to retrieve her balance, her grasping fingers spun the steering wheel. The white boat began to turn then, as the full strain of the turning force conflicted with its momentum, it skidded violently away across the water to crash, completely out of control, into the rushes of the bank.

Peggy saw the fate of her rival and shuddered, knowing that if Camilla had had her way it would have been she who crashed thus. Deeply thankful that she had slowed down, Peggy turned the marker buoy and accelerated down the finishing straight.

As she raced over the line she became conscious once again of the cheers of the great crowd. They were shouting and cheering wildly as she shut off her engine and let her speedboat drift, too exhausted to do more. Dimly the realization percolated into her tired brain. Slowly she realized why they were cheering. The great race was over. She had won the coveted Shellgrove Cup!

She smiled wanly at her father as he lifted her from the speedboat. "I've done it, Daddy," she whispered. "Now we're safe from trouble at last."

THE SECRET OF THE PHANTOM WRECKER

by Anne Gilmore

Stella Berriwick was horrified to hear there were tales of mysterious wreckers on the island next to the one where she lived. Soon, the ghostly ringing of a bell and a frantic SOS message led her into a desperate adventure in the Pirate's Cave.

"Ugh! Gosh, this is creepy!" decided Stella Berriwick. "Why am I reading this when I'm all alone in Rockcliff Castle?"

She looked up from the open book on the desk before her. It was a large, heavily bound volume entitled "The Legends of Rockcliff Castle." Stella had taken the book from the ancient library into her cosy sitting-room on the ground floor because she was enormously interested in the castle which she had inherited; she wanted to know all about it. But perhaps she had not chosen the best moment to pursue her enquiries. It was now dusk. Except for herself the castle was empty. Her young bailiff, Lance Millerchip, who looked after the castle and its affairs when she was at school, had gone to the village. Every servant was out, having been given a ticket by Stella to attend the circus which had pitched in the nearby seaside town of Cliffborough. She was entirely alone.

"Perhaps I'd better stop reading," thought Stella. "Or am I getting silly and nervous just because I'm on my own?"

For a moment she sat thinking over the legends she had just read–most of them eerie and mysterious.

"Of course, none of them is true," she told herself. "They're jolly creepy, though. I'll read on," she resolved.

She smiled at her vague apprehensions; then she rose and switched on the light. She sat down again, opening the book at random. She blinked as she read the title on the page which confronted her.

THE LEGEND OF THE WRECKERS ON GREEN ISLAND.

"Green Island!" she thought–for the island was barely a quarter of a mile out to sea and belonged to the castle. "How odd, when Green Island is the very spot where I'm taking the village children for a day's picnic outing on Saturday –"

She dipped back into the book with interest. It was an absorbing story which was told there–how, two hundred years ago, Green Island had been the haunt of wreckers–a gang of scoundrels who used a fake bell buoy to lure ships on to the rocks, then attacked the helpless crews and looted the ships. Among those wreckers was a bearded ruffian known as Red Steve who, posing as the Sergeant-at-Arms in the castle itself, gave the wreckers the signal when a ship was approaching.

"Jolly exciting," Stella murmured as she finished reading. "But I'm glad there are no such villains in these days!"

She closed the book. Outside the rising wind howled more loudly, a note of menace in its voice and through the dark, racing clouds fitful beams of the full moon came and went. Outside the old white owl croaked again. She went to the window, intending to draw the blinds. She glanced out over the high cliff on which the castle stood. It was practically dark now. The sea, running out rapidly on the ebb tide, glistened sulkily in the light of the retreating and returning moon and rolled and boomed with a growling voice. Only by staring hard could she make out the vague hummock which was Green Island. Mechanically her hand reached up for the cord with which to pull the curtains to. But even as she touched it she tensed. What was that? For faint and far off, from the direction of Green Island, came the sound of–a bell!

"The wreckers' bell!" Stella caught herself thinking, and then, deciding that the legend she had just read was affecting her nerves, shrugged crossly. "But no–of course not. What can I be thinking about?"

However she found herself going rigid, as faint, but clear, the notes of the bell boomed out again.

She looked round, her heart thumping a little. Stella was by no means a nervous type. There must be quite a simple explanation.

Perhaps somebody was merely ringing a bell on the unseen beach below. She drew the blinds, but as she did so the bell clanged out again. A little agitatedly she turned back into the room. She caught up the book, thrust it into her bureau and closed the lid. Then she swung round as there came a sound at the door.

"Who is that?" she breathed. "I heard someone –"

She listened. She could still hear the distant clang of the bell. But now something nearer engaged her startled attention. For, from the hall outside, came a shuffling step.

"Some–someone is in the hall!" Stella breathed.

Her immediate and instinctive action was to switch off the light. Then, with her heart jumping a little, she pulled open the door which led into the great old hall with its shining armour, its brooding pictures and the wide gallery which surrounded it. She peered out. The hall was shadowy in the growing dusk. Then she stood rigid, her eyes popping wide. For out of the room in which she stored the Berriwick relics and which she called her "Museum" came a figure. It was a figure the first sight of which sent a chill down Stella's spine.

It was the figure of an old-time sailor, jackbooted and bearded; wearing a three-cornered hat and a red tunic. In eerie fashion the figure glowed like some luminous, coloured shadow. In its hand swung an old-time ship's lantern which gave out ghostly light. Stella clung to the door.

"It–it looks like the phantom wrecker!" she whispered, gazing at that eerie figure in the castle hall.

For a moment she was frankly terrified. She ought to have cried out, but she didn't. Curiosity, as well as fright, seemed to hold her spellbound. She waited. Swinging the lantern the spectral figure moved to the main doors. It threw them open. Then, leaving them still wide, it disappeared.

Stella gulped a breath of relief.

"But who is it?" she asked herself. Obviously this was no ghost! No, it was somebody dressed up in phosphorescent garments and playing a trick, she decided. But why play the trick here–in the very castle itself? Then she thought of the lantern. It was one of her own museum specimens–yes, dating back to the time when the legend must have been invented.

"But who–and why?" Stella drew a deep breath. If this was some attempt to scare people in the castle, then she was going to do something about it–at once. Swiftly she hurried across the floor. From the stand she snatched down her coat. Quickly she belted it tightly; then stepped into the night, groping her way in almost pitch darkness towards the Barbican. The fresh wind hit at her face and blew back her hair. From the unseen Drummer's Tower to her left the white owl hooted throatily. But Stella hurried on–into the darkness of the Barbican and into the outer court beyond. And then again she saw the ghostly, luminous figure moving across the cliff top towards the gulch, a narrow, ditch-like trackway which led down the cliffside. The lamp, swinging in the figure's hand, threw an eerie, glowing shadow about it. Then the figure had reached the gulch and disappeared.

Stella, drawing a deep breath, followed cautiously. She reached the top of the gulch. She peered down. She could hear steps crunching upon loose stones below and realised that she dared not follow, for the loose stones would also betray her presence. She stopped, watching. The footsteps ceased. Stella moved to the edge of the cliff and peered over. She could see nothing at first, but suddenly a weaving patch of light moved across the sands heading for the sea, and she knew that was the phantom figure. She watched as it advanced with hurrying steps into the sea itself.

"Whatever is it going to do?" Stella asked herself wonderingly.

Now, suddenly, the figure faded. At the same moment the moon broke through the scudding clouds, floodlighting all around. She stared out to sea, marking the hump of Green Island. Plainly she could make out its sandy beach, for the tide, at this time, was at its lowest ebb. And then suddenly she saw the figure of the wrecker again. She gave a startled, incredulous gasp. There it was, a small moving silhouette in the moonlight, plodding its way to the island. It was in the very middle of the channel that separated Green Island from the mainland and–

"Oh gosh! Am–am I seeing things?" Stella thought shakily.

But no–there was the figure, actually walking towards the island, the sea leaping about its feet. Tensely Stella watched, filled with amazement as it made its way slowly through the waves until at last it reached the shore of the island and the trees swallowed it up. Stella stood there, quivering and a little scared. What should be her course of action now?

"There are boats in Rockcliff Creek," she said to herself. "Shall I row out to the island–now–and investigate?"

The very thought of it made her shiver a little. But throwing off her nervousness, she hurried down to the creek.

"That figure – whoever it is–must be on the island still," Stella told herself. "I'll row over and–and challenge him!"

Brave words! And Stella would have carried them out, but even as she stepped into a boat and seized an oar she realised how impossible it was. A thick white mist, like a blanket, was enveloping Green Island and the sea around it. Such a mist, as Stella knew, was always liable to come down suddenly. It might stay like that for hours–perhaps till dawn–shrouding the island, although the mainland itself would remain quite clear. Impossible to hunt for anything– or anyone–on the island now. Shaking her head, she made her way back to the cliff-top.

"Stella!"

She turned with a violent start. Then she laughed shakily. In the moonlight her young bailiff, Lance Millerchip, came hurrying towards her.

"Stella, I was just going back into the castle. Then I saw you standing here–like some statue in the moonlight, gazing out to sea. What's the attraction?"

"Lance, I don't know. Either I'm seeing things or legends have started coming true."

And then rapidly she told him of her experience of the last hour, starting with the tolling of the ghostly bell.

He glanced at her sharply.

"You're sure, Stella?"

"Yes, Lance, I'm guite sure."

"M'm!" he frowned. Then he took her arm. "Let's go back and look in your museum. If your old lantern has gone, then obviously the wrecker–whoever he is–came to steal it."

They went back to the castle and into the museum. Sure enough, the old-time lantern was missing from its accustomed place.

"So that was it," Lance said. "He wanted that lantern. But why should he dress up like that?"

"Ask me!" Stella said feebly.

"You say he left the castle by the main doors – along the cliff-top and down to the gulch?" Lance asked.

"Yes!"

"Righto! Wait here while I get a torch, then we'll have a hunt round."

Stella waited while Lance rushed upstairs to his own room. In two minutes he was back, a powerful torch in his hand.

"Now let's go and see what we can find."

His eyes were very steady and keen as he led the way outside, Stella following rather wonderingly, but not afraid any more. The moon was still bright, but in spite of that Lance persisted in shining his torch on the darker patches of the ground as they went.

"Look! You can see his prints here and there."Lance said.

Then, as they searched for clues to the mystery, he suddenly stopped.

"What is this? Look, Stella!" he exclaimed, shining his torch on the ground. "Is it a clue to the phantom wrecker?"

Stella stared down and then gasped, hardly able to believe her eyes. She blinked and looked again. Yes, there could be no doubt. What she and Lance were looking at was a rather big and rather comic false nose!

"How did that get there?" he demanded, picking it up.

"I'm sure I don't know," Stella returned. "Unless–" with sudden enlightenment "it was dropped by one of the village children the other day. You remember–one or two of them dressed up at the party we had."

"I remember," Lance said. But he shook his head. "No. It wasn't dropped by one of the youngsters. If it had lain here all that time it would have been damp. Remember, it rained this morning. But it's bone dry, which means that it was dropped here not so long ago. This false nose, Stella, was dropped by your ghostly wrecker! I shouldn't think it was part of his disguise, otherwise he'd have missed it. So–he must have lost it accidentally."

Stella nodded. That was very clear.

"It's a comic nose," Lance pointed out. "So it's possible that the man was just a practical joker. Or–" he suddenly stopped. "Gosh!" he breathed excitedly.

She looked at him with wide eyes.

"Lance–what?"

"I don't know. But I've half an idea–more than half," he said, rapidly. "I'll tell you about it–later." He looked at her. "Stella, will you go back to the castle? The servants will soon be back."

"Yes," she answered, wonderingly. "But–but what are you going to do, Lance?"

"I'm following up the clue of this fake nose," he said a little surprisingly. "I'll tell you all about it later. Don't say anything about what you've seen, will you? Don't do anything until you hear from me again. And don't worry about me, Stella. I may be a little late getting back."

"Lance, won't you–"

But Lance, in that impetuous way of his, had turned. With a wave of the hand he went striding off–not in the direction of the gulch as she had thought he would–but in the entirely opposite direction–towards the village. Puzzled, Stella retraced her steps towards the castle. Still vastly mystified she hung up her coat. Half an hour later the castle servants returned. They had all enjoyed the circus, they said, but one or two of them appeared strangely nervous. Stella sensed at once that something had happened. After they had gone for a meal she asked Janice Crowe about it.

Janice was more than a maid. She was Stella's sincere friend and companion.

"Janice, what's wrong? Some of the maids seemed a little scared about something."

Janice bit her lip.

"Well, Miss Stella–"

"What is it, Janice?"

"Well, perhaps they–they are a bit scared." Janice herself looked by no means assured. "You know that Rockcliff Castle hasn't had a very good reputation in the past because of all its ghosts and legends. We all thought they had been cleared up, though, until this afternoon–"

"Oh?" Stella looked at her quickly. "Janice, tell me!" she urged.

"Well, we got mixed up with a crowd of people from the village," Janice said. "And–and they were all saying that the wreckers have come back to Green Island."

"The wreckers? You mean–" Stella drew a deep breath. "Red Steve?"

"Yes, miss. They say he's been seen–all ghostly and glowing. They say that the bell buoy sounds again, though there is no bell buoy these days at Green Island. They say that Red Steve has been seen hanging around the castle."

Stella paused, compressing her lips. But she decided not to tell Janice what she herself had seen. She said:

"But–but surely they don't take these tales seriously."

"I don't know," Janice said haltingly. "Some of them do, I think." She paused. "And–and–I'm sorry it's me who has to tell you this, Miss Stella. But you'll soon have to know. The parents of the village children for whom you were planning the picnic outing on Saturday are fair scared of Green Island now. They–they say that while the wreckers are about they won't allow the kiddies to go to the island!"

That came as something of a blow to Stella, for she had made great plans for the kiddies on the Green Island picnic day. The ghostly figure of the wrecker was now more than a baffling mystery. It was definitely proving a menace. If he was reported to have been seen again, there was little doubt that half the servants would leave the castle. Also, there was the mystery of the ringing bell buoy.

"But perhaps," she thought, "Lance will come back with news. Where did go–and where is he now? And how, I wonder, could that false nose he found have any bearing on the mystery?"

She sat up until midnight waiting for Lance and then, as he had not returned, she went to bed determined to discuss the matter with him on the morrow. But tomorrow came and Lance had still not turned up–nor had any word come from him. Stella's wonder turned to worry as the morning wore on. Had something happened to him? After lunch Stella had a visitor. It was Miss Chase, the teacher at the village school.

In her brisk way she came bustling into the hall . . . that same hall through which, last evening, the phantom wrecker had made his eerie way.

"A bad business, my dear," Miss Chase exclaimed. "I'm more than sorry, because I know you'd set your heart on it. But there it is–it's off!"

"Off?" Stella queried.

"The picnic!" Miss Chase cried. "I've just had a kind of–well, deputation of parents at the school, Stella. And they've asked me to let you know that, while grateful for your kindness, they just can't let the children make the trip to Green Island on Saturday–because of these rumours of wreckers' ghosts and phantom bells."

Miss Chase patted Stella's shoulder.

"All nonsense, of course," she declared. "But you know how superstitious the folk are around here. I argued, but they won't change their minds. And, between ourselves, my dear–"

The schoolmistress paused.

"There is *something* odd going on," she confessed. "As I lay awake last night I heard a bell, Stella–ringing faintly from seaward–from the direction of Green Island. No phantom bell, of course, but–well, it's queer."

Stella nodded.

"It's certainly queer," she replied. "And thank you for coming to tell me about the picnic decision, Miss Chase. It just can't be helped."

All the same, it was a keen disappointment. Stella had made such wonderful plans for that picnic. There was to have been a fabulous tea, and a treasure hunt–she'd spent hours working out the clues–with games and sports of all kinds. It was to have been an outing that the village kiddies would have remembered for years. Now it was all washed out, Stella sadly reflected, as she watched Miss Chase's sturdy figure bustling away. No picnic, and–no Lance!

"Surely I should have had word from him by now," Stella worriedly thought. "He'd know I'd be feeling jolly anxious. He wouldn't keep me in suspense, if he could help it. And yet he–"

Hours rolled on–still no Lance. Teatime–and still no word from Lance. Restive and uneasy, and fearing she knew not what, Stella went for a walk on the beach at dusk when the tide was out again and gazed towards the island. With a little shiver she remembered the figure which had walked on the water last night. The dusk thickened. Soon it would be night. She was turning away when from the island came the sudden booming sound of a bell.

The bell buoy! The buoy which, legend said, had lured ships to their dooms in the past. A shudder went through her. She stared at the island again. But nothing was to be seen except the moon flinging spangled silver patterns on its slopes and trees. Then again the bell clanged.

Who was ringing it–and why?

"Well–" she came to an immediate decision. "I'll find out!"

The bell was still ringing when she jumped into one of the two boats which were kept in the Rockcliff Creek for visits to the island.

The tide was well out, but a deep rivulet carried her into the open sea. And there, resolutely, she headed towards Green Island.

But suddenly she paused.

What was happening to the bell? It was changing its note.

For now, surprisingly, the chimes came rapidly. They were coming–not from the sea, but from the island itself. So, thought Stella, somebody's actually on the island sounding the ghostly bell–no wonder that the buoy itself had never been seen. Resting on her oars she strained her ears trying to detect from which part of the island the sound came.

"It's stopped!"

For a few moments there wasn't a sound save the swish of the moonlit sea and the monotonous boom of the breakers. But now, clearly, the chimes came again, in a series of uneven ringings. Clang, clang, clang–a pause. Then a single clang. Pause again. Clang–pause. Clang–pause. Then clang, clang, clang again. A sudden excitement shot through Stella as she recognised the significance of those sounds.

"SOS! The morse code!"she breathed. "Somebody is signalling with the bell from the island–"

She stopped, listening intently again as the signals commenced once more. Now she spelled out other letters, her pulses leaping as she turned them into the highly significant words:

"P-R-I-S-O-N-E-R L-A-N-C-E—"

Lance. *He* was ringing the bell! He was sending out the message. And Lance was a prisoner on the island. That accounted for his non-appearance at the castle all day. But now–Stella felt her finger-tips tingle. She realised at last that she was at grips with the mystery. What lay ahead on the island she did not know. She only knew that she must hasten to the aid of the boy who meant so much to her-and Rockcliff Castle. Swiftly she dipped the oars again, thrusting her craft through the water. It was not easy rowing, for often she scraped the bottom. At low tide the rocks formed a sort of causeway between the main shore and the island and were only a little way below the surface. But she pressed on.

At last she had reached the island, beached her boat and stepped ashore. As she did so there came another clang. And again the signal spelled itself out:

"P-I-R-A-T-E C-A-V-E–"

Stella's heart bounded. She knew the Pirate Cave–just a hundred yards inland. But who might be watching–ready to pounce? With heart thudding, she stole up the bank, taking advantage of all the dark cover she could find. Her nerves twanged as a disturbed bird suddenly flew from under her feet with a hoarse cry and a metallic flutter of wings. Had that given her away?

She stopped, tensely listening. But there was no sound.

She crept on, looking from right to left. On through bushes and bracken, through tall rush grass which scratched her legs. At last she came to the dip in which Pirate Cave was situated. She crept towards it. Near the entrance she stopped.

"Lance!" she called softly.

"Stella–thank goodness!" came a hoarse voice from inside. "It's all right–for the moment at least. Come inside."

Flashing the torch she had brought with her, Stella entered the cave. As she did so she saw suspended from the roof a largish brass bell, hanging by a slender length of rope. The wind shifted and it gave out a faint chime.

"So that was how it was done," she muttered. "Somebody hung the bell here so that every time the wind blew it would ring. I–" and then moving the beam of her torch downwards, she gave a gasp.

"Oh, Lance!" she cried.

"Thank goodness you've come, Stella!" he burst out.

Lance was bound, but not gagged. A trail across the floor of the cave showed how he had dragged himself from its farther end to get to the bell. In a few moments Stella had untied his bonds.

"That's better. Thank you!" Lance breathed, rubbing his wrists. "I wondered if anyone would ever find me. But–"

"But, Lance, what happened? Who did this to you?"

"Well, you know I found that comic nose? It gave me a clue. I followed it up in Cliffborough and came back to the island. But I was slugged by the phantom wrecker while I was exploring this cave–"

"But, Lance," said Stella in puzzlement. "He tied you up. So– so how were you able to peal the bell as a signal?"

For a moment Lance grinned, and Stella smiled too.

"I know! You used your teeth!" she cried, and Lance nodded.

"But come on now," he said urgently. "I think I've got something to show you."

Bewildered Stella followed as he caught her hand, tugging her back through the bushes and the undergrowth. In a few minutes they had reached the shore again. There Lance picked up a long length of timber–flotsam from the sea.

"Now–watch!" he breathed.

Stella looked across the causeway, her heart thudding as she wondered what Lance had in mind. And then she tensed as a shining, luminous figure, carrying an old ship's lantern, appeared on the opposite beach.

"The wrecker!" she breathed.

"Wait!" Lance whispered tensely, and pulled her down behind a large boulder.

She watched as the figure came walking into the sea. And once again her unbelieving eyes widened as she saw that he was walking apparently on the very surface of the water. But he walked strangely, slowly, as though dragging one leg after the other, his lantern swinging and jerking at his side.

"That lantern." Lance breathed. "I can't decide whether he stole that to complete his costume, or whether he came to the castle hoping to scare the servants–for of course he didn't know they had all gone to the circus."

Stella was still gazing with fascinated eyes at that strange, eerie figure, as slowly, steadily it drew nearer. Now it was within a few yards of the island. Suddenly Lance straightened up.

"Don't move," he breathed.

In his hand he gripped the length of wood. Now he swung it back. The next instant it left his hand to go whistling across the intervening space. It shot true to its mark. It caught the surprised wrecker across the chest. With a screamed "a–aha–a!" he went backwards, toppling into the water.

Immediately Lance ran forward, plunging in towards him. Stella cried out: "Lance!"

But Lance was on the wrecker before he had risen. Palpitating with anxiety Stella watched the brief fight which followed. But Lance was strong and tough. A sudden blow to the jaw sent the wrecker splashing back. Unheeding the water Stella floundered knee–deep to help Lance.

"O. K." Lance grunted. "I've got him this time. Help me drag him to the shore, Stella. Then we'll tie him up."

Stella caught one of the wrecker's arms, Lance the other. The man was still dazed when finally they dragged him in to dry land. There Lance tied him up and then plucked the false beard from his face.

Stella stared.

"Gosh! Who is he?"

"A clown–from the circus at Cliffborough," Lance answered.

"A clown–"

"Yes and a clown who's got a few bagfuls of smuggled jewels back in that cave. We'll get those later, Stella. It was while I was examining them that he crept up and slugged me."

"But how did you find out all this?" Stella asked in amazement.

"Because, as I told you, that false nose gave me the clue. I was flummoxed at first. Then I remembered the circus at Cliffborough. It was a clown's nose and I felt certain there was a link. So–as you know–I rushed off immediately to investigate."

"I went to the circus," Lance went on. "There I learned that one of the clowns–Alf Griffiths, this fellow–was missing. He was famous," he added significantly, "for stiltwalking."

Stella gave a start. In a flash one big mystery became clear.

"So–so that's how he crossed the causeway–walking on stilts! That's how he appeared to be walking on the surface of the water?"

"Exactly," Lance agreed. "Look, you can see the stilts floating there." And for the first time Stella saw the two long stilts that drifted a dozen feet away.

"I put two and two together," Lance went on. "I came back here to find out things. In the cave I found little packets of jewels–also some papers which proved clearly that Alf Griffiths was in the habit of meeting a boat here and taking from the captain packets of jewels which had been smuggled over from the continent. You see," he added, "Alf Griffiths had an idea. He knew all about the legend of the wreckers and brought it back to life by faking the ghostly bell buoy and disguising himself as Red Steve so as to scare off any people from this island."

"So that's the explanation," Stella breathed. "Oh, Lance, how clever you are! One more ghostly mystery at Rockcliff Castle has been cleared up."

"It sure has," Lance said cheerfully. "And that means you'll be able to have your picnic without any fear of the wrecker, Stella. Now help me to bundle this chap back into the boat and we'll row him to the coastguard's station."

Stella willingly obeyed, grateful to Lance, her faithful friend, who again had helped her to remove a threatened shadow of fear from her beloved castle.

THE WANDERING SANDS

by Denise Kerry

Carol Peters, a young teacher at a school in the Australian bush, took her school girls on a picnic. When a fierce wind arose, they became lost on the wandering sands, without water or food. Rescue came to them in an unexpected way.

Cla-ang . . . cla-ang.

The cracked sound of the Myrtle Wells school bell rang out across the open, rolling country of the Australian outback. Steadily Carol Peters pulled the rope that rang the bell, summoning her pupils from the cattle stations that were scattered distantly about. The school stood alone, in the centre of the cattle stations, so as to be convenient for all the pupils. Though the building was built of weather-beaten planks, and looked more like an old barn than a school, Carol was proud of it. It was her first school, for she had only recently qualified as a teacher–in the city of Sydney to the south–and she was in complete charge.

A city girl herself, everything was still new and strange and wonderful to her, from the lizards that darted about the sun-soaked walls to the call of a distant kookaburra, or laughing jackass. Suddenly, there was a movement at the side of the building and a girl came trotting shyly into sight. She was an aborigine, her skin was very dark. But her eyes were bright and intelligent and though the dress she wore was very old and much patched it was scrupulously clean. She halted, seemingly overcome by the sight of the young teacher and she stood on one leg, rubbing the other big toe in the dust.

"Hello," smiled Carol. "Are you coming to school?"

The aborigine girl smiled with a flash of white teeth and nodded her head.

"What's your name?" asked Carol. "What name b'long you?" she added in pidgin English.

"My name–Muramati," was the girl's answer.

Where had she come from? Carol wondered. There were other aborigine children at the school, the daughters of cattle workers at the stations–as ranches are called in Australia–but Carol had never seen Muramati before.

"Well, let's get you on the register," Carol smiled. "Come along inside and we'll get you some books, too. Can you read or write at all?"

The girl did not answer. She was gazing round the bare, shabby schoolroom in awe, as if it were a palace. It was almost as if she had never been in a building before. Carol entered her name in the register and allocated a desk to her. While she was doing this she heard the growing sound of many hoofbeats. Her class was coming. There were a score of girls at the school, some white and some aborigine. From every direction they came riding on their hardy, cattle-trained ponies.

"What a happy-looking crowd they are," Carol thought as she watched them arrive and turn out their mounts in the shaded paddock at the rear of the school.

The class thronged into the schoolroom. They were of all ages from ten to fifteen. The oldest was Joanna Bigtoe, an aborigine girl whose father was chief stockman on the Tumbling Trees station. Carol was marking the register when she heard Joanna's voice raised in anger.

"What are you doing here? This is no place for you!"

Joanna was standing over Muramati, scowling down at her. Carol quickly asked what was wrong.

"This girl," said Joanna indignantly. "What is she doing here? This is school for civilised people. She is only walkabout girl."

"She's from one of the wandering tribes," explained Margot Johnson, a white girl.

Though most of the aborigines were now settled, working on cattle stations or in the towns, there were still a few who lived in the old way, wandering wherever they wished, hunting and fishing for their food. And Carol's new pupil came from such a family.

"We don't want savages in our school," Joanna blustered. "Send her away."

Angrily Carol rapped her desk. "You must not talk in that way," she told the big girl. "Muramati may belong to a wandering tribe–but she's fully entitled to an education. I think it does her great credit that she should even wish to come to school. I know a lot of girls who would be glad to avoid it."

There was a little laughter at her joke and some of the tension eased. But Carol noticed that the others kept as far from Muramati as they could. And in the break, while the others chattered or played in eager groups, Muramati was left as a wistful outsider.

"I must get the others to be more friendly," Carol told herself. "It's not fair that she should be shunned just because her people live in the old way."

Hardest of all on the new girl was Joanna Bigtoe. Carol could understand what was in her mind. Joanna had been brought up in the civilisation of the cattle station. She thought of herself as an Australian, not a tribal aborigine. But the colour of Muramati's skin was a continual reminder to her that they both shared the same history–a history of which Joanna was ashamed.

"She thinks that Muramati's presence will make the white girls look down on her," Carol realised. "But that's just nonsense. Nowadays it's what people are that counts, not the colour of their skins or how they live."

Carol tried to make Joanna understand. But it was useless. "She is only a savage," the big girl snorted. "It's a waste of time letting her come to school at all."

And Joanna's attitude seemed to affect the whole school. They all ignored poor Muramati.

Muramati had been with the school for about a month when Carol decided that they all deserved a holiday.

"We'll have a picnic" she declared. "At the Wolomola River. We can swim and we can have a nature lesson, too."

In her mind was the halfthought that this outing might help Muramati. In the open the aborigine girl should know more than any of the others. The announcement was received with delight by the class, save for Muramati, who did not know what a picnic was.

"We all bring tucker," Carol explained. "And–"

"Please, no!" Joanna cried. "Do not tell her. If she brings tucker, what will she bring? Those walkabout people–they eat anything, grubs and worms and–"

There were shudders at her words. Muramati had not seemed to understand. For a moment Carol's eyes sparked indignantly at Joanna's contemptuous words. But then her anger went. Perhaps there was a grain of truth in what Joanna said.

"At any rate," she told the girls, "the picnic will be tomorrow. You know what to bring."

It was a merry group that gathered at the school the next day. All were mounted–for the river lay some ten miles away. All carried a basket or box of food. Everyone was there–but Muramati. Carol asked for her.

"Pooh! She would not like a picnic," Joanna declared. "Why should she go on a picnic when all the time she eats outdoors. Besides–she has no horse."

Carol had a shrewd suspicion that Joanna herself might have something to do with Muramati's absence. But she had no proof of this. Presently the cavalcade set off from the school towards the distant river. None of the girls knew that a sad-eyed, wistful figure watched them leave . . .

The route to the river bordered an area of dry, sandy desert that none of the cattle stations had been able to bring under cultivation because nothing would grow there.

"I should have thought that with all the latest methods they have now they would be able to grow grass on it," Carol remarked.

"Grass on the Wandering Sands!" laughed Joanna, who was acting as guide because her home station ran closest to the river. "Oh, Miss, you should not say that. Often and often they have tried but–"

"The Wandering Sands?" Carol echoed. "What a strange name. Tell me–why do they call it that?"

The aborigine girl shrugged and slowly shook her head. She did not know.

"It's the old abo name for it," Margot Johnson explained. "I guess maybe some of the tribes did some wandering in the sands."

The explanation did not satisfy Carol but no one knew of a better one and the school members trotted on their way. At last the cool, shaded waters of the river came in sight. The girls dismounted and tied up their horses. The weather was hot and the pleasure of swimming was even greater because of this. It was a pleasure that the girls had not been alone in seeking for as they approached the stream several great kangaroos went splashing out of the water and bounded away.

"This is wonderful," Carol breathed as she swam in the clear, cool water. "We must do it more often."

After their first swim, Carol set the girls to gathering nature specimens.

"A good job Muramati's not here," sniffed Joanna as she brought a big, handsomely marked caterpillar. "She'd probably want to eat this."

They had another swim and then they lit a fire and began their picnic meal. It was while they were doing this that Carol noticed the clouds gathering in the west.

"It looks like rain," she remarked.

"Rain!" scoffed Joanna. "It never rains this time of year. This is the dry."

Yet as she saw the dark mass of clouds piling up, Carol grew more uneasy.

"I didn't think the wind ever blew from the west here," she remarked.

"It doesn't," Joanna answered, eating greedily. "Never ever has it come from the west."

"It did in my father's time," Margot objected, and some other girls agreed with her.

"The day of the Big Wind," Margot went on. "The old folk still talk of it sometimes."

Flocks of birds flew low overhead, moving eastward, and this added to Carol's dismay.

"Perhaps we should make for home," she said.

There were groans of protest from some of the girls. But Carol's mind was made up.

"We're going," she insisted.

As she spoke there was a sort of moaning in the air. An instant later the wind came, fiery hot and filled with stinging particles of sand.

Inside moments no one could see more than a foot or two. It was hardly possible to stand.

"Get down the bank," Carol cried. "Shelter there."

She dragged the girls to the river's bank. There they would get some protection from the fearful strength of the wind. Ankle deep in shallow water, they crouched together while the wind roared overhead. Even protected by their towels, the girls found it hard not to breathe in the choking sand that filled the air. While the sandstorm raged, Carol passed back and forward along the line of girls, encouraging the younger ones, keeping them all close and in the shelter of the bank. A great crashing sound told her that she had chosen well in making the river bank their shelter and not the trees, for the fury of the gale was bringing the trees down bodily.

How long the dreadful storm lasted none of them knew for the sand had penetrated even into their watches, stopping them. But very gradually at first then quite quickly the wind's roar faded to a grumble, then a moan. Then the storm was passed and the sun was shining again.

"Oh thanks goodness," breathed Margot Johnson. "Wasn't it dreadful?"

For the girls the first thought was to wash the sand from their faces and then to drink deeply of the river water. Carol climbed the bank, followed by Joanna. The aborigine girl gave a great cry.

"The horses! Our horses are gone!"

It was true. The spot where the animals had been tethered was now empty. The frightened animals must have torn up their tether pins and fled for safety. How would the girls get home? It was a disconsolate little group of girls who gazed round them at the wind-swept landscape.

"My poor Neddy," wailed little Tina, the youngest of the class. "He's lost."

"I wouldn't worry too much about the horses," Carol smiled. "I'm sure they'll all find their own way home."

"What about us?" asked a girl.

Carol had already been considering this carefully.

"I think we should wait here," she said. "Someone's sure to come and help us."

"But–but it might be hours before anyone comes," Joanna

"Get down the bank," Carol cried. "Shelter there."

protested. "Why, they might not even be able to come tonight. The cattle will be scattered and everyone will be looking after them."

"It would be a long walk home," Carol warned.

But it was at once plain that all the girls wanted to head for home. Many were thinking of the worry of their people. None was willing to wait the night beside the river.

"All right," Carol agreed. "We'll go then–if you all feel up to it."

They set off at once. And almost at once they met a new worry. For the country seemed completely altered since their arrival at the river. Familiar landmarks had vanished. Now a sea of rolling sand seemed to cover everything.

"So that's what they meant by the Wandering Sands," breathed Carol. "They have certainly wandered in the last few hours. But–but how are we to find our way now?"

"Pooh," said Joanna. "it will be easy."

She seemed to have recovered her confidence completely. She stared straight ahead.

"Are you sure?" Carol asked. "It–it doesn't look too easy."

"We have lived here all our life," said the big aborigine girl. "Of course we can find our way."

Carol hesitated. But after all, as Joanna said, they had lived there all their lives. She was only a city girl. Probably there would be no difficulty in finding the way. And surely an aborigine girl like Joanna would be even more skilled at path-finding than the others. Yet she was not completely happy as she gave the order for the march to continue.

At first the girls laughed and chattered among themselves but as they plodded on they began to fall silent. The wind had blown the sand in every direction. They had to cross the new-made, rolling dunes. They had no other choice. It was very hard going with feet sinking at every step into the loose sand. The pace grew steadily slower.

"I wish I had a drink," a girl croaked. "I–I feel as dry as the flue of a fire."

Carol had some paper-wrapped sweets in her pocket–fruit drops–and she passed them round the schoolgirls. They helped a little. But as they moved on, Carol was growing more and more worried. Were they going in the right direction? Surely there should be some familiar landmark in sight by now. Carol let herself drop to the rear where she could help the younger girls along. Though they struggled on bravely, they were plainly tiring rapidly.

"It can't be so very far now," said Margot Johnson. "We should see the trees round the school soon."

They were nearing the top of a long, sloping dune as the girl spoke. But Carol scarcely heard her words. Nor did she look ahead for any sign of the school trees. Instead, she stared at the ground before her. For on the slowly shifting sand she could see two bits of paper. Dropping to one knee, she picked them up and stared at them in dismay, for they were sweet wrappers–the very wrappers from the sweets Carol had given the girls! They had returned to the spot where they had eaten those sweets some time before. They had been travelling in a circle!

There came frightened cries from the girls as they saw the pieces of paper Carol was holding.

"We've just been going round and round," someone whispered. "We're–we're lost!"

Every gaze turned to Joanna.

"You said you knew the way," a youngster said accusingly. "And–and now we're lost–lost in the Wandering Sands–"

Carol could sense the wave of anger and fear that swept the girls. In a moment it could become panic.

"That's enough," she rapped crisply.

"Joanna tried to help us all. But she didn't realise how bad it would be, how the movement of the sands had changed everything. You mustn't blame her."

As silence fell, Carol's gaze swept the horizon. What should they do now? Which way should they go? The girls looked hopefully at her. Her mind was hard at work. It might not be wise to press on during the fierce heat of the day.

"First," she said, "we'll all have a rest. Everyone lie down on the shady side of the dune. Try to sleep."

"And–and when we waken?" a girl demanded. "What then?"

"It'll be near sunset," said Carol. "Or getting on that way. The sun sets in the west. That'll give us our direction. In fact, if our watches were going we could get the direction from them and the sun."

"But what happens after sunset?" Joanna demanded. "We will have no direction then."

"We'll use the stars," Carol explained patiently.

The girls settled down on the shady side of the dune. Carol's face was anxious as she looked at them. Would her plan really work?

"If only we had some water," she thought, growing a little drowsy. "It would help the youngsters especially."

Despite herself, she dropped off to sleep for a little, still thinking of the water that was so vitally needed. She had not slept long, she thought, when she awoke. But the sun was already low in the west when her eyes blinked open again. Immediately, her eyes widened in surprise. Almost at her side there lay a two-gallon can. Surely it had not been there when she lay down? She lifted it. It was full. With trembling fingers she unscrewed the cap. It was full of water. *Water!*

Carol gazed at the can, hardly able to believe it was really there.

"Water," one of the girls groaned.

Carol rose and went quietly to her. Gently she poured a few drops of the precious water between the youngster's lips. The taste of the liquid brought the girl to wakefulness at once. And her cry of delight wakened the others. In a moment there was a surging crowd of thirsty girls round Carol. Not until their parched throats were satisfied did any of them think to ask where the water had so wonderfully come from. And Carol could not tell them.

"I can't believe that anyone would come along and leave us water without wakening us," she said. "The only explanation I can think of is that the water was there all the time. It might have been hidden by the sand when we lay down and our movements while sleeping disturbed the sand enough to uncover it."

It was a poor explanation, but it seemed the only one possible, especially as the girls could find no sign of any tracks of a stranger. Carol wasted no time now. From the sun she had got a direction. The little party moved on. As the sun went down and they waited for the stars to rise after the brief twilight, Carol made a line in the sand that would give them their direction when the stars could be seen. And again they moved on. Though thirst was no longer a worry, Carol was still anxious. Would the strength of the youngster last out till they reached safety?

"The girls need a good meal," Carol thought. "They're hungry. But just a little food would keep them going."

Yet there could be no hope of food in that barren waste. Nothing grew there. Nothing moved, not even a goanna, the little lizard of the outback. On plodded the schoolgirls and their young teacher. But all the time they were moving slower. It was Margot Johnson who first caught the odour that came drifting down the gentle breeze.

"Miss Peters," she gasped. "I–I could swear I smell something cooking–stew, it's like."

"We're still a long way from anywhere there's likely to be food," Carol answered a little sharply. "You shouldn't raise–" She broke off. She, too, could smell food cooking. "Follow the smell," she ordered.

They did not have to follow it far. Soon they could see the glint of a fire through the night. Eagerly they all broke into a run, shouting in delight. It must be a rescue party. It must! Then, as they neared the fire, silence fell on them all. For the fire was deserted. There was no one near, no sign of anyone–only the fire blazing merrily in the midst of the desert–and a big, battered cooking pot steaming above the flames. It was an eerie sight.

Whose could it be? Who could have left their camp like this? For a moment an almost superstitious silence fell on the girls. They huddled closer. Then one of the youngsters burst forward.

"I don't care who left it," she cried. "It–it smells wonderful. And–and I'm hungry."

Carol had already made up her mind. Whoever owned the fire and the food would not grudge it to the lost schoolgirls. "Let's tuck in!" she cried.

It was easier said than done, for the stew in the pot was hot and among them all they could muster only one spoon and one fork–Carol's, which she had slipped into her pocket at the river.

With spoon and fork each of the girls took their turn at the stewpot. And all too soon it was empty. There was a new spirit in the party as they moved on. But Carol was thoughtful. An idea had begun to build up in her mind. They had walked for less than an hour when something happened that made Carol's idea harden into certainty. From ahead there came the whinny of a horse. The girl's first thought was of a rescue party. Then, as they drew nearer, they found that there were horses, but no riders. The horses were tethered to picket pins of rough wood.

"Who can have left them here?" cried Joanna.

She broke into a run. Then, as she neared the horses, she halted in bewilderment. "B–but that's my horse!" she cried.

"And mine!"

In wonder and delight the girls cried out as they saw their own mounts.

"They–they must have kept together," gulped Margot Johnson. "And–and halted here when the wind stopped."

"And do you think they tethered themselves, too?" asked Carol. "As you see, they're firmly staked."

"Then – then who could have done it?" demanded Joanna.

Carol did not answer. The girls mounted and rode on, relieved at no longer having to walk yet murmuring their wonder among themselves. On horseback, less than an hour ended their ordeal. But yet another surprise awaited the girls as they neared the school. For lights burned brightly in the building. Many horses were tethered round it. A few cars were parked in the yard.

"Our parents!"cried Margot. "Our people are all here."

Wonderful was the relief on both sides as the party entered the school yard. Mothers and fathers rushed to hug and greet them. At last the hubbub subsided, however. Margot's father held his hand out to Carol. Joanna's father, Horatio Bigtoe, was just behind him, delight beaming on his dark face.

"We've certainly got to hand it to you, Miss Peters," said Mr. Johnson. "When that sandstorm blew up we guessed what would happen. We were all set to start searching the Wandering Sands. Then you bring them all out, cool as a cucumber. For a greenhorn, you did a wonderful job."

"You mustn't thank me." Carol said, shaking her head. "I could have done nothing without help."

"Which of them helped you?" Mr. Johnson demanded. "Joanna I guess she'd be able to find her way all right."

"It was none of us," the big aborigine girl mumbled.

"Who was the helper then? I've got to thank him," said the cattle station owner.

"We don't know," one of the girls said.

But Carol was looking round, out into the darkness that surrounded the school.

"Muramati," she called. "Muramati, will you come here, please?"

There was a moment's pause. Then the aborigine girl came trotting into the circle of the light. But she was not alone. Three aborigine boys followed her, looking round uncertainly at the circle of cattlemen.

"Muramati!" gasped Margot. "It was Muramati who saved us? Muramati who brought the water–the food–the horses–"

"Brothers help too," said the aborigine girl, smiling shyly and indicating the lads with her.

"Yes," said Carol. "It was Muramati's knowledge of the wild that saved us all."

"But–but why didn't she show herself?" Margot asked. "She – she could have led us to safety."

Carol eyed the crowd of schoolgirls.

"I think you'd all shown her that she wasn't wanted," she said. "That she was looked down on by you–despised. She didn't want to invite any more rebuffs."

Horatio Bigtoe, who for some minutes had been looking closely at Muramati with increasing disbelief on his face, suddenly gave a gasp. Now he threw himself forward to gather up the child.

"It is!" he cried. "It is the real Muramati. It is the daughter of my brother."

He turned on his own daughter. "Why did you not tell me that your own cousin was at the school?" he demanded. "The daughter of one of the greatest men of our people."

At last Carol began to understand why Joanna had been so harsh to Muramati. She was ashamed of her primitive kinsfolk. She wanted to be thought of as civilised. She did not want anyone to know that she had any relations among the walkabout people. The crowd was dispersing at last. But as she watched Muramati leave, her hand in her uncle's, and as she saw how downcast Joanna had become, Carol knew that in future things would be very different for the young aborigine girl. Never again would anyone look down on the heroine of the Wandering Sands.

THE LONELY HOUSE

When darkness fell on the bleak moorland, Hazel and Monica knew that they were lost and would have to lie down until morning. But the night turned out to be one of great adventure instead.

The two girls had to face it: they were lost. They crouched in the shelter of a rough stone wall and peered at their crumpled map by the light of a torch.

"The Youth Hostel *ought* to be here, if my map-reading's right," said Monica doubtfully.

"Since there's nothing but howling wilderness all round us," sighed Hazel, "it's pretty certain your map-reading's wrong!"

Darkness had overtaken Hazel Hill and Monica Drayton much earlier than they had expected on their week-end tramp across the wild hills. "Perhaps we could pick out some landmarks and fix our position on the map," said Monica hopefully.

Hazel laughed. "Landmarks? Gosh, I can see the outlines of a lot of hills against the sky but they all look alike! Monica, you may be a genius in some things, but as a map-reader you're a washout!"

"No need to rub it in," Monica grumbled. "Anyway, we'd better keep pressing on."

"Monica, how do you feel about sleeping out under a wall, or under one of those huge rocks we saw?" said Hazel, as they started to walk along a narrow, stone-walled lane.

Monica shivered. "Clot! Don't make it worse!"

Neither fancied the prospect of a night out on the moors. Silently they trudged on, thinking of mugs of hot tea, blazing fires, everything that didn't happen to be out there with them in the baffling darkness. Then, as they came to a rise, Hazel clutched Monica's arm.

"Look! A light! It must be a house, or a cottage, maybe a farm!"

The lane seemed to lead away from the light. Striking across country, stumbling on tussocks, keeping the light as a beacon ahead, they struck another lane. The light was now hidden by trees, but they came to a wide gateway and saw a drive curving away between a plantation of firs and cypress trees. They hurried on and came to a long, low, stone house, dark except for the one lighted but curtained window.

"What a lonely house," Monica whispered. "It must be miles from anywhere."

Hazel was already knocking on the heavy door. There was a pause, then it opened, slowly, and a man peered out. "Well, what d'you want?" he snapped.

His face was broad, sun-tanned, with a small scar over his left eyebrow. His eyes were small, grey and unwinking, yet Hazel was sure he was nervous.

Smiling at him, despite his hostile manner, Hazel explained what had happened. "Sorry, I can't help you," he said brusquely. Their hopes of being asked in, perhaps being found accommodation for the night, faded.

"Oh!" said Monica blankly. "Well, perhaps if you could point out on our map exactly where we are."

Grudgingly, without asking them in, the man bent to look at the map. His finger stabbed at a house by itself in the hills, shown as a small, square blob. There was a village about four miles away.

"But that's miles from where we thought we were!" Monica groaned.

"Well," he shrugged, "that's where you are! Best make for the village." And he shut the door.

"Come on. Let's hop it," Monica muttered. "I don't want to stay round here, and besides . . ." Her voice trailed away, with a puzzled tone, as the two girls walked away. "Hazel, that house he pointed out has a stream running near the front. There's no stream here!"

Hazel halted. "What d'you mean?"

"Either he made a mistake, or he deliberately pointed out the wrong house on the map! Not only did he want to get rid of us quickly but he tried to make us go even farther astray! He wants to make sure we have no idea where we are!"

"You could be right! There's something strange about this. Oh, what can we do?"

Monica, hurrying along, stumbled suddenly and almost fell. "What's that? I tripped over something." She switched on her torch and both gasped. A dog, a big bull terrier, lay on its side near the edge of the gravel drive.

"Is–is – is it dead?" whispered Monica.

Hazel was examining the dog. "No, still breathing," she said with an angry ring in her voice. "Poor thing! Know what, Monica? This poor dog's been drugged!"

"Then that man–" Monica gasped.

"–Has got no right in the house!" said Hazel. "I'd say this was a watchdog. He drugged it so he could get in – maybe with a bit of doped meat! He must be a – a burglar!"

"Look here," said Monica shakily. "That lane we came up–does it lead to a road? Must do, sometime. We'll have to leave the dog–thank heavens he's not dead–and get help if we can! Come on!"

"Look! A car! What luck!"

Stumbling, bumping into each other, they had come along the lane and reached the road. At first there was nothing in sight. Then they saw the flash of headlights against the sky as the car came out of a dip. Hazel stepped into the road, flashing the torch. The car drew up beside them.

"Anything wrong?" said a deep voice.

Swiftly Hazel explained. The pleasant-faced, burly man at the wheel and the woman at his side glanced at one another. "But it wasn't until we came across the dog–" Hazel went on.

"The dog?" said the man sharply, and Monica explained.

"The scoundrel!" the man continued. "If he's harmed Bruce–"

Hazel gasped. "It's *your* house?"

"It certainly is, young lady! Jump in! By the way, my name's Hayes, and this is my wife."

Soon the car was speeding up the lane and turning into the drive. Mr. Hayes stopped where Hazel and Monica had seen the dog, and

Mrs. Hayes jumped out with the girls. Mr. Hayes got out, too.

"See how Bruce is," he said. "I'm going up to the house."

To their relief, the powerful dog had begun to recover from the effects of the drug. He was still dazed, but could lick his mistress's hand. Hazel and Monica, their hearts pounding, ran on up to the house. Mr. Hayes had let himself in, and he had switched lights on everywhere.

"All right, they've cleared off," he said.

Mrs. Hayes arrived with the car, and helped Bruce, on tottering legs, into the house, where the dog flopped down, panting, to be fussed over by the two girls. A shout from Mr. Hayes attracted them to the lounge, where he stood frowning by an open wall safe.

"Molly, they've taken the formula!" he snapped.

"Oh, no, Tom!"

He nodded, explaining to Hazel and Monica: "I'm a metallurgical chemist. My works have been developing the formula for a new alloy. It's most important; so important that I was going to place it in the hands of the Government."

"And that man stole it?" cried Hazel.

"Probably had an accomplice working on the safe while he was talking to you," said Mr. Hayes grimly. "But there's a chance yet, if you can give me some sort of description of the fellow."

"Well, he was shorter than you, square-shouldered, with a broad, flat sort of face, little, grey eyes and, yes, a scar over his left eyebrow!"

"Bertram!" exclaimed Mr. and Mrs. Hayes together.

"You know him?" said Monica.

"He worked for us as a chauffeur-handyman, until I fired him for laziness and insolence," growled Mr. Hayes. "No wonder Bruce let him get close; the dog knew him well."

He hurried from the room and they heard the car start up and race away.

"We've no phone here," said Mrs. Hayes quickly, "but Tom will contact the police in the village."

It was an hour later when Mr. Hayes returned, and he was smiling.

"Caught 'em red-handed! They took another lane at the back of the house. I knew they couldn't have gone the way we came, or we'd have seen 'em. The police just got patrol cars out and their car was stopped near Wendle. Thanks to you two girls, the formula's safe."

"I'm so glad," said Hazel, then said hesitantly: "Well, I suppose Monica and I had better be on our way. We might yet find that Youth Hostel."

Mr. and Mrs. Hayes exchanged smiles. "You're not going anywhere tonight," said the big man. "You're staying here!"

So that night, after a splendid meal and a merry evening with their hosts and the dog, which was now fully recovered, Hazel and Monica slept in comfortable beds.

Mrs. Hayes was preparing breakfast when their host invited the two girls to take a stroll in the grounds. He took them along a winding path through a plantation of firs and pines, and suddenly, as they came out into the open, they saw a collection of huts, with smoke rising from chimneys, and heard young voices.

"I thought you'd like to see the Youth Hostel," said Mr. Hayes.

"The h-hostel!" gasped Hazel.

"Actually in my grounds," grinned their host. "The Army put the huts up first as a base for training commandos, and the Youth Hostel took over."

"But why didn't Bertram send us here?" said Monica. "We'd have come along happily, and not suspected a thing!"

"Ah, but you might have mentioned something here, and the people would have known he had no right to be in the house," smiled Mr. Hayes. "So he sent you away, and hoped you'd get more lost!"

"Lost!" said Monica indignantly. "Why, we were bang on top of the place all the time! *Now* who can't read maps, Hazel?"

PAMELA TAKES THE PLUNGE

Pamela's fear of horses caused Beryl to fall in the river when she visited her friend's farm house for tea but she soon discovered that Ruby, the old bay mare, had her uses after all.

Pamela Green picked her way carefully over the muddy path which led to Broadmeadow Farm. It took her all her time to keep her footing on the rain-soaked track. 'If this is country life, anyone can have it!' she thought. 'We've been living here a fortnight and it's done nothing but rain every day.'

The river in the nearby meadow was running in full spate. It had long since broken its banks and the surrounding fields were deep under water. In the distance she could see the roof of the farmhouse, but there was no sign of Beryl, the farmer's daughter, who had invited her to tea and had promised to come to meet her.

Pamela was already half-way across the long meadow, when she stopped suddenly. A bay mare, which had been sheltering near the hedge, gave a whinny and came cantering towards her.

There had been a time when Pamela loved riding; but ever since an unfortunate experience at the riding school, she was terrified of horses. Her heart began to thump. She waved her hands and shouted, but the horse only quickened its pace. With its hoofs squelching on the soggy ground, the mare was bearing down on her.

Pamela screamed and turned to run, but she had no chance on the wet turf. Clutching her basket, she tried to get clear, but the mare stretched her long neck, and with her muzzle, sent the apples flying over the field.

Dropping her basket, Pamela threw a frightened glance over her shoulder. The mare, nosing among the apples, started to munch contentedly. Thankful for the respite, the frightened girl reached the fence and clambered on to the lower branches of an old oak tree.

"Pamela, what on earth has happened?" Beryl had reached the meadow just in time to see Pamela running to safety. She hurried to the oak tree and looked up with concern.

"It's that awful horse." Pamela's teeth were chattering. "I'm terrified."

Beryl gave a hearty laugh. "Frightened of old Ruby? She wouldn't harm a fly. She's been pensioned-off for years, only I persuaded Daddy to keep her on. She's too old for anything but a few odd jobs."

"But she came running up to me," Pamela began.

"That's an old trick of hers." Beryl moved across to her. "She usually shoves her muzzle into your pocket to see if she can find a lump of sugar or an apple."

While Beryl was speaking, the old mare had come trotting up to her, and Beryl ran her hands over her warm, satin neck. "Come on down and make friends" Beryl called.

"But you don't understand. I'm simply terrified of horses," Pamela cried. "I was thrown off my horse at the riding school in town. It's different for you. You've always lived in the country."

"But you're going to live in the country now. It's up to you to cure yourself. Come on down. It's getting dark. You can't perch like an owl in a tree all night."

"All right." Pamela managed a weak smile. "But you send that horse away first. Don't let her come near me."

Beryl gave Ruby a sharp slap on the flanks, and the old mare backed away. Pamela stood up on the bough and balanced herself, while her friend reached up to help her down.

"Bother! My foot is stuck." Pamela tried to free herself, but her heel was firmly wedged into the fork of the tree. She tried to free her shoe, but it was no use.

"Let me have a go!" Beryl climbed up the tree beside her and tugged at her foot. She pulled with all her strength, and all at once, the foot was free.

"Look out!" Pamela screamed. As the shoe came off in her hand,

Beryl fell backward. She flung out her arms, but before she could recover her balance she had rolled down the sheer bank and landed with a splash in the swirling flood.

In a flash, Pamela had jumped down from the tree. The rush of water had quickly carried Beryl out of her depth, but she was now swimming strongly in the current. Pamela stumbled along by the fence in an attempt to keep up with her, but Beryl, evidently a powerful swimmer, was already struggling against the swift flow of the river.

Pamela clenched her fists with a feeling of complete helplessness. Then she gave a shout of relief. Beryl was slowly drawing diagonally across the water. She saw Beryl's arm reaching out for a fence post which stood above the level of the water. She drew herself up, with the water swirling around her knees. She was back again on the solid ground of the meadow, and as long as she gripped the fence, she would be free from the pull of the current.

"Hold on, Beryl," she cried breathlessly. "I'll run for help."

She could not tell whether her voice carried over the flooded field, but as Beryl waved back, she felt she must have heard. Pamela set off across the field towards the farmhouse, barely noticing the thud of hoofs as the old mare ran behind her. By now it was getting dusk. Even if Beryl's father were at home, it would take time to get out the flat-bottomed boat and row it across the water. Meanwhile Beryl would be left shivering in her soaking clothes, clinging to the wooden fence.

Pamela stopped in her tracks, and the old mare came to a sudden halt, her breath warm upon the girl's neck. She hesitated a moment, then she set her teeth. Even though her knees were trembling, Pamela flung herself on Ruby's back and turned her head in the direction of the river.

"We've got to do it, Ruby. It's our only chance." She bent her head over the flying mane. The sturdy horse responded gallantly and went straight into the flooded field at a gallop.

When her hoofs lost their grip on the river bank, Ruby began to flounder, but Pamela, her arms around the mare's neck, urged her on. Ruby's head swung round in the force of the current, but soon she was swimming with the strong strokes of her legs. Pamela's arms were stiff, and the water splashed into her eyes, but she held on grimly.

"Good old Ruby! I knew you'd do it."

The old mare lifted her head at the sound of Beryl's voice. Then Ruby's hooves buffeted on the solid ground. She stopped swimming and plodded through the water to the drenched girl, perched on the swaying fence.

"And what do we do now?" Pamela gasped.

"You just stay where you are."

Beryl quickly climbed on to Ruby's broad back, and clasped her arms around Pamela's waist. Pamela turned Ruby's head back into the foaming water. Again she felt the mare struggle as her hoofs lost their grip, but Ruby was swimming as strongly as ever. Snorting against the current, and with the girls urging her on, the old mare crossed the swollen river. In a short time, they were on solid ground and the girls slid off her back.

"I never thought I could manage it." Pamela hid her feelings by shaking the water out of her dripping hair. "Still, I so wanted to help you that I quite forgot my fears."

"Not a bad remedy." Beryl gave her a warm smile. "But we mustn't waste time talking. The vote of thanks must wait till we get out of these wet clothes. Come on, let's make for home."

LITTLE DANCING STAR

by Esmé Nolan

Stella loved ballet dancing and she knew she was very lucky to be taught by the great teacher, Madame Tanya, but nothing she could do seemed to please the great lady. One day, she learned the secret of why Madame Tanya always bullied her.

"Stop!" Madame Tanya's shrill voice rang through the hall. "You are like ze elephants! Clomp! Clomp!"

Her pupils tittered as she imitated them, and some of them grimaced behind Madame's back. "I want butterflies–not cart horses. Again, please!"

Madame's cane tapped and the piano jingled wearily as for the seventeenth time the girls of the ballet class went through their Pas de Bourree. The old lady was in one of her worst moods that morning, and they had already been kept behind for half an hour. Their feet were aching and one or two of them had a stitch.

"The old dragon!" one of the girls whispered, as once more the music stopped and Madame's voice filled the hall. "She gets worse and worse. I don't know why I go on with her."

The others were silent. They knew that for all her severity, Madame Tanya was the finest teacher in England. Nobody liked her, but they all knew of her genius.

"Very well!" Madame screeched. "Ze class dismiss!"

With a sigh of relief the girls shuffled into the changing room, and there was some wincing as they drew off their shoes. But as they sat there exhausted, Madame's tiny figure appeared in the doorway, her hard black eyes darting round the room.

"Just one moment!" She snapped her fingers. "Stella, I want you. You will stay here with me!"

A pale, slightly-built girl with large, expressive eyes rose to her feet.

"Hard luck, old thing," her friend Rosamund whispered sympathetically. "Looks as though you're in for it again."

Nervously Stella followed Madame Tanya back into the hall, wondering what was coming. Her heart was fluttering strangely and her lips were dry. Madame seemed agitated, for she jabbed fiercely at the floor as she walked, leaning awkwardly forward. She could never walk without her cane, for she suffered badly from arthritis in one leg. When they reached the platform she turned to Stella, her eyes glittering.

"Stella, you dance ze disgrace!" she stormed. "You will stay behind after every class for half an hour with me–and work."

Stella's heart sank. Though she would never have admitted it to her friends, she was a little afraid of Madame Tanya. There was something demon-like in the old lady's appearance–the jet-black, glistening hair piled high on top of her head, the thin, bent fingers, almost like the talons of an eagle, clenched round the top of her cane, and those piercing eyes–eyes that never left you for a moment.

"Now!" Madame rapped on the floor with her cane. "We will begin."

And the music from Coppelia streamed out from a gramophone. Later that evening, when Stella slipped away, Rosamund and some of her other friends were at the corner of the street, waiting for her.

"Why, Stella, whatever happened? We thought you were never coming!" exclaimed Rosamund.

"What did she want you for?" Marion's eyes were like saucers. "Has she been beastly?"

"She says–" Stella's voice faltered, "she says my dancing's disgraceful. I have to stay behind with her every day."

"The horrid thing!" Pauline expostulated. "What's got into her?"

"I don't understand!" Rosamund frowned, twisting the tapes of her ballet shoes round her fingers. "You're easily the best in the class, Stella. Everyone says so."

"Oh, I'm not," Stella shook her head sadly. "And Madame certainly doesn't think so!"

"But you are!" Rosamund persisted vehemently. "And she must know it. Do you suppose . . ." Her voice trailed away, and again she frowned.

"What?" chorused the other three.

"Do you suppose she's secretly jealous of Stella? An awfully odd look came to her face the other day, when Stella said it was her ambition to dance like Natasha Ninsky, the famous Russian ballerina."

The others were silent for a moment, staring at each other with wide eyes. The thought had never occurred to them before, and now they began to wonder. Madame Tanya was a bit of a mystery. She was indeed the finest teacher of ballet in the country, but little was known of her background. Nobody seemed to know where she had come from. Perhaps, like Stella, she had longed to be a prima ballerina and had been unable to achieve her ambition, owing to her bad leg. Perhaps, fully aware of Stella's talent, she bore her a grudge. The girl's minds raced back to the time when Stella first joined the Tanya Ballet School two years ago.

"If you remember, Stella, she didn't seem to like you even then. She was always picking on you," Marion said.

"She's just a jealous old woman!" Rosamund declared, decisively. "I suppose we should feel sorry for her, really."

The days that followed were full of anguish for Stella. Whatever she did, however hard she worked, Madame's voice haunted her.

"Go on, again! Again! Higher, higher! No, zat is terrible! Ugly, do you hear, hideous! Again!"

Sometimes Stella would even dream about it at night. She would wake up trembling, the tears running down her face. Everyone she met, every face she looked at, seemed to turn into Madame Tanya. Often, when she was at home alone, she fancied she could hear the angry tap-tap of that cane across the floorboards, and she would get up from her chair, half expecting to see Madame's small, wizened figure in the doorway.

"I don't know how you stick it," Marion said, when late one night Stella appeared at the stage door, almost in tears. "I couldn't."

"Nor could I," agreed Rosamund with a solemn face. "You've certainly got pluck, Stella."

"It's the only thing, when you've made up your mind what you want in life," Stella said quietly.

Her friends looked at her with curiosity and a new admiration. Everyone liked Stella. She didn't say much, but she was the most determined girl in the whole school. Dancing was her life and her one thought was to get right to the top. It was quite obvious that, without ballet, Stella's life wouldn't be worth living.

So the days wore on. Stella had never worked so hard in her life. She was up early every morning and the other girls arrived at the school to find her already there, hard at work, practising, practising, practising. Marion and Rosamund watched her anxiously.

"She'll crack up, as sure as eggs are eggs, if she carries on like this," Rosamund said worriedly.

And Marion, noticing the wistful and faraway expression on Stella's pale face, could only agree with her.

"If only Madame Tanya wouldn't drive her so hard. She's working fit to burst and yet the old lady just gets madder all the time and gives her no praise at all. It's cruel!"

One evening Madame Tanya appeared for evening class with a face like thunder, and the girls knew they were in for a difficult lesson. Stella, of course, was the one who suffered most.

"You get worse!" Madame raged, banging her cane on the barre. "You are not even in time. You will practise for an hour tonight, until you get it right. As for you–" turning to the rest of the class, "you do not yet know the steps!"

Somehow, that night, a demon got into Stella. Tired as she was, she danced more furiously than ever before. The louder Madame scolded, the harder her pupil worked. All her favourite music was played–Swan Lake, Giselle, Coppelia. With all the extra practice Stella had been doing, she felt right on top of her form. Her limbs were lithe and supple and she glided from one movement to the next with the ease of a prima ballerina who had years of experience behind her. Somehow the magical music seemed to become part of her. Even Madame's shrill instructions cutting through her thoughts ceased to bother her. She danced for all she was worth, dismissing everything else from her mind. When at last the hour was up, Stella felt she had really danced well, and turned expectantly to Madame. But not a flicker crossed the old lady's face. Her mouth was tight, her eyes like slits.

"Zat will do!" she said finally.

And without giving Stella another glance, she turned her back. Almost without realising what she was doing, Stella strode up to the platform, and took the old lady by the arm.

"I've something to say to you, Madame Tanya," she said in a low voice. "It won't take long."

Madame swung round and faced her without a word. But she wore a strange expression, one that Stella couldn't fathom, and her eyes never left the young girl's face.

"However much you jeer and rage and bully me," Stella said, her face pale and her eyes bright and glistening, "I shall never give up ballet as long as I live. If you keep me up all night, I shall still become a great dancer–as great as Natasha Ninsky–or die. Goodnight, Madame!"

And Stella swept out of the hall.

Alone in her bedroom that night, Stella glanced at the picture of Natasha Ninsky pinned to her wall. The famous Russian ballerina smiled down at her through a garland of faded roses. It was a strange little smile; Stella could never quite make it out. It was the smile of the Mona Lisa–bewitching yet mysterious. Tonight Stella wondered if that smile was not one of mockery.

"Perhaps Madame was right about my dancing," she said to herself. "Perhaps I'm no good after all!"

Perhaps her great belief in herself was nothing but a dream. Her eyes filled with tears. Was it, after all, useless to go on? But then, in any case, Madame would most certainly dismiss her from the school, after what she had said to her.

"I've done it now!" she told her friends the following day, as they changed for a dress rehearsal of a ballet they were to dance in a concert. "She'll never allow me to stay after last night."

"You were brave," Rosamund whispered. "I wonder what will happen?"

As the class assembled Stella waited, trembling, for Madame to appear. She was waiting to be told that Madame Tanya never wanted to see her again, and the suspense was almost unbearable. The room swam round her, and the faces of her friends seemed unreal. She felt tears pricking her eyelids, and blinked them furiously away.

"I mustn't break down!" she kept muttering to herself. "I mustn't!"

When at last Madame appeared, unusually late for once, something that was almost a smile lurked at the corners of the old lady's mouth. Her voice was calm and quiet as she took them through the rehearsal. After the class had finished, and the girls stood waiting for Madame to give them leave to go, the long-awaited moment arrived.

"Stella! I would like to see you in my room," Madame Tanya said. "Please go there, and wait for me."

So this was the end! Stella felt strangely numb and listless as she walked along the corridor. It seemed an eternity standing there in Madame Tanya's blue sitting-room, hung with portraits of famous dancers of the past. Suddenly, on the bureau, Stella caught sight of a superb photograph of Natasha Ninsky, in a gilt frame. Forgetting everything, she picked it up and gazed at it. She was so enraptured that she did not hear the door open and Madame come into the room.

"Well?" a voice demanded slowly.

"Why do you gaze at that photo? What do you know about Ninsky?"

Stella started, and swung round. Still clutching the photograph, she faced her teacher.

"I remember –" she stammered, "I remember seeing her when I was very small. She was fifty years old then, and I've never forgotten her performance. She danced Swan Lake, Madame."

"You couldn't have been more than six!" Madame said, raising her thin, arched eyebrows.

"I wasn't," Stella said, "but I remember it vividly. Her extraordinary lightness. She seemed to be dancing on air."

For a moment Madame was silent, then she took the photograph from Stella's hands.

"So you think I am trying to put you off ze ballet, by bullying you?" she exclaimed.

Stella blushed, not knowing quite what to say. This wasn't what she had expected at all. She watched the dark eyes narrow, and suddenly the old lady came very close to her, peering into her face.

"You poor silly child! Do you really think I would waste night after

Suddenly, Stella caught sight of a superb photograph of Natasha Ninsky.

night of my precious time coaching you if I didn't think you were my most promising pupil?"

Stella gasped, and stared blankly at Madame. She tried to speak, but the words wouldn't come.

"You have a great gift, Stella–a very great gift," Madame said gently. "That is partly why I bullied you. You see, I wanted to be sure–sure that you loved and wanted ballet enough to suffer anything for it. For that is the sign of a true artist."

Madame Tanya clasped her hands together.

"That was a terrible moment last night, my child, when I thought you were going to give in ze notice. But how happy I was when I learn ze truth! And now–" Madame brought a letter from her pocket, "here is your reward. I have a letter from Paul Savlon, Maitre de Ballet of the Savlon Ballet Company in France. At my recommendation, you are to join his company in April."

At first Stella was dumbfounded. She seemed unable to take it in for a moment, and stood staring at Madame as though she were dreaming. Then at last she found her voice.

"Paul Savlon! But he's one of the most famous Maitres de Ballet in the world!"

Madame nodded. "I–I just don't know what to say," Stella began in happy confusion. "But surely Monsieur Savlon wants an audition?"

"He is quite satisfied with my word," Madame replied. "Why," she continued softly, "don't you think ze word of Natasha Ninsky is enough?"

Natasha Ninsky! The little blue sittingroom, crowded with all its memories of the ballet world, seemed to spin around Stella. She was utterly bewildered. Was Madame really trying to tell her that she and Natasha Ninsky were one and the same?

"You–" Stella breathed, scarcely able to find her voice. "But–but–"

Madame smiled a little sadly

"Ah, it is hard to believe, my child? But it is true. Once I was Natasha Ninsky, though today I am nothing but an old and crotchety teacher of ballet."

She read the unspoken question in Stella's eyes.

"Why do I choose that the world should know me as Madame Tanya? Because ze past is over and done with. To all ballet lovers–those old enough to remember her and those who only know my name–Natasha Ninsky is a legend."

There was a moment's silence. And through Stella's mind flashed visions of that unforgettable experience of seeing the great Ninsky dance Swan Lake. Then Madame continued.

"It may be ze whim of a silly old woman, but I prefer to keep it like zat. I feel it would give people more pleasure to remember the ethereal Ninsky in the glorious past, than a bad-tempered old woman crippled with arthritis. I wonder if you understand, my child?"

Stella nodded, her eyes filled with sudden tears.

"Paul Savlon is ze only one who knows my secret, besides you," Madame said gently. "And I trust you to say nothing."

"I'd sooner die," Stella whispered.

Madame smiled. And with that smile everything clicked into place in Stella's mind. She was suddenly reminded of her picture at home–Ninsky looking down from her garland of roses. The dancer's appearance had changed with the years–but that strange, unfathomable smile was the same.

Madame–Natasha Ninsky–took hold of her and kissed her on the cheek.

"And you, my little one, what better name could you have? For Stella means a star. Stella–my little dancing star!"

THE LIGHTED WINDOW

Laura and her young brother were fascinated by the still, silent figure which sat motionless at the window opposite their house but their investigations led to a rather surprising outcome.

Laura sat at her bedroom window, staring out into the darkness. The street below was quiet and deserted, and a fine rain spattered the pavements. Her young brother fidgeted beside her.

"Nothing seems to be happening," he said.

John glanced at his watch. "Half-past nine. I'm getting sleepy."

"All right," smiled his sister. "You go to bed. I'll call you if anything happens."

John slipped away to his own room. He was tired of waiting, and Laura often imagined things. But Laura was not tired. She felt curiously excited, and full of a growing conviction that something strange was about to happen. The minutes ticked by, but the silence was unbroken and the rain fell steadily. Suddenly Laura stiffened. A light snapped on in a window across the street.

He was still there!

For a moment she hesitated. Then rushing to the door, she called softly: "John. Come quickly." Her brother flew into the room.

Together they stared at the window across the street. Silhouetted against the light was the figure of a man. He appeared to be sitting motionless with his back to the window.

"He's never moved," breathed Laura excitedly. "For three nights he's been sitting there in exactly the same position."

"Perhaps he's reading," suggested John, "or just sitting still."

"He wouldn't sit so still," argued Laura. "He never moves a muscle. You watch."

The figure indeed remained absolutely motionless, as though he were carved out of stone. "He looks sort of – stiff," John said.

"Exactly," answered Laura. "It's most unnatural. Something must be wrong."

"What do you think?" asked John, with mounting excitement.

"He might be ill, and unable to move–"

"He might be bound and gagged!" John cut in.

"Yes," agreed Laura, her eyes widening. "He could be a prisoner in a den of thieves. He might even be–"

"Dead!" finished John. "I say! Supposing it was a murder?"

"It's too horrible to think of," said his sister, shuddering.

"Shall we ring the police?"

"No. We haven't enough evidence. There might be quite a simple explanation, and then we should look silly. Besides," Laura smiled secretly, "I'd like to do a little detective work on my own."

"What are you going to do?" asked her brother.

"I'm going over there," said Laura, suddenly making up her mind.

"All right. I'll come with you."

John fetched a raincoat, which he flung hastily over his dressing-gown. A few moments later he and his sister had crept downstairs and out of the house. Laura shivered as they crossed the street. The house opposite looked dark and sinister except for the one lighted window. There was a side entrance to the house with a list of names on the door.

"There are four flats," Laura said, reading the names. "Our window is at the top. That must be the fourth floor."

John tried the handle. "The door's open," he whispered in surprise.

"We're in luck," returned Laura. "Now listen carefully. I'm going up to the fourth floor. You stay here, and if I'm not back in ten minutes ring the police."

"I want to come, too," said John indignantly. "Why should I miss all the fun?"

But Laura was firm. "I'm older than you," she pointed out. "And I don't want you mixed up in anything–well–unpleasant. Besides, we must have someone to give the alarm if necessary."

Laura pushed open the door and found herself at the foot of a dimly lit staircase. Swiftly and silently she reached the first floor. There was no light, and she crept on in the darkness, feeling the wall with her hands. Past the second floor and the third; the stairs were getting steeper now and she paused for breath. There was no sound in the house except the occasional creak of a board under her feet.

"Everyone must be out," she thought. Everyone, that is, except the man in the top flat. She shivered again, and as she started to climb the last flight her heart pounded madly. What would she find behind that lighted window?

Scarcely daring to breathe she crept on to the top of the stairs. Then she stopped dead. A door stood half open and a stream of light filtered across the dim landing.

That was the door. What lay inside it? She thought wildly of running back down the stairs to the safety of the street. But the moment of panic passed and curiosity overcame her. Carefully and cautiously she tip-toed across to the open door.

What she saw was so unexpected that she could scarcely stifle an exclamation! At one end of the room a man was painting a picture. He seemed completely absorbed in his work. In the window, propped up in a chair, was a life-size wax model! And this was what he was painting!

Laura felt relief and disappointment. There was no bound-and-gagged victim, or murder. Just a man painting a picture. She sighed. She must slip away quickly before she was discovered.

As she turned to go the man said quietly, without looking up: "Do come in."

Laura jumped. "I – I – you see, I . . ." Then she stopped and blushed scarlet.

"Come in and sit down," said the man, still intent on his picture. "I don't often have visitors."

Laura hesitated. Then shyly she walked into the room.

"I – I'm not a visitor," she stammered. "I don't know how to explain. It sounds so silly. You see, we – we thought something terrible was happening."

The man looked up and smiled charmingly. "Tell me about it," he said.

He was quite young, and rather untidy. But Laura liked his smile and soon she was explaining about the lighted window and the figure in the chair. The young man was highly amused. "Anyway, it was very brave of you to come up here by yourself," he said.

"I left my brother downstairs," Laura told him. Then she cried: "Oh, gracious! He'll be telephoning the police."

"Oh, no, he won't!" said a voice from the landing. And the next moment a small figure in pyjamas and mackintosh appeared.

"I wasn't going to miss all the fun," grinned John. "I decided to come up, too." He stared disparagingly at the figure in the chair. "Who would have thought of a wax dummy!"

"I'm sorry you don't like Horace," smiled the young man. "He's a good type really and my only friend, even if he is made of wax. By the way, I'm Robert Strang, and I'm delighted to meet you both."

"I'm afraid we're disturbing you," Laura said. "I'm sure artists don't like being interrupted at their work."

"Don't worry about that," said Robert Strang, and he threw down his brush wearily. "It's not much use trying to paint a wax model. What I want is a real live one."

"Why don't you paint Laura?" suggested John promptly. Eyeing his sister rather doubtfully he added: "She's supposed to be pretty."

Robert Strang looked at Laura. "She is pretty," he declared, as though seeing her for the first time. "She's very pretty. But I can't afford to pay models you see."

"Laura wouldn't want paying," said her brother indifferently.

The young man smiled. "And what has Laura got to say about it?" he inquired.

"Of course I'll sit for you, if you really want me to," Laura replied.

"Want you to? Why, this is a heaven-sent chance. And all brought about by old Horace sitting in the window. Now let me see. How shall we paint you?" Suddenly he was all excitement and enthusiasm.

After that, Laura turned up each day to sit for her portrait. Long hours in one position made her stiff and tired, but Robert Strang said she was an excellent model, and he worked like a man possessed.

When at last the picture was finished, the artist could scarcely conceal his excitement. "It's the best thing I've ever done," he told Laura. "I'm taking it to an exhibition tomorrow."

A week later Laura heard the astounding news. Her picture had won first prize.

"Mr. Strang is taking me to see it tomorrow," she told John excitedly that evening. "And then we're going out to celebrate."

"That's better than solving a mystery," grinned her brother.

"But I did solve a mystery," said Laura.

And she stood for a long time gazing out across the street at the lighted window.

SECRET OF THE HOLIDAY SNAPSHOT

by Doreen Gray

Why were Jill and Ann made prisoners in an old tower while they were on holiday? And why were their holiday snapshots mysteriously stolen? Finding the answers to these questions brought the two schoolgirls face to face with great danger.

"This is a very good snap of you, Jill," said Ann Perry admiringly. "But-oh, help! Look at this one of me! I look as if my face has slipped sideways. Or do I always look like that?"

Jill Thorne looked at the snap and shrieked with laughter. "You must have moved, duffer!" she said after a bit. "You don't usually look quite so queer–at least, I don't think so," she added with a grin.

"Grr!" said Ann. "You're jealous of my fatal charm, that's what it is. But come on, let's see the rest of the snaps–since it's only by luck that we've got them."

What Ann said was true. Not only had the two friends, who were touring Devon in a horsepulled caravan, nearly been prevented from taking some of the photographs, but one of the spools of films had narrowly escaped being stolen. At the moment they were camping near some high cliffs on the coast, and it had been after they had undertaken the perilous climb down to the beach that a fisherman had attempted to cut short their photographing, urging them to clear off on the plea that there was danger of falling rocks. Later, they had gone into the nearby town of Lindridge, where the annual fair was to take place the next day, to get the snapshots developed, but suddenly a man had darted forward and made a snatch at Jill's handbag which had contained, not only her money, but also the spool of film. The attempt at theft had failed, and until now the schoolgirl caravanners had thought no more about it.

Suddenly Jill looked up from the holiday photos she and Ann were going through, to glance across at the enormous bonfire on the cliff top which tomorrow was to be set alight by the villagers as part of the celebrations. Until a few minutes ago Patch, their Cocker Spaniel, had been playing around there, but now there was no sign of him.

"Where can he have got to?" Jill asked.

As if in answer to the question, Patch appeared. In his mouth he held a felt schoolgirl's hat. He was shaking it frantically from side to side and growling at it. Then, spotting Ann, he wagged his tail furiously, darted forward and dropped the hat into her lap.

"Thanks very much," chuckled Ann. "It's just my style, and–"

And there, suddenly, she broke off, her eyes widening in surprise. For as Patch made a playful dab at the hat he bowled it over. Pinned to the inside was a piece of paper–rather tattylooking now after the way Patch had shaken the hat around–with some scrawling writing in pencil, suggesting it had been written in great haste and agitation.

Quickly Ann snatched up the hat, unpinned the note and read: "Please come to the old Tower. I need help. Please hurry."

"Golly!" Jumping to her feet, Ann thrust the message towards Jill. "Some schoolgirl exploring and had a fall, I suppose. I'm not surprised. It's so dangerous that people are warned not to go there."

"I suppose she spotted Patch and gave him her hat with the message in it to bring to us," said Jill. "Good thing she didn't know Patch very well or she wouldn't have felt so confident. It's only by sheer luck he managed to bring it here with the message intact."

A few moments later they were hurrying as quickly as they could across the uneven ground towards the old tower that stood gaunt and derelict on the headland. Twice Ann had to call Patch sharply to heel for, with his flash of brilliance apparently very quickly vanishing, he persisted in plunging into the bushes near the caravan and barking furiously. He was still whining and growling and showing great reluctance to accompany them when Ann, growing exasperated, grabbed his collar and almost dragged him along with her. Immediately they reached the tower and Ann released her hold, however, he was off again like a flash with a defiant and joyful "wuff!"

"Oh, let him go!" said Ann rather crossly, as Jill began calling Patch back. "He'd probably only get in the way. Hallo, there!" she shouted, as they approached the door of the tower. "Is anyone in there?"

There was no reply, so they entered. There was a rickety flight of stairs leading to the upper floors. They climbed them and on the first floor called again. There was still no answer, but from below came a sudden slamming crash. Ann darted to the head of the stairs and peered down.

"It's the door-it's slammed!" she cried. "But–golly! How could it? There's no wind. And it's much too heavy and stiff to swing shut of its own accord. We – Jill!"

Her voice rose sharply as she stared around the floor, thick with dust, faintly lighted by the shaft of sunlight streaming through the small, slatted window.

"Jill, somebody's playing a joke on us. Nobody's been here for ages, otherwise the dust on the floor would be disturbed. Downstairs, quickly–but be careful."

Puzzled and growing worried, they hurried downstairs and grabbed the iron ring handle of the door. They turned it and tugged. But nothing happened. The door would not budge an inch. For some reason, someone had tricked them to the old tower by means of a false note and, having got them there, had made them prisoners.

"If this is a joke, it's a pretty feeble one," said Ann grimly. "Locking us in this dangerous old place! But if whoever it is thinks we're just meekly going to sit here and wait for them to let us out again, then they're jolly well mistaken. Come on, Jill!"

Ann was really angry now as she led the way back upstairs. She was worried, too. In their hurry to answer what they had taken to be a genuine call for help, she and Jill had not bothered to lock the caravan. All their stores were there–and their handbags with all their money. True, they were tucked away in a secret place, but a determined thief ransacking the caravan would be sure to find them.

For the first time Ann was very glad that Patch had broken away from her. He might not be terribly clever in some ways, but he would guard the caravan with his life. And thinking of that, she suddenly gave a start. Had Patch spotted someone lurking near the caravan when they had started out? Was that why he had kept running back

The caravan was a shambles!

barking so furiously? Was that why he had taken the first opportunity of dashing back? It seemed so.

"What are we going to do, Ann?" asked Jill, as they once more reached the first floor. "Have you thought of a way to get out?"

"We'll try the window," she answered. "Those slats look pretty flimsy."

They pulled off the wooden slats that were nailed across the window, then clambered through. For a moment they hung by their hands from the sill, then dropped to the ground. Luckily some bushes broke their fall.

"Now for the caravan!" cried Ann, leading the way forward.

Vaguely worried because they could hear no sound of Patch, the two girls plunged on until they came to the caravan. Up the steps they dashed. Then Jill pulled up with a sharp cry. At first sight the caravan seemed a shambles. Cushions, the pretty bunk covers, magazines were strewn around. And slumped in a corner–

"Patch!" screamed Ann. "Oh, Patch!"

Patch, who had looked so lifeless as Ann shouted, raised his head rather dazedly and feebly wagged his tail. Running a hand over him, Ann hugged him with relief.

"Oh, poor darling! He's had a biff on the head," she said, with tears in her eyes. "But he'll be all right–"

"He gave a jolly good account of himself, anyway," said Jill proudly, "even if he did get knocked out in doing it. And whoever attacked him didn't get away unscathed."

That was obvious, as they discovered when they began to tidy up. Patch must have returned and surprised a man in the caravan. He had sprung for him. The man had raised his arm to defend himself. Patch had grabbed at the arm, tearing away a piece of the faded navy-blue jersey.

"But what was he after?" asked Ann, after they had found their handbags and stores intact. "Nothing seems to have gone, does it?"

"No –"began Jill doubtfully, as she began collecting the scattered snapshots. Then: "Yes, Ann–yes! Our snapshots–some of our snapshots and their negatives have gone."

It didn't take Ann long to see that Jill was right. It took the two girls even less time to check up on just which snapshots were missing.

Every one that they had taken among the rocks after their scramble down the cliff. Ann grew curiously still as that realisation struck her. For the first time things began to add up–things that had made no sense before. The man who had shouted at them to be off! The attempted theft of the undeveloped spools from Jill's handbag!

"So, for some reason, someone didn't want us to take snapshots in that particular spot," said Ann at last. "When they discovered we had done so, they tried to steal first the undeveloped spools, then the prints. And this afternoon they succeeded."

"Too bad that they didn't know we had two prints of each spool taken," said Jill, "so that we could send them home to our people. Here they are, Ann, sealed in this envelope. And talking of those snaps on the rocks below, I did spot something peculiar just before Patch came up with the hat. I intended to mention it, but I forgot in the excitement. There seemed to be an opening in the cliff, where it just didn't seem possible there could be an opening. And I'm sure there was a boat nosing out –"

As she spoke, she scrabbled beneath the table for the envelope which had been knocked on the floor in the struggle. When she emerged, she had the envelope and something else as well.

A piece of carefully-folded, thin, pale yellow, foreign-looking paper. She opened it out, and she and Ann read it together. In strange, pointed-looking writing, it said:

"Fishing becoming impossible. Last haul Friday this week. Be ready to receive consignment usual place at midnight."

It had obviously fallen from the thief's pocket. But what did it mean?

Ann and Jill were still puzzling that out when they went to bed that night. A glance at the snapshots had shown them that Jill had seen right. One of the holiday photos clearly revealed that there was an opening in an apparently solid cliff, and there was the glimpse of a boat just nosing out. It had been by the merest chance that the two girls, unknown to themselves at the time, had got that view into their snapshot. But somebody must have feared they had got it–somebody who had a vital reason for wanting to keep it a secret.

Despite the danger of coming up against their unknown enemy, Ann and Jill had desperately wanted to set off there and then to explore more closely the opening in the cliff that the holiday snapshot had revealed. But the climb down the cliff, hazardous in daylight, would have been extremely dangerous, if not impossible, in the dark. They would go at first light tomorrow, they decided. But, tired as she was, the puzzling events of the day kept churning over in Ann's mind, keeping her awake. She could hear the slap of the waves on the rocks below and the sound of a boat's engine as it whined around the point. She had heard that particular engine so often at night that she now recognised it as the coastguard cutter. All night and every night it kept up its ceaseless search for some sign of the outbreak of smuggling that had flared up recently.

Smuggling! Ann sat up abruptly as that thought shot into her mind. With her heart beginning to thump with excitement, she pulled her torch from beneath her pillow, then stretched out a hand for the piece of yellow paper that lay on the table. Being careful not to disturb Jill, she stared at the paper, then held it up and shone the torch through it.

The smugglers were operating from the French coast. And this paper had a French watermark! And the writing was foreign. Then suddenly that message began to make sense.

It made sense if the word "fishing" was changed to "smuggling". "Smuggling becoming impossible. Last haul Friday this week. Be ready to receive consignment usual place at midnight."

This was Friday! The usual place–of course that hidden cleft in the cliffs, probably widening out beyond into some sort of passage, a kind of backstairs up which the smuggled goods were carried to safety. And the time – Ann glanced at her watch and gave an exclamation. Midnight! And it was now half-past eleven! No time to get into Lindridge and tell anyone of her suspicions–for they were still only suspicions. Yet if there was smuggling going on, the coastguards should know about it! It was then that Ann had a daring idea. She woke up Jill and confided in her.

"I'm going to climb down the cliff," said Ann determinedly. "I'm going to watch and see if there is smuggling going on, and if so, then I shall wait there until the coastguard cutter comes along again and signal to them with my torch. Even if they don't actually catch the men unloading the boat, they'll be able to follow them into the cliff passage and catch them there."

"You're crazy climbing down that cliff in the dark," said Jill, very dubiously. "But if you do it–then so shall I. Come on!"

Pulling on dark jerseys and jeans, taking a torch each, and leaving Patch in charge of the caravan, the two girls set off. Later, it was only with a shiver of horror that they remembered that climb down the precipitous cliff in the fitful light of the moon. Time and again their feet could find no hold and they were hanging only by their hands. Sometimes they just clung there, terrified of continuing their scramble down, but even more terrified of trying to make their way back.

At last trembling and soaked with perspiration, they reached the rocky beach, too exhausted even to congratulate each other. By then, it was five minutes to twelve. With great caution, but with many a slip and much grazing of their ankles, they made their way towards where they had been taking their snapshots, to the place where they knew the fissure in the cliff to be. There was no one in sight, not a sound.

"You're sure it was tonight, Ann?" whispered Jill. "I can't–"

Ann's hand grasping her wrist stopped her saying anything else. From just out at sea a light flashed once–twice. A moment later there was an answering flash only a few yards away. Immediately Ann and Jill sank down behind a rock, frozen into immobility, straining their eyes to stare into the darkness. The minutes seemed like hours before a boat came into view, nosing into a narrow channel between the rocks. A figure darted in front of the two watching girls.

"Heave up the net!" came a hoarse whisper. "Steady now!"

The fishing-net was swung up on a small derrick. And, as Ann strained forward, out on to the rocks poured a stream of silvery fish. Fish! Were these men just fishermen, after all? Had she and Jill risked broken bones just to watch a catch landed? But that was ridiculous! Why would the men be landing fish in this outlandish spot at this time of night? And why the secrecy? Even as Ann asked herself that question, another man leapt on to the rocks from the boat, plunged his hand among the fish and drew out of the net on oilskin bag.

"Here we are–safe and sound!" he whispered jubilantly. "Must be a couple of hundred watches there, besides other things. And we've–"

He stopped short, swinging round. Jill, in an effort to ease her cramped position, had shifted slightly. And the slight movement had sent a pebble rattling down. Instantly the man swung a powerful torch round in that direction. It was too late for Jill to duck. The man was upon her, grasping her arm.

For a moment Ann lay frozen and horrified. Her first instinct was to leap forward and help Jill. But what sort of a fight could she put up against these powerful men? She could help Jill more by remaining free to give the alarm somehow. Perhaps that was what Jill would have done, too, or what she was trying to tell Ann to do. For she made a great deal of scuffling with her feet, struggling violently and giving muffled cries, that all helped Ann to creep away without being heard. Ann hurried towards the cliff, heedless now of scraped ankles. Her heart was beating furiously. She wondered how long it would be before the men began to ask themselves whether Jill would have come on this expedition alone and would start looking for her friend. And as she asked herself that question, she knew the answer. The search for her had already started. It was bad luck that just as Ann started her climb back up the cliff, the moon should come out from behind the clouds, lighting the whole cliff up in a white glare. A glare in which she was only too painfully visible. Immediately two men were after her. Ann had a start, but they knew this cliff better than she did. And even if she reached the top first, she would never keep ahead of them in a race to Lindridge for help.

Up and up Ann scrambled, gasping and sobbing with the effort. The men were coming closer. She felt, rather than saw, a rough hand reach out to clutch her ankle, and just in time drew it out of the way. She was at the top now. She could hear the hum of the engine of the coastguard cutter. But she hadn't time to stop and signal. In less than a minute the men would be upon her – And in that instant Ann's eyes fell upon the enormous bonfire, already soaked with paraffin in readiness for tomorrow's celebration. With a shaking hand she drew her little petrol lighter from her pocket and flicked it on. Then, as the two men scrambled over the edge of the cliff with triumphant cries, she threw it into the bonfire.

For a second nothing happened. Then with a boom the tinder-dry brushwood, soaked with paraffin, burst into flame. It illuminated Ann and the two men on top of the cliff. It cast a glow on the scene below, with Jill still kicking and struggling as she was thrust towards the boat. And it illuminated the coastguard cutter just coming round the point, adding its own powerful searchlight to the already bright glare.

In a matter of minutes it was all over. The two men wheeled away from Ann and raced off, to be picked up later. Those in the boat were caught red-handed and Jill was freed. It was very much later that the two girls once more crawled into their beds.

They had been very regretful that the townsfolk had lost their bonfire, but the cheer those people gave them the next day proved that they bore the two girls no grudge because of that. They all set to work with a will to build a new bonfire and that evening they insisted on Ann and Jill being guests of honour at Lindridge Fair–a wonderful end to their adventure for the Schoolgirl Caravanners.

MOUNTAIN RESCUE

by Denise Kerry

In spite of Hazel's and Fiona's warning, two young American mountaineers tried to climb a treacherous Scottish peak in bad weather and this led the two girls into organising a dangerous mountain rescue attempt.

In the big, open grate of the Glencorrachie Hostel a huge fire of logs hissed and crackled cheerfully. Hazel Hall came staggering in with an armful of fresh fuel and set it down on the hearth.

"There," she chuckled. "That should keep us going for the rest of the day. Now I'm going to sit here and see them all burned."

"And I'll be helping you," Fiona Mackenzie, her cousin, chuckled. "Losh, Hazel, isn't it a change to have nothing to do and all day to do it in? This'll be the end of the season now. We'll have no hostellers this weather."

The North-East wind howling over the moors drew a deep, drumming note from the chimney. The hostel, which Hazel helped her cousin and her uncle to run, was a snug haven of comfort.

"Look at the time," Hazel commented with a glance at the clock. "Uncle must have decided to stay in the city overnight. If he'd caught the train he'd be here by now . . . "

Mr. Mackenzie was away on a business trip, but the thought of a night on their own did not worry the girls for they had often been alone before. A dog barked not far away, and stepping to the window Hazel saw a tall, tweed-clad figure moving up the glen with deceptively slow-seeming strides behind a flock of black-faced mountain sheep. A lively sheepdog trotted at his side.

"It's old Donald, the shepherd," Hazel cried. "I'll call him in. I'm sure he could be doing with a warm drink." And indeed, the old man was glad of it and of the chance to warm his bones before the fire.

"I'm just at shifting the beasts," he explained. "For there's snow in the air and I wouldn't want them to be caught out."

When snow threatened he liked to have his sheep as close at hand as possible, for snow on the mountains could be dangerous for the flock. The trouble was that they would seek what shelter they could find from the wind–in a glen perhaps, or behind rocks. Huddled together, they would let the snow drift over them until they were unable to move. Then it might be days before the shepherd could find them and set them free, and many would die.

"If only they had the sense to understand that their thick coats would protect them," sighed the shepherd, "I'd be saved a lot of work. But I'll be at it all day tomorrow, too, gathering them in."

Old Donald was still sipping gratefully at his steaming drink when there came a loud rap at the front door. To her astonishment Hazel found two youths in mountaineering garb standing there. Each had a heavy pack on his back.

"Say–is this the Glencorrachie Hostel?" asked the taller of the two in an American accent. "Gee, that's great. We were sure figuring we'd missed it and were in for a night in the open. Wouldn't have worried me any, but I guess Harry might have found it a bit hard." He grinned down at his partner, who shrugged his shoulders a little sheepishly.

Hazel led the two lads into the hostel and with Fiona hurried to the kitchen to prepare a meal for them. "You're very late in the season to be hostelling," remarked Fiona.

"Hostelling? Heck, we're not hostelling," snorted the taller lad, who had told them to call him Hank. "We're climbing. Yes indeed. We've got a nice little schedule of Highland peaks just about finished. In the morning we'll climb the Corrach and I reckon that'll be it."

"The Corrach!" It was old Donald who gasped the words from his seat by the fire. "You'll never be thinking of climbing the Corrach in this weather?"

"Why not, Gran'pop?" Hank demanded. "Say, if you'd seen some of the peaks we have climbed . . . "

"Aye–but the Corrach with the snow on it . . . there's not

half-a-dozen climbers in Britain would attempt it," answered the shepherd.

"Check," said Hank confidently. "Make that eight . . . me and Harry. Yes, sir, the Corrach's down on our schedule, and climb it tomorrow is what we're going to do . . . Besides, there won't be any snow. The weather forecast says so."

Anxiously Donald tried once again to persuade the boys not to climb the Corrach. Harry, an English boy from his voice, might have been convinced. But Hank was determined to make the ascent. He was even a little scornful about the warning.

"Back home we climb any weather," he said. "And when it snows there, boy, it snows. Don't worry, Gran'pop, we'll be all right."

Apart from his brashness, Hank seemed a nice enough lad, and as he ate his meal he told the girls a little about the tour he was making of the Highlands, the tour which was due to end the next day. He particularly wanted to climb the Corrach, which was last on the list he had made, before he started.

Old Donald had to go then, but as Hazel took him to the door he spoke to her earnestly. "Whatever you do," he said. "Don't let those lads go climbing. Maybe their weather forecast is right. But if I ever saw snow coming it's coming now. If they try to climb the Corrach they'll be lucky to see another day dawn."

After Hank and Harry had gone to bed, Hazel and Fiona sat by the dying embers of the fire and discussed the old shepherd's warning.

"We've tried persuading them not to be going," Fiona exclaimed. "What else is there that we can do? I'm sure old Donald's right. There'll be snow . . . and . . . "

"There's only one answer," Hazel replied. "And that's to make it impossible for them to go climbing. We'll hide their gear tonight and not let them have it back until they promise to give up the idea . . . Unless, maybe, it's extra fine in the morning and no sign at all of rain or snow."

There and then they decided to put the boys' packs in the hostel coal cellar. "They'll be furious," Hazel mused. "And they'll try to get round us. But we mustn't give way, Fiona. It's for their own sakes. They don't know the Corrach. They don't understand the dangers they're tackling."

Carrying out their resolve, the girls went to bed. Hazel was resigned to an early wakening, for she knew climbers usually started before dawn. But to her surprise the sun was well up when she did awaken, and there had been no sound from the lads. Had they changed their minds? Or had they just slept on?

"Just as well they're not going, anyway," she told Fiona as they hurried downstairs to start breakfast cooking. "The sun's shining now, but the wind's still strong and there are nasty banks of cloud working up. I think Donald's snow warning is going to be justified."

The smell of frying bacon usually awakened any hostel guest, but there was no sign of the climbers by the time breakfast was ready. Fiona went to call them. Almost before she heard her cousin's racing feet on the stairs, Hazel guessed the message she would bring.

"They . . . they've gone," gasped Fiona. Hazel was already dashing for the cellar. In it there was only coal. The boys' climbing gear had vanished! And as she gazed in dismay at the heaps of coal, Hazel felt the first soft flakes of snow!

Both the girls turned to look at the looming mass of the Corrach, bleak and forbidding against the grey of the sky. Was it their fancy, or could they see two small figures plodding up the lower slopes of the mountain that gave the glen its name? Then with a flurry the snow fell like a curtain, blotting out the landscape, and all they could see was the stretch of moor immediately in front of them.

It was Hazel who spotted the note fluttering on the cellar floor.

"Don't worry," it said. "We'll be all right . . . And next time you plot–don't do it at a fireplace."

"Losh," exclaimed Fiona. "They must have heard every word we said. It would carry right up that chimney. Oh, they have the laugh on us all right!"

"Laugh," said Hazel. "It's no laughing matter. Gosh, Fiona, they could get in terrible trouble on the Corrach on a day like this!"

What should they do?

"Hank may be all right," Hazel went on. "But what about Harry? A climbing party is only as good as its weakest member. And Hank made it pretty clear that he didn't think much of Harry's ability."

"But what can we do, Hazel?" Fiona demanded. "I–we–neither of us is a climber –I mean, apart maybe from scrambling about the rocks.

What can we do to help them? That is if they need help?"

Hazel was staring grimly into the snow. It was thickening, and the wind was strengthening.

"There's only one hope," she decided. "Perhaps Hank has decided to wait for the snow to stop before he starts to climb. We'll get after them and find them, and somehow we'll stop them going up that mountain if we have to hold on to them to do it."

Dressing warmly and wearing heavy shoes, they set off into the swirling snow. Hazel had slung a coil of rope across her shoulder in case it should be needed. That was their only equipment. With their knowledge of the moors, the girls had no trouble in heading in the right direction, even though they could at times see only a few yards ahead. The snow showed no sign of stopping, and Hazel's hopes rose. Surely the boys would be forced to abandon their attempted climb? She began to feel that they would find them waiting disconsolately at the foot of the Corrach.

Soon they could see the dark loom of the mountain, even through the snow. The Corrach was shaped like a cone with one side sliced away, forming a sheer cliff that rose almost to the summit. It was this cliff that drew the climbers to the mountain, for its relatively gentle slopes on the other three sides could be climbed easily enough. Indeed, sheep grazed there at times. But the cliff was a real challenge.

The girls headed along the base of the cliff, looking for the two or three spots where climbers usually began their ascent. These were funnels that bit into the sheer face of the rock and led up to ledges and the start of the climb proper. Hazel was sure they would find Hank and Harry sheltering at one of these points, waiting for the snow to clear. But there was no one there. Each starting point was deserted. And because the wind was coming from the other side of the mountain, there was no snow on the ground and so no tracks for the girls to follow.

"Either they've given up the idea altogether and headed back for the hostel, in which case we must have passed them in the snow, or else they've already begun to climb," Hazel said.

But which was it? Could they turn for home ignorant of whether the boys were safe or not?

"We'll go back along the foot of the cliff," Hazel decided. "And we'll look even closer at the starting points this time. If they've gone up, then their nailed boots will have left some sort of mark on the rocks, I should think."

Once again the two girls moved along the base of the huge cliff, scanning with their keen eyes each spot where the boys might have started to climb. There were two places where the rock was scored with the marks of climbing boots, but to Hazel it seemed that they were old ones for there had been climbers on the mountain a week before. Yet it was hard to be sure. The girls stared upward in perplexity. What on earth should they do? They were still standing there when, from far above them, they heard a faint sound. A moment later there was a crashing noise.

"Right up against the cliff!" shouted Hazel.

Just in time the girls flattened themselves against the sheer rock face. Over their heads whistled a shower of stones that went crashing and thudding to the ground. In mounting alarm the girls looked at each other. Then they stared upward again, trying desperately to pierce the swirling mantle of the snow.

Was there someone up there? Was it Hank and Harry? Had they knocked those stones down?

A moment later there was a sound that seemed to put the matter beyond all doubt. It was a high-pitched cry, almost drowned by the howl of the wind. And it came from up the cliff!

For a moment the girls stood transfixed. "It–it's them!" groaned Fiona. "Oh, Hazel, they–they're in trouble. What are we to do?"

But already Hazel's mind was hard at work.

"We've got to get up to them," she said.

Fiona looked upward at the frowning cliff. She shivered.

"Oh, we're not going to try to climb," Hazel said quickly. "Not up there. Come on."

Another faint cry sounded as Hazel led the way along the base of the cliff. Soon she had reached the end of it and the beginning of the more gradual slope on the other side.

"We can climb this way," she cried above the howl of the wind. "We'll have to lower a rope from the top."

As they began to scramble up the steep heather-clad slope, Hazel blessed the foresight which had made her bring the rope. There was snow here in plenty, covering the bushy heather with a smooth white coat, making the going hard.

They had been climbing for only a few minutes when a movement in the snow ahead brought a spurt of hope to their hearts. But hope faded, for it was only a sheep which bleated and went bounding away up the slope.

At last they were close to the peak. Cautiously they approached the edge of the cliff, crouched low so that the wind would not hurl them over. In the snow they could see nothing beneath them. But even as they peered down they heard again that wailing cry.

"They're shouting for help," groaned Fiona. "They must be stuck on a ledge, not able to get up or down."

Looking down that sheer cliff was a nerve–racking experience in itself. To think of the two lads trapped there was worse. What must they be thinking? How they must be suffering! It was no consolation to think that they had only themselves to blame.

"Hal-loo-ooh," called Hazel, cupping her hand to her mouth. "Are–you–all–right . . . "

The wind seemed to snatch the words from her lips, but they were heard, for there was an immediate answer from beneath, a loud cry which echoed eerily round the cliff and blew away indistinguishably.

"Hal-loo-ooh," Hazel called again.

She listened intently to the reply, trying to fix its position.

"They must be about three-quarters of the way up," she said. "Come on . . . "

She led the way back down the slope a little, halting at last at a ledge that led out across the cliff face.

"I'm going out there," she told Fiona. "You take the rope. Tie one end round that rock and pay it out slowly as I go. Keep it not quite tight!"

"But–but Hazel," her cousin protested. "Suppose–"

"I'll be all right," Hazel answered. "The ledge is pretty broad. I've seen deer walking along it. Climbers don't use it because it doesn't lead upwards. But I think it should take me pretty close to where the cry came from. If I can see the boys I'll be able to judge how to help them."

Then, before Fiona could argue–or her own resolution fail –

Hazel began to edge her way out along the ledge. It was not as bad as she had expected. The cliff sheltered her from the force of the wind, and the swirling snow screened the ground beneath–giving her nothing to look at. For, as Hazel knew, looking down was the greatest danger to the inexperienced climber.

As she moved along, Hazel called again, and hearing the answer she knew she had guessed aright. She was coming closer to the stranded victims. They must be isolated close to the ledge, she thought, probably secured by their own ropes–quite safe, but very uncomfortable. She hoped she would find them beneath the ledge. It would be easier to pull them up than to get them down.

The ledge moved out round a big buttress, and she called again.

The answer came from just around the buttress.

"I'm almost with you!" Hazel called.

She rounded the buttress carefully–and almost met disaster.

For a length of the ledge had crumbled away, and her leading foot stepped suddenly into space! Her hands had a good hold in a crevice and she withdrew her foot, breathing heavily and feeling her heart thump furiously. She had shut her eyes tightly as her foot slipped, but now, cautiously, she opened them, wondering to find herself still alive.

An instant later her eyes opened much wider. For ahead of her were the victims of the cliff. And they were not the two boy climbers. Instead Hazel saw two sheep on the ledge! They were trotting back and forth on their tiny ledge as if it were a prison cell, and as they saw Hazel they bleated mournfully.

The girl could hardly restrain a smile of relief. Sheep! It had been the bleating of the sheep she had heard, distorted by the wind and the echoes.

Hazel remembered what old Donald had said about his charges. These two animals must have sought shelter on the ledge. They had come along so far, and the ledge had given way behind them. That shower of stones that had so nearly hit the girls–

But Hazel's relief did not last long. They might be only sheep–but she could not abandon them there.

"I'll have to go back and get a plank to bridge the gap," she decided.

But as soon as she started to move, the bleating of the sheep rose to

Instead Hazel saw two sheep on the ledge!

a new pitch. They crowded forward, right on the very edge of the gap in the ledge, seemingly almost willing to leap the chasm, so anxious were they not to be left behind.

"I've got to do something," Hazel told herself.

And there was only one thing she could do–go to them. She would have to cross that gap.

Steadily she pulled on the rope until she had a few feet of slack. Above her there was a knob of rock, and she put the rope over this. Then she edged her way out over the gap. Only an inch or two of the ledge was left to give her a toe-hold, but higher there were two crevices to put let her fingers in. Clinging tightly, Hazel worked her way slowly across that spine-chilling gap until she was standing on the ledge beyond. This was her moment of greatest peril. The excited sheep were bumping round her legs, nuzzling her eagerly. She had already decided how to get them across. Now she loosed the rope from her waist and tied it about the shoulders of the first sheep. She used a slip-hitch with a long length dangling free.

"Now then," she breathed. "Off you go."

And the bleating sheep was given a shove which swept it from the ledge. It swung out and across the gap, suspended from the high knob of rock which brought it swinging right on to the other ledge. But it landed safely, and Hazel jerked back the rope. Filled with elation she swung over the second sheep which went scampering after its companion into safety. Then she swung herself after them.

She made a perfect landing and ran after the sheep. Then, suddenly, she saw Fiona rushing to meet her.

"Oh, Hazel," she cried as she leapt to embrace her. "You–you're all right–

Hazel looked round in surprise. The girls were not alone. Harry was there–and Hank–and old Donald himself!

Afterwards, as they gathered round the hostel fire, Hazel learned all that had happened.

"I guess I'm not as crazy as my talk," confessed Hank. "When we saw what the climb was really like–and the weather–well, I guess I put my pride in my pocket. We decided to head right back here."

He flushed as he went on.

"And right then, I found I wasn't as smart as I thought I was. I led the way–and lost it. We wandered the moor for a long time until we happened on Gran . . . on Mr. Donald, here. He was hunting some of his sheep, so we reckoned we'd give him a hand. I owed him that after the way I'd talked about his weather sense . . . "

"And a right good help you were," chuckled Donald, taking up the tale. "'Twas the dog that brought us up the hill, for she insisted there were sheep there. And once up the hill we saw the sheep pouring down the ledge."

Hazel smiled. Hank was a greatly changed lad after that day's experiences. And so was Harry. She thought, rightly, that they would both be more inclined to listen to good advice in future.

CRUISE IN THE SUN

by Janet McKibbin

Stephanie and Sue had a very glamorous life working as hair-stylists on a luxury cruise liner. But when they went ashore at Naples in Italy, they found some excitement which they did not expect.

"A day ashore in Naples! Gee, aren't we lucky, Sue?" Stephanie Ross said happily.

"Yes, rather, but – But I can't understand why Miss Brent wants us!" puzzled her shipmate, Sue West.

They were hurrying across the quayside in the brilliant sunshine of Naples. Both were assistant hair-stylists aboard the luxury cruising liner *Marina* lying here in port. Both had expected to be on duty till lunch-time. Instead, they had been told mysteriously to report ashore to Miss Brent, one of the first-class passengers who had disembarked earlier that day.

"I know Miss Brent's here on business. But what is her line, Sue?" chatted Stephanie.

"I haven't the foggiest idea. But she brought a lot of stuff with her on the ship, and they say she's a leading business woman, and very well-to-do," said Sue.

"It sounds intriguing!"

"So did the address she gave us! What was it again?"

"The house with the green door. Number 7 Via Sorrento," Stephanie said, obviously excited at the mysterious background to their trip ashore.

They crossed the sunny square, inquiring their way of the vivacious girl flower-sellers, and they came to a quaint, old-world street that looked as if it hadn't changed in centuries.

"The green door! Here's the house!" exclaimed Stephanie, eagerly ringing the bell of number seven.

An Italian maid in frilly apron and cap curtsied them in.

"Ah, my dears! So nice of you to come!"

Miss Brent greeted them with real pleasure. She had a brisk, businesslike charm, and she was still surrounded by cabin-trunks, cases and boxes she had brought with her off the ship.

"You sent for us, Miss Brent? Can we help you in some way?" Stephanie asked, mystified.

Miss Brent smiled from one to the other, but she still did not satisfy their curiosity. "Come into the next room, my dears. I cannot go into reasons just yet," she said mysteriously, "but I promise you a very happy day in Naples if you will do what I ask!"

Stephanie and Sue followed her into an ante-room, and they saw two open boxes lying on the table, their contents covered with tissue-paper.

"I have some things here you might like to wear today," said Miss Brent. "Will you? It will make a change, and they will suit you beautifully."

Astonished, the chums watched her uncover the boxes. One contained an outfit of light blue pants, with an attractive tunic-style top, sleeveless and with a frill at the waist. There was a dainty pair of sandals with it. The other box held a pink, fullskirted frock with a white candy stripe, trimmed with matching ribbon–and a handbag and shoes to match.

"Do you like them?" Miss Brent murmured.

"Yes, rather, but–"

"They're lighter weight than your own frocks, and more suitable for a hot sunny day in Naples. I suggest you wear the slacks, Stephanie, and Sue the frock!"

"You mean–wear them–to go out in, Miss Brent?" dithered Stephanie.

"For a day in Naples, yes," nodded Miss Brent. "You can leave your own things here till you come back, but I do want it to be a happy day for you in every way. I have arranged for a guide to take you round, and I will speak to him while you are changing."

She bustled out in her brisk way, leaving the girls gazing at each other blankly.

"Change? But why do we have to change?"

"Because they're cooler than our own clothes. Looks as if we've got a lot of walking to do–but I don't mind!" Stephanie said, her eyes longingly fixed on the new outfits.

They changed eagerly. Their simplicity made the clothes very comfortable to wear. The pants suited Stephanie fine, and the frock fitted Sue a treat. Even the shoes for them both were a miraculous fit.

Miss Brent came back when they were ready and looked at them with bright approval.

"Splendid! Absolutely right for Naples!" she declared. "Now come next door and meet Guiseppe. He's going to be your guide."

Guiseppe was a cheery, handsome young Neapolitan in a white suit. He had dark curly hair and laughing southern eyes.

"Guiseppe has his instructions, my dears," Miss Brent said enigmatically. "He is going to bring you to meet me later when you have enjoyed the sights of Naples."

"Come!" said Guiseppe.

He led them out through the green door. Then the chums blinked dizzily as he ushered them into a gleaming silver car–the very last word in sports models.

They sank down on to the cushions beside him, and he let in the clutch and went whirring off through the street to the bay.

"Where are you taking, us, Guiseppe?" Stephanie asked breathlessly.

"Vesuvius!" answered Guiseppe with pride. "All who come to Naples must visit Vesuvius!"

They flashed round the bend of the bay and the chums gazed spellbound at the extinct volcano of Vesuvius, towering majestically above the famous, breathtaking, bay of Naples.

"Can we . . . can we really climb to the top?" thrilled Stephanie.

"It ees a *must,*" grinned Guiseppe, "as you say in English!"

The car whizzed on through the old fishing-town of Naples, to the foot of the mighty mountain itself.

"Is this where we get out and walk up the mountain?" began Sue excitedly.

"Walk?" chuckled Guiseppe. "When here is ze autostrada?"

He swung the nose of the car up the most breath-taking motorway in Europe, the "autostrada" of Mount Vesuvius. Up it spiralled like a corkscrew round the mountainside, growing steeper at every fresh turn. Stephanie looked down and her head swam. So she fixed her gaze upwards on the blue summit.

They had to leave the car some way from the summit where the road ended–and they took a spectacular ride by funicular railway, to the rim of the crater. Beautiful views lay below them on every side. Now all the mystery surrounding their tour was forgotten in their excitement.

"What are all those people doing at the top, Guiseppe? Can they see right down into the volcano?"

Guiseppe was gazing intently at the crowds of visitors above–almost as if he were looking for someone he expected to meet there.

"Si, si. It is many years since the volcano's last big eruption. Now–she is quite safe," he said. "We stop, and you shall look down!"

They climbed from the railway to the mountain summit. Guiseppe led them to the safety rail, and the girls gazed down, fascinated and awestruck, at the pit where years before eruptions had left fantastic shapes and patterns in the molten lava now covering the volcano's vent. As they did so, Guiseppe made a mysterious sign to someone. A young but bearded sightseer with a camera moved closer.

"Click!"

The girls swung round, stupefied. The camera was pointed straight at them. That stranger had, for some reason, taken *their* photograph!

"Who . . . W-why did he do that, Guiseppe?" gasped Stephanie.

"Pardon?" murmured Guiseppe.

His face was sublimely innocent as if he had noticed nothing . . . But they had seen him beckon secretively to the photographer!

"Who was that man, Guiseppe? Why did he take our photo?" asked Stephanie, flabbergasted.

The stranger was gone even as she spoke. He was no working photographer, touting amongst the tourists. He looked like a young artist or professional man.

"Did he photograph you?" Guiseppe asked innocently.

"You know he did–"

"It ees because you make so charming a peecture!"

"You got him to do it. You signalled him!"

"I?" Guiseppe's eyes widened. "I was looking down at the mighty volcano."

The girls exchanged tantalised looks.

Guiseppe helped them back into the car, leaving them still guessing as he drove round below the lip of the great crater of Vesuvius and down the other side of the mountain.

"Where are we going now?" they clamoured, more and more intrigued.

"Pompeii," said Guiseppe. "It is very–very interesting–ze ancient ruins of Pompeii!"

Pompeii! The ancient city, which many years before had been swallowed under ash and rubble from an eruption, spread beneath them on a ridge of lava high above the sea. Guiseppe pointed out to them the historic sights, as they left the car and walked slowly along the paved roads between the excavated ruins.

The bright sunshine perpetuated the beauty of the marble colonnades and triumphal arches, still standing majestically amid the ruins of Apollo's Temple, the Basilica, the great Roman amphitheatre, and the villas of the Roman elders.

"I could stay here for ever!" sighed Stephanie enchanted.

"We would," teased Guiseppe. "But now we must lunch."

The lunch, in a sumptuous hotel, was a dream, and the bill when it came was just staggering. Guiseppe paid it casually and said something to the waiter about a motor-launch.

"Motor-launch?" asked Stephanie, catching the gist of those few words of Italian. "Did you tell him we want a m-motor-launch?"

"Sure!" said Guiseppe. "We are going now to the Island of Capri!"

The girls met his teasing eyes and smiled at each other helplessly.

"And there we shall visit ze Blue Grotto," said Guiseppe. "For Capri has nothing more beautiful than ze Blue Grotto!"

The girls lay back against the cushions in the motor-launch and felt sleepy with the wonderful lunch, the sun and the gentle roll of the boat.

"Don't pinch me, Sue, or I shall wake up!"

"Me, too," echoed Sue.

They took a baffled look at Guiseppe's bland and inscrutable face . . . then turned their gaze seawards, over the bows of the speeding boat, to the distant isle of Capri rising up in the sunshine.

"Now," said Guiseppe, as at last they drew inshore, "we must change to a leetle boat! I tell you why."

"So you're going to let us in the secret at last!" exclaimed Stephanie. What's the answer, Guiseppe?"

"Because this boat is too big for ze Blue Grotto," chuckled Guiseppe.

He hired a small rowing-boat at the jetty. The girls scrambled in, and Guiseppe took the oars.

They seemed to be striking out towards the sheer face of the rocks, when suddenly he gave a soft warning.

"Dip your heads down. Low!"

They saw a low arch breaking into the rocks, scarcely three feet high. Stephanie ducked down beside Sue, and the boat glided into the dark cavern of the Blue Grotto.

It was so dark that at first they could see nothing. Then little by little their eyes grew accustomed to the dimness, and a kind of bluish rainbow began to appear. The colour deepened, growing steadily more luminous as the minutes passed and the boat glided on.

The light deepened to an exquisite sapphire blue, and now they could see the rocky walls of the grotto, rising to the roof of the cavern forty feet above their heads.

Presently a low ledge, like a platform, began to appear, sloping up from the edge of the water. A broken stairway, out into the rock, led from it.

The stairway, said Guiseppe, had once led up to a villa of ancient Tiberius, built high above.

"Climb the steps, and who knows what you will see," he teased them.

They scrambled out on to the ledge. They stepped on to the wide, broken stairway at the foot of the tunnel–

"Oh!" they gasped, dazed.

A flash of light lit the stairway, momentarily dazzling them, and they heard the click of a camera. Stephanie caught a fleeting glimpse of a young, bearded face–then it was gone, vanishing literally into the darkness above them.

"It was that photographer again–the same chap we saw at Vesuvius!" she gasped, and whirled round, all thoughts of the view from the end of the tunnel forgotten. "Guiseppe!"

Guiseppe's face was as innocent as a cherub's.

"You put him up to that, Guiseppe. You knew he was going to be here! Why? What's all this mystery–and these photographs–about?"

"No-one could resist so charming a picture–"

"But why does he want *ours* in particular, though?"

Guiseppe was a master of evasion, however.

"I think we should be on our way now," he murmured, glancing at his wrist-watch. "It is time we had a rest and some refreshment."

There was nothing to be got out of the tantalising Guiseppe. He rowed them back to the jetty. Then he took them to the tea-garden of what seemed to be the biggest, most expensive and smartest hotel on the island.

A dress display was in progress when they arrived. Stephanie and Sue watched–fascinated–from their table, while Guiseppe ordered tea and big portions of the superb Italian ice-cream.

Glamorous models were parading on a carpeted platform by the lake in the hotel gardens. They were displaying up-to-the-minute fashions from Paris and Rome.

While the public applauded, a group of business-like people sat in rows, watching shrewdly.

"They're the buyers. They represent the big shops, and they order the dresses they want," said Sue.

They were finishing their ices when someone came across to their table. The girls gazed in surprise. It was Miss Brent.

"Are you having a nice day, my dears?" she greeted them. "I want you to do something for me now, if you will."

She led them to the side of the platform and whispered something to the lady announcer at the microphone. Then she turned to the friends again.

"All I want you to do, dears, is to stroll up and down the platform. As naturally as you like."

Stephanie's senses spun. She looked completely blank. Neither of them had time to think. The models had all withdrawn, and Miss Brent gently edged them on to the platform.

They heard her voice ring out over the mike:

"Ladies and gentlemen. These girls are not professional models, nor did they even know that they are modelling the clothes they are wearing now. They have been wearing them all day, and you will see how fresh and trim they still look."

Her word were translated into Italian for the audience, by the lady announcer, as the chums paraded dizzily on the platform.

"Stephanie is wearing sailor-cut slacks with matching sandals, and a sleeveless tunic-top in England's very latest design. Her complete outfit may be bought for just under seven pounds."

An excited buzz came from the teenagers as the price was translated into Italian money.

"Sue is wearing a light, cool candy-striped frock, in England's very latest non-iron fabric. Her matching shoes and handbag give a gay, bright touch to the outfit, which, complete with accessories, costs only nine pounds."

The teenagers chattered excitedly, and the chums saw the buyers all writing briskly now in their notebooks.

"I repeat, Stephanie and Sue are not models, but ordinary active girls I chose to demonstrate how serviceable these new lines from England are," concluded Miss Brent. "They have worn them all day to go sightseeing, as you will see by their photographs taken for the Press. Thank you, my dears!"

Stephanie and Sue walked off the platform amid hearty handclapping from the audience.

"Darlings, you were wonderful–so natural! I knew you would show off these inexpensive lines much better than the models would. That's why I didn't explain to you!" enthused Miss Brent.

"B-but is that all you want us to do?" gasped Stephanie.

"All? My dears, you've helped me get a splendid order for the British dress trade!" declared Miss Brent. "Now off you go with Guiseppe to enjoy yourselves! He's bringing you back to me tonight, and we'll all dine and dance together in Naples! You'll see your photos in the newspapers by then!"

"Then that m-mystery photographer was a Press man–" Stephanie and Sue gasped together.

But Guiseppe was beckoning them now as he paid for the ices. It wasn't the end. It was only the beginning of their wonderful, unforgettable day in sunny Italy!

PAT'S HOUR OF PERIL

by Susan Morris

Pat Wilson was friendly with a boy in the seaside village where she lived but his parents had forbidden him to see her. Then, one day, Pat found a dangerous mine on the beach which might explode at any moment and destroy the whole village. What could Pat do to save the village?

The sky was cloudless with a hint of haze over the estuary as Pat Wilson ran down the beach at Thorhaven, the sea breeze blowing back her sun-bleached hair.

Pat always tried to fit in an early-morning swim, for after that she was too busy. The rest of her day was taken up with catching lobsters and selling them in the nearby town.

Usually Pat had the beach to herself, but this morning she saw that there was someone else there. A boy of about her own age was standing on the little wooden jetty from which Pat always began her swim. He waved to her.

"Come on, lazybones!" he called gaily. "The sea is lovely this morning."

Pat recognised him as Bob Hood, and she waved back happily as she ran to join him. Bob's father owned the Thorhaven fleet of trawlers, and the boy went to an expensive public school. Pat attended the local school, but she and Bob both loved swimming, and they saw a lot of each other during their school holidays.

"Hallo, Bob," Pat said and a warm smile shone on her sun-tanned face. "I didn't expect to see you this morning. You don't usually get up so early the first day of your summer holidays!"

Bob grinned.

"I thought I'd take you by surprise," he chuckled. "Have you been keeping up the swimming practice whilst I haven't been here to keep an eye on you?"

"Yes – and if you don't believe me I'll race you to the harbour mole," Pat challenged, promptly slipping off the old mackintosh which covered her swimsuit.

"Right!" said Bob. "I'll give you twenty yards start."

"I can beat you without a handicap," Pat chuckled, a teasing glint in her clear blue eyes. "Are you ready?"

Bob nodded, and they chanted One, Two, Three in unison. Then, at the word Go, they dived simultaneously into the sea, and struck out for the stone mole which protected the little harbour.

Pat was as good as her word, for she reached the end of the mole and scrambled up a flight of stone steps whilst Bob was still some twenty or thirty yards behind her.

"I say, Pat, you *have* improved," he exclaimed admiringly, when he reached the steps and clambered up beside her. "You ought to win the Junior Five Hundred Yards at the Gala."

"I'm going to have a shot at it," Pat replied with a smile; and they sat talking for a little while in the warm sun. Then Pat jumped to her feet.

"I'll have to be getting back," she said. "After breakfast I'm going out to fetch in our lobster-pots."

Then they swam back to the wooden jetty, and were making their way along it when they caught sight of a horsewoman cantering across the smooth sands which the ebb-tide had laid bare.

"Look!" exclaimed Bob. "Here's my mother out for an early morning ride."

Mrs. Hood checked her little chestnut mare when she reached the jetty. She was a handsome woman, but rather haughty-looking.

"Hallo, mother, this is Pat Wilson," Bob said, drawing Pat forward to be introduced. But Mrs. Hood gave Pat only the briefest of nods. She didn't speak to her. Pat felt a flush rising to her cheeks as she realised she'd been snubbed.

"Good-bye, Bob," she said hurriedly, and walked briskly up the beach to where she had left her mac and a towel. As she gave her face and arms a quick rub down she couldn't help overhearing what Mrs. Hood said.

"Robert, I'm annoyed with you. Your father is sending you to an expensive school, and we don't expect you to hobnob with fisher girls. Surely you can find someone more suitable as a friend than that girl?"

Pat didn't hear Bob's reply. She was too angry to listen.

"What a cheek," she thought indignantly, as she slipped into her mac. "We may not have a lot of money but we're as good as the Hoods, any day."

And she ran up the beach, and across the road to the little white-washed cottage where she lived with her widowed mother. As she reached the front door the postman was passing.

"Morning, Pat," he greeted her in his friendly way, and handed her a letter addressed to Mrs. Wilson.

"Golly, this looks important," Pat exclaimed, for the address was typewritten.

She gave the letter to her mother, who was in the kitchen preparing breakfast, then went to her own room to finish drying herself and get dressed. When Pat came downstairs again Mrs. Wilson was staring at the letter with a worried face.

"What is it, Mum?" Pat asked anxiously.

"It's from Mr. Hood," her mother answered in a distressed voice. "He says we're not to take any more lobsters from the Shallows."

"WHAT!" Pat cried, and read the letter which her mother handed to her.

It was addressed from Mr. Hood's office in Thorhaven, and stated very curtly that he had recently bought up most of the foreshore. "My rights extend to the Shallows from which you have been taking lobsters," the letter continued. "And I must warn you to discontinue this practice forthwith, otherwise I shall be forced to prosecute. Yours faithfully, Josiah Hood."

"Oh, but he can't do this," Pat cried. "Thorhaven people have always caught lobsters in the Shallows, and even if Mr. Hood has the legal right to stop us I think it's awfully mean of him. A few lobsters are nothing to anyone as rich as he is, but they mean a lot to us."

That was true. Pat's father had been drowned two years ago, and Mrs. Wilson had only a widow's pension; so the lobsters which Pat caught and sold in the nearby industrial town of Oldcastle were a big help.

"I don't suppose Mr. Hood has considered that," Mrs. Wilson said with a sigh. "Wealthy people don't always understand what a difference the money can make."

"Suppose I go and see Mr. Hood, and explain," Pat suggested impulsively. "Perhaps then he will change his mind."

Mrs. Wilson didn't think there was much likelihood of that happening, but she said nothing to discourage Pat. Soon after breakfast Pat set off for Mr. Hood's office. It was near the harbour, facing the quay where the Thorhaven trawlers unloaded their catches. Pat's heart was thumping as she neared it, and she almost turned back.

"He can't eat me!" she told herself; but she was still hesitating when a car drove up and a tall, burly man got out. Pat recognised him as Mr. Hood, and she stopped him as he was striding towards the building.

"Excuse me, sir, may I speak to you?" she said, and wished that her voice didn't sound so wobbly.

Mr. Hood frowned.

"Hey?" he asked sharply.

"It's about the letter you sent to my mother," Pat said; and began to explain. But Mr. Hood soon interrupted her.

"You're wasting my time," he snapped impatiently. "My rights extend to the Shallows, and I intend to enforce them. So don't let me catch you putting down lobster-pots there again."

Pat's plea had failed. Mr. Hood marched on to the swing doors which led to his office. But as he was entering he suddenly turned and addressed Pat again.

"Haven't I seen you with my boy?" he asked.

"We sometimes go swimming together during the holidays," Pat replied.

"Hum!" Mr. Hood grunted, and his frown deepened. "Well, in future I'll thank you to keep away from him," he said angrily. "I'm spending a lot o' brass making Robert into a right gentleman, and I want him to have the right sort of friends. So keep away from him in future."

And before Pat could think of an answer, he thrust his way through the swing doors and was gone.

"Oh, what a beastly thing to say!" Pat thought indignantly as she turned and walked away.

"Never mind, my dear," Mrs. Wilson said, when Pat told her what had happened. "We shall manage, I daresay. But perhaps you had better not see anything more of the boy," she added gently.

Pat flushed. "I shan't," she said; and forced a smile so as not to let her mother guess how miserable she felt. "And now I think I ought to go out and fetch in our lobster-pots."

"Perhaps you had," her mother agreed; and Pat went down to the beach where their dinghy was tied up at the end of the little wooden jetty. As she was casting off she heard a shout, and Bob came hurrying along the jetty. He was looking serious.

"I say," he began in an embarrassed voice. "Dad has told me what he said to you. I – I'm awfully sorry, Pat."

"It isn't your fault," Pat answered quietly. "But since both your parents object to us being friends I don't think we had better go swimming or rowing together, any more."

Then she pushed off quickly from the jetty lest Bob should see the glint of tears in her eyes.

"Hey!" he called after her. "Come back! We can't part like this, Pat! Come back! Please!"

"It's no use," Pat answered, with a little break in her voice. "It will be best if we don't meet again."

But she felt very depressed as she rowed away, for she had grown to be very fond of Bob.

Helped by the ebb-tide, Pat soon reached the Shallows near the mouth of the estuary, and found the buoys which marked the lobster-pots. They were blocks of wood, each with a little flag flying from a couple of feet of stick.

Leaning over the gunwale, Pat grabbed one of the buoys, and began to haul in the line which was fastened to it. Presently a dripping cage of bent hazel-sticks came up out of the water, and Pat tumbled it down into the bottom of the boat without stopping to examine the catch. Then she seized another line, and repeated the process.

One by one Pat hauled in a dozen lobsterpots, rowing from buoy to buoy. As she worked she noticed that a thick mist was drifting in from the sea, and blotting out the coastline; but she didn't worry because she had often been out on the estuary in a fog.

She finished getting in the lobster-pots, and began the long pull back to Thorhaven. Luckily she didn't have to row against the tide, for it had turned by this time and was flowing strongly. Except for the occasional faraway mournful blare of a ship's siren it was very quiet out on the estuary, and the water had the still, oily look which it often does have in a sea-mist.

Pat hadn't rowed far when a big metal sphere loomed in the mist.

"It must be a marker-buoy that's broken loose from its moorings and is drifting with the tide," Pat thought.

But as it came nearer, rolling sluggishly from side to side, she saw that it was not the right size or shape for a buoy. The black paint had peeled off in places to show the rusty iron plates below, and there was a red ring painted round the top, and four spikes or horns sticking out from the sides.

Pat's heart gave a sudden wild thump, and then seemed to miss a beat. The sphere was a floating mine – a relic of the war!

"Oh! If it hits my dinghy, it'll explode!" she gasped in horror. For she knew that if one of the horns came into contact with anything solid, such as the hull of a ship, the mine would explode and blow the vessel out of the water. Once before a mine had been washed ashore near Thorhaven, and the coastguards had had to explode it from a safe distance with rifle-fire.

"I – I must get away from the beastly thing," was Pat's first thought and she bent to her oars.

Then she thought of something that sent a chill up her spine. The fishing fleet was due back in Thorhaven that morning, and it was quite possibly one of their sirens she had heard sounding a little while before. If the mine drifted out into the fairway one of the trawlers might easily hit it in the thick mist for they would not be thinking of such a danger.

"Oh, gosh!" Pat gulped. "There isn't time to row back to Thorhaven and get the harbourmaster to send out a radio warning, and if I row out to meet the fishing fleet I may easily miss them in this fog. But unless I do something one of the boats may easily hit the mine as they head for the harbour."

Pat almost panicked as she realized her own helplessness. Then she had an idea that set her heart thumping wildly again.

"It–it's a wild idea–and dreadfully dangerous," she thought, hesitating, for her plan involved a fearful risk to herself.

And then Pat remembered that her father had been the bo'sun of the Thorhaven lifeboat, and his father before him.

"They risked their lives lots of times to help vessels in distress," she told herself firmly, and she hesitated no longer.

She turned the dinghy and rowed cautiously back towards the floating mine. Yes, as she had thought, there was a metal ring in the side, below the deadly spikes.

Pat selected the longest of her lines and made it fast to a cleat in the dinghy's stern. Then she shipped one oar, and sculled with the other, standing upright and holding the free end of the line in her left hand.

As she neared the floating mine a wave hit it, and the rusty iron sphere rolled over towards the dinghy. Pat gasped fearfully, and thrust clear with her oar just in the nick of time – indeed, one of the deadly horns seemed almost to scrape the dinghy's gunwale!

"Oh, I've never been so scared in my life!" Pat whispered.

But she persevered with her plan. As the rusty sphere began to roll upright again, she grabbed the ring and tried to thrust the end of her line through it. But fright made her fingers all thumbs, and before she could make the line secure the mine came rolling over towards her a second time.

Once again Pat thrust the dinghy clear; and now she was tempted to give up the hazardous attempt to take the floating mine in tow. But then it was almost as though she heard her father's voice encouraging her.

"Nay, lass! Thee cannot give up. Try again."

"Yes, I've GOT to succeed," Pat whispered; and suddenly her hands ceased to tremble.

She sculled alongside the mine again, and this time she inserted the line through the ring, and made it fast before the rusty sphere began its slow backward roll towards her. Then she was clear, and sculling for dear life.

As she picked up the slack in the line and it grew taut Pat took both oars and started to row with all her strength towards the shore.

It was hard work towing the heavy metal sphere, but fortunately the tide helped her. Pat's heart was in her mouth with every stroke she took, and she kept a fearful watch on the mine as it rolled and wallowed in her wake. Suppose she exploded it? . . . Pat tried not to think of that. But it was a nightmare experience.

Presently she heard the sound of surf. The mist was thinning slightly, and when Pat looked over her shoulder she saw the waves breaking in clouds of flying spray over a long reef of jagged rocks some way out from the shore.

"I'll cast the mine loose here," she thought "Then the tide will carry it on to the reef, and it ought to explode when it hits a rock."

Shipping her oars, Pat quickly untied the line, and let the mine drift free. As she expected, it began to drift with the tide towards the reef, and Pat gave a little gasp of relief to be free of her dangerous companion.

"But I had better start rowing again," she told herself. "Or I shall be on the rocks myself."

But Pat was getting very weary after her long row, and the tide was setting very strongly towards the reef. She didn't seem to be getting any nearer the seashore which she could glimpse through a break in the mist. Indeed, after a time she seemed to be nearer the reef than ever. She began to grow alarmed.

"I'm being swept on to the reef," she thought. "Gosh! I didn't realize the tide would be so strong. But I MUST get clear before the mine goes off."

She tugged desperately at the oars, although her shoulders ached and her arms felt heavy as lead. But it was no use; she was fighting a losing battle with the strong tide. Once again Pat felt a chill at her heart. Even if she wasn't killed when the mine exploded, the jagged rocks would tear the bottom out of the little dinghy. Then, good swimmer though she was, she would stand no chance in that cruel tide.

Pat was in despair, but she went on rowing desperately, and kept a fearful eye on the floating mine. It was now so near the edge of the reef Pat expected it would be detonated any moment.

And then, when she had given up hope, she heard the throbbing of an engine. Some motor vessel was passing in the mist. Pat stopped rowing.

"Help!" she shouted desperately. "Help!"

But there was no answering hail, and the sound of the engine grew fainter. Pat could have wept for despair. She thought the vessel was

"Jeepers! What was that?"

going to pass without hearing her cries. But then she heard the sound of the engine returning, and a motor-boat came out of the grey, swirling mist.

"Help! Help! I'm drifting on to the reef," Pat cried.

And even as she shouted Pat saw that the solitary occupant of the motor-boat was Bob Hood. He shouted back to her, and put his tiller hard over, and the motor-boat glided gently alongside the dinghy.

"Get in, and I'll take your dinghy in tow," he cried.

Pat dropped her oars, and grabbed the dinghy's painter. Then she scrambled into the motor-boat, and Bob opened his throttle wide. The motor-boat surged away from the reef, and a curtain of mist came down over it.

"What were you doing so near the reef?" Bob asked, as Pat slumped in her seat, feeling shaky with relief. "It's jolly lucky I came to look for you in our motor-boat."

But before Pat could reply there was a blinding flash of saffron-yellow flame that tore a great rent in the fog, and a roar that seemed to shake the heavens.

"Jeepers! What was that?" Bob asked in a startled voice.

"It–it was a–a floating mine," Pat answered shakily; and gave a rather breathless account of her adventure.

Bob gazed at her in stunned silence as she finished.

"Gosh! You've a lot more nerve than I have," he said at last in an awed voice. "I should never have dared take a mine in tow."

"I had to do something to save the fishing fleet," Pat answered simply.

Bob, of course, gave his father a full account of Pat's adventure, and that evening Mr. Hood's car drove up to the Wilsons' cottage, and he and Bob got out. Pat and her mother were sitting by their front door repairing some lobster-pots.

"Good evening, Mrs. Wilson," Mr. Hood said rather awkwardly. "I've come to thank your lass for the plucky way she saved my trawlers. And I also want to apologise to you for being so rude this morning," he added to Pat.

Pat flushed. "There's no need to do that," she answered, rather embarrassed.

"Hum! I'm not much good at this kind of thing," Mr. Hood went on, smiling rather wryly. "But I want to say that both Mrs. Hood and myself would like you and Bob to be friends again. I reckon pluck and intelligence, such as you've got, lass, are a lot more important than money, or even an expensive education. And, of course, you're welcome to take as many lobsters from the Shallows as you like. By the way," he hurried on, before Pat or her mother had a chance to reply, "Bob has something for you, lass."

Bob grinned cheerfully, and patted a square box which he had lifted out of the car.

"It's something for the dinghy, Pat," he said. "Come on–I'll show you."

He raced down the beach to where the Wilsons' dinghy rested on the shingle.

"What is it?" Pat asked, intrigued, as she ran after him.

"An outboard motor," Bob smiled, putting the mysterious box on the dinghy's thwarts, and opening it. "Dad wanted to make you a little present, and I said an outboard motor for the dinghy would be jolly useful."

"Oh, Bob! It's a lovely present," Pat cried in a thrilled voice. "It's what I've always wanted."

Then she slipped a slender brown hand into his.

"But best of all I like your Dad saying that we can be friends again," she smiled happily.

JO OF HAWTHORN STABLES

by Enid Boyten

When Jo Hathaway was riding her beautiful chestnut horse, Beauty, over the moors, she thought she saw the phantom huntsman with his long cloak. If this was the one of which she had heard, she knew he could be a danger to her stables. Trying to solve the mystery, she found herself in the midst of some strange adventures.

"So it's true! Or–am I dreaming?"

The startled words broke from Jo Hathaway, the young owner of Hawthorn Stables, as she reined in her horse on the dark moorland track.

It was a misty winter's night. Jo had ridden over to Moorstone to buy horse fodder and other things she needed, and she had been delayed there longer than she had expected. It was quite late as she rode her splendid chestnut, Beauty, along the track that led towards Hawthorn Cottage.

She had happened to glance over her shoulder across the mist-wreathed moors, where the moonlight shone in fitful gleams. It was then that she reined Beauty in, with that gasp of amazement.

"The–the phantom huntsman!" she whispered.

Were her eyes playing tricks? Some distance off, a glowing shape had emerged from a bank of mist. It was the figure of a horseman in a flowing cloak, bathed in an eerie light as he rode across the moor towards the distant cliffs.

Only for a few seconds did Jo's eyes rest on him. Then, almost before she could blink in amazement, that distant, weirdly glowing rider had vanished in the mist again, and echoing across the misty moors came to her ears the distant sound of a huntsman's horn.

Jo sat for a moment as if turned to stone, her thoughts racing. Everyone in that district knew the legend of Jeb Towers, the phantom huntsman.

It was said that Jeb had been huntsman to a nobleman in the eighteenth century. One day he and his horse and his hounds had gone astray in a terrific storm that had covered the moors with darkness. They had ridden clean over the cliff, never to be found again.

The legend said that on certain moonlit nights Jeb Towers could still be seen, sounding a phantom horn and galloping towards the cliffs.

Until a few days ago that story had been only a legend. But just lately rumours had reached Jo that the phantom huntsman had actually been seen.

"I thought Mrs. Bond was just imagining things when she rang me up this morning," mused Jo. "But she wasn't–unless I've jolly well been imagining things myself."

Mrs. Bond was a rather nervous lady who had a twelve-year-old daughter, Roberta. For some time past Roberta had been one of Jo's pupils at the riding-school. But that morning Mrs. Bond had rung up, cancelling the rides for the time being.

"Of course, I don't believe in ghosts," Mrs. Bond had said. "But something queer is happening on the moors, Miss Jo. There are strange rumours about a phantom figure. Roberta is a highly strung child, and she just doesn't care to ride on the moors now, even in daytime."

Jo didn't believe in ghosts either, but all the same, that phone call had worried her. She loved her life at Hawthorn Stables. But it wasn't easy to make a profit, week after week, especially in the winter; and she couldn't afford to lose any of her clients. She couldn't afford to have them scared off the moors.

And now–Jo had actually seen the phantom huntsman herself. Or–had she? Was it possibly some trick of mist and moonlight?

"Beauty! If it was clearer, we'd gallop over there and search," Jo exclaimed, speaking aloud to her horse, as she often did. "But the mist is closing in–we'd probably get lost if we left the track."

It was a very puzzled Jo who arrived at the little white-walled cottage, with the stables clustering beyond. And that puzzlement had not grown less by the time she dropped off to sleep that night. When she did so eventually, it was only to dream of a phantom rider in flowing cloak, gliding across the moors to the sound of a ghostly horn. And then, in the morning–came another disturbing phone call.

This time it was from Dan Verity, a genial farmer who was one of Jo's nearest neighbours. His two nieces, Kay and Muriel–who lived with him–often came to Hawthorn Stables for rides.

"Reckon you'll say I've been listening to old wives' tales, Miss Jo," came his booming voice over the wire. "But those two nieces o' mine have been a bit scared-like by all these yarns o' the phantom huntsman. One of our farmhands vows he's actually seen the feller, flowin' cloak and huntsman's horn, and all the rest of it. Utter moonshine, of course–and so I told him. But Kay and Muriel–bless their hearts!–feel they'd rather stop ridin' on the moors for a while, anyway."

Jo's forehead was worriedly puckered as she put down the receiver. Two more of her young clients lost, because of the so-called phantom huntsman!

"Gosh! I've got to do something about this!" Jo murmured.

She was having a specially difficult time just now. For one thing, Tom Chubb, her loyal old groom, was away with influenza. And last week the weather had been so bad that riding was practically impossible, and Jo's stables had earned very little.

"And now, because of the phantom huntsman, I've lost Roberta, Kay, and Muriel as clients," thought Jo. "I can't afford to lose any more. So to-night I'm going to keep watch. And if that person who's dressing up as a phantom huntsman appears again, I'll jolly well tell him what I think of him.

"Quiet, Beauty! Steady, boy!"

Jo rested a gloved hand on her chestnut's silky neck, as they waited that night, concealed in a little copse. Although she had only seen that glowing figure for a few seconds the previous night, Jo knew, within a little, just where the mysterious rider had appeared. And now she and Beauty were hidden in a small copse near the spot.

The moon was rising. Once again those wraith-like patches of mist clung to the frosty ground here and there.

"Maybe we're on a wild-goose chase, Beauty," whispered Jo. "Maybe I didn't really see that ghostly horseman last night at all. But we had to take the chance, Beauty, old fellow, for the sake of the stables, and–ah-h-h!"

She whirled, with straining ears. A sound had echoed through the mist-wreathed night. The ringing notes–faint, yet clear–of a huntsman's horn. There was a brief pause and then it sounded again, much nearer this time.

"Just as if a rider's coming on through the mist," quivered Jo. "But the ground is frozen as hard as iron. If a rider was coming, surely I would hear the clatter of hoofs. Last night I was too far away, but to-night–"

In spite of herself, she felt her heartbeats quicken. For the third time that eerie horn echoed through the night. Then from a patch of mist, emerged the rider.

Again he was bathed in that weird glow. Wearing a flowing cloak, he was bent low over his horse's head. And though he was galloping over the frozen ground not very far from Jo, not a sound of hoof-beats could she hear.

"It's just as if–as if he's gliding over the ground!" panted Jo.

She felt an odd tingle of fear. Then, with a shake of her brown curls, she threw it off.

"Beauty! We must follow!" she panted.

In a twinkling she was in the saddle. A touch of her heels on Beauty's flanks, and he was whirling out of the copse.

Again the weird, echoing notes of the huntsman's horn rang in her ears.

And then–disaster!

As bad luck would have it, a fox started out from under the frosty grass, almost at Beauty's feet. No horse–however well trained–could be blamed for taking momentary alarm at such a happening. Beauty checked, and reared. Jo, startled, lost her grip and pitched to the ground.

Like the good rider that she was, she kept hold of the reins. Unhurt, she pulled herself gasping to her feet.

"Oh, Beauty! That was hard lines!" she breathed. "Steady, old fellow–steady. The fox has gone, and–"

The words died in her throat. She stared ahead, wondering again if this was some eerie dream. For in a clear patch of moonlight she had seen the phantom rider heading straight for the cliff. Then, before her eyes, he vanished, just as if he had plunged over the brink, as Jeb Towers–his lordship's huntsman–was reputed to have done two hundred years ago.

Staring in blank amazement, Jo climbed back into the saddle, urging Beauty forward. A breeze had rolled back the mist a little, and yet she had a clearer view of this area of the moor, which was bounded not very far ahead by the cliffs and the sea.

"There's that small fisherman's cottage," Jo murmured, "and a haystack nearby. But no stable or shed–no place, surely, where a horse could be hidden."

She rode right round the tiny cottage. She dismounted again at the edge of the cliffs, gazing down their sheer surface to the sea creaming in foam far below.

"It's just as if the phantom horseman vanished into thin air!" she told herself.

A little farther back she saw an object on the hard-frozen earth, and picked it up. It was a scrap of cloth with a nail embedded in it, and thoughtfully she slipped it into her pocket.

Was it a clue? She couldn't tell. And, after further search, she felt it was useless to remain any longer, especially as the mist was beginning to creep in again.

"There may be something I've missed," she told herself. "I must come back in daylight when I can get a clearer view. I mustn't give up–whatever happens!"

No, she mustn't give up. For the mystery of the phantom huntsman was still unsolved. The threat to her beloved stables still remained.

The stone-walled cottage–the lone haystack–the cliffs with their wheeling gulls–how different it all looked in the wintry sunshine, thought Jo, compared with the eeriness of last night's happenings! And yet how clearly it seemed to prove that there was no hiding-place for a horse here, no explanation as to how the phantom huntsman and his mount had vanished.

After giving early morning feed to her horses and grooming them, Jo had cycled out here again. It was as if a magnet drew her to the spot, as if she could not rest till she had solved the problem.

Slowly she walked forward, scanning the ground on each side of her.

"That piece of cloth with the nail," she mused. "Was it linked with the phantom huntsman in any way? Was it–"

She paused, heartbeats quickening, a glint in her brown eyes. From the haystack a length of fencing ran crookedly towards the cottage. And across its topmost bar, close to the stack, hung–a saddle and bridle!

Here, surely, was vital evidence! Jo hurried noiselessly towards them, lifted and examined them, turning them about in her hands.

"Just an ordinary saddle–an ordinary bridle," she told herself. "But, gosh! What are they doing here? Could they be the ones used by the phantom huntsman?"

A footstep sounded from beyond a clump of frost-starred brambles. Hastily Jo put the harness back on the fence, and stepped away–to confront a youngish man in jersey and shabby blue trousers, with untidy hair, who had evidently come from the cottage.

Jo had always thought that the cottage was empty. She never remembered seeing this young man before. He threw a careless glance at the saddle.

"Well, miss! Nice to see a human face around these lonesome parts," he muttered. "It's getting real scaring. Maybe you heard it last night? Maybe you saw it?"

Jo stared. "You mean–"

"I mean Jeb Towers, the phantom huntsman!" he burst out. "He's riding again, just as the legend says. I saw him last night–and the night before that. I heard his horn wailing like a banshee. I watched him–with my own eyes–vanish over the cliff yonder. And he'll come again to-night, for it's the night of the full moon. I tell you, miss, it's more than flesh and blood can stand."

He seemed to check himself, thrusting his hands in his pockets, gazing at Jo with nervous deep-set eyes.

"Sorry to let off steam like that, miss," he went on, more quietly. "But after I broke a leg and couldn't go to sea any more, I was trained as a leather-worker. Thought to earn a living by making leather articles, repairing saddlery and such-like–that saddle on the fence there is one I've been working on these past few days. I took this cottage, thinking to settle down quietly at my work."

Sombrely he shook his head.

"It's no use," he went on. "Ghosts–phantoms–visions in the night. Jeb Towers with his ghostly horn! I'm packing up today and clearing out, and if you've any sense, miss, you'll keep of the moors. It's a place of bad omen, miss. And Bill Hargraves, for one, has had enough."

He slouched to the fence, picked up the saddle and bridle, and–with a nod to Jo–walked back towards the cottage. And Jo, her thoughts confused, moved away to where she had left her cycle.

"So that," she mused, "explains the saddle. It wasn't an important clue at all."

And here, she reflected uneasily, was someone else who was being scared off the moors. On her return home Jo wheeled her cycle into the shed where she kept it and it so happened that a breeze blew the door shut behind her, leaving her in momentary darkness.

She raised her hand to open the door again. And then–a choking little cry broke from her. She raised her other hand before her eyes, gazing amazedly at them both. Her hands were empty. Yet, nevertheless, they held vital proof.

"I–I begin to understand!" she whispered.

That proof–that amazing evidence she had seen when she looked at her hands–had set her thoughts flashing in a new direction. She began to put two and two together. She began to make plans as she made her way to the little cottage.

"Thank goodness that the twins are coming to-day!" she murmured.

Those loyal young helpers from the village, Maureen and Martin Archer, had a day's holiday from school. They loved nothing better than to help their admired Jo at Hawthorn Stables.

"I'll have to leave them in charge, to some extent," she thought. "Because I must make a trip into the town, and–and plan a hundred things for to-night. And I'll have to phone Farmer Verity and Mrs. Bond, too. I'll be taking a big chance, for the sake of the stables. Oh, if only it works out as I hope!"

After dark that night, a shooting-brake was being driven along the moorland track, as the full moon swung high above the cliffs. Genial

Farmer Verity was at the wheel. Beside him sat Mr. Bond, while Mrs. Bond and their daughter Roberta were in the back, together with Kay and Muriel, the farmer's two nieces.

"Mummy! What's going to happen?" inquired Roberta, throwing back her fair pigtails.

"My dear girl! I just don't know," Mrs. Bond replied. "I must confess I'm a little nervous myself. Everything looks so eerie out here on the moors at this hour. If Miss Jo hadn't been so insistent, I hardly think I should have ventured, even with daddy and Mr. Verity to look after us."

The farmer chuckled as he puffed at his pipe.

"Well, Mrs. Bond, ma'am! It was the least we could do," he said. "We took our youngsters away from Jo Hathaway's riding-school because this legend of the so-called phantom huntsman was scarin' them. And now Miss Jo sends us an urgent message to come out on the moors, where she'll demonstrate just what this phantom is. So–bless my prize porkers!–here we are!"

He brought the shooting-brake to rest under the shadow of some trees on rising ground near the cliffs, where Jo had asked them to wait. Tense, silent minutes passed. Then–

"Mummy! Mummy!" Roberta suddenly cried. "W-what's that?"

"Only the waves on the shore yonder," reassured the farmer.

But Roberta sprang to her feet, clinging to her mother.

"It isn't! It's the huntsman's horn! Listen–all of you!"

There was no mistaking it now. Weirdly it echoed over the moors.

"And–and look!" Muriel Verity was on her feet now. "That glow of light over there. It's the huntsman!"

Yes! Once again the weirdly glowing horseman was gliding over the frozen ground. No sound of hoofs; nothing but the eerie wailing of the horn. The little party in the shooting-brake gazed in wonder-struck silence.

And then–

"Great guns!" Farmer Verity half-rose in his seat. "Here's another one! Are we dreaming?"

It was true! From a clump of bushes to their right, between the first horseman and the cliffs, came a second rider. Straight towards the first phantom-like figure it sped, equally noiseless, with no sound of hoof-beats. It wore the same type of flowing cloak, and the same weird glow shone from it.

No wonder the occupants of the shooting-brake gazed as if turned to stone as those two riders drew closer together. The second one, they saw, had raised a glowing arm. And now a hollow, ghost-like voice floated through the shadows.

"Who comes here?" it called. "Who dares to impersonate me–Jeb Towers, the huntsman? Who is this masquerader? Woe to him! Woe–woe–woe!"

A cry–a shout of fear–broke suddenly from the first rider.

He checked his horse so suddenly that the animal reared and plunged. And next moment he tumbled headlong to the ground.

And now a voice rang out again.

"Farmer Verity! Mr. Bond! Quick–quick! Help me hold him!"

Never had the burly farmer moved so fast.

"By Jingo! It's Miss Jo!" he boomed.

Like a human cannon-ball he hurtled out of the brake, Mr. Bond close on his heels. And next moment they had grasped that panting, scared figure who had fallen from the saddle.

"I thought as much!" came Jo's voice again. "It's Bill Hargraves–the man who lives in that cottage on the cliff. He's the phantom huntsman!"

Mrs. Bond and the girls were coming forward now, and in amazement they gazed at the scene.

Jo had thrown open the plastic cloak she was wearing. Attached on a belt underneath it were several electric bulbs, attached to a small battery, and it was these which had helped to throw out that weird glow. Jo had been riding Beauty, and his harness had been treated with luminous paint. Jo had, in fact, used much the same ghost-like disguise as the scowling, shivering Bill Hargraves.

"You see, I found a saddle hanging on the cottage fence this morning," Jo explained. "This man pretended he was engaged in leather work and repairs, and I believed his story. But when I stepped into a dark shed at home I found my hands were glowing. Luminous paint had stuck to them when I picked up the saddle. And that proved, of course, that the saddle had been used by the phantom huntsman!"

Jo's brown eyes danced suddenly.

"I thought Bill Hargraves was the type of ignorant fellow who might be scared if he saw another phantom figure. I guessed he'd think it really was the ghost of Jeb Towers," she went on. "So I decided to dress up, just as he did and confront him while you were watching. It was my only chance to catch him!"

Jo's first clue, of course, had been the scrap of cloth and the nail, which she had recognised as coming from a horse-shoe. It had suggested to her that the "phantom" horse might have had its hoofs muffled in cloth, to create the soundless effect.

She had done the same with Beauty's hoofs.

"But–but why?" cried Mrs. Bond. "Why did this man go to all that trouble?"

A letter in Bill Hargraves' pocket gave them the reason. He was in league with two men who were smuggling along that part of the coast. By playing the ghost, Bill Hargraves had hoped to scare people away, so that the smugglers could work undisturbed.

"But I still don't know how the ghostly horse and rider disappeared so suddenly as they neared the cliff, when I saw them last night," confessed Jo.

It was Farmer Verity who cleared up that point. Something about that haystack behind the cottage struck him as odd. And when they investigated, they found that it was, in fact, a shed, cleverly camouflaged as a stack, with thatched roof and straw sides. It was in here that Bill Hargraves kept his horse.

A phone call to the coastguard station resulted in Hargraves being taken in charge, and his accomplices rounded up.

"And to-morrow, Miss Jo, I reckon you're going to have three girl pupils coming back for their rides," boomed Farmer Verity. "Roberta, Muriel, and Kay. Eh, girls?"

"Rather!" they chorused.

Jo smiled happily. Never again would the phantom huntsman of the moors be a threat to Hawthorn Stables.

NURSE POLLY AT THE CIRCUS

by Ann Larvin

When Nurse Polly Martin took her little girl patients on an outing to the circus, she had to go backstage and soon found herself dramatically trying to save a girl acrobat.

Nurse Polly Martin saw the notice on the staff announcements board as she waited in the main entrance of St. Vincent's hospital for her friend, Liz Blake, to join her, going off-duty.

VOLUNTEERS NEEDED.

A party of convalescent patients will attend a matinée performance at the Grand Theatre, Camberford, as guests of the Friends of the Hospital, on Thursday next.

Extra escorts are urgently needed. Will any nurses, off-duty at that time, please volunteer to help?

(Signed.) Matron.

Liz's voice interrupted her reading. "Sorry I'm late, Polly. Sister was talking to me about my pet patient."

In the Children's Ward, Liz's special charge was six-year-old Linda Rivers who had been admitted to St. Vincent's after a car crash in which her aunt, her only relative in England, had been killed.

"Has Linda managed to speak today, Liz?" asked Polly eagerly.

Liz's face clouded. "Not a word yet. And it's three weeks now since the accident. Sister says Linda's X-ray shows no head injury. So her loss of speech is due to shock. And unless she recovers soon," said Liz unhappily, "it could be very serious."

Polly sighed. "If only her parents were here, they might help."

Linda's father was an explorer. His wife had accompanied him on his latest expedition. Now they were deep in the forests of the Amazon, out of touch with civilization.

"It might be weeks before they even know Linda's ill. I've got to help her *now,*" said said Liz desperately. "There must be some way to encourage her to talk again. If she'd only give a smile even!"

Polly's face suddenly brightened. "There is a way, Liz!" She pointed to Matron's notice. "Let's volunteer as escorts!"

"But how will that help Linda?" asked Liz.

Polly chuckled. "Don't you know what's appearing at the Grand this week? A circus. Youngsters always yell and laugh their heads off at a circus."

"And so might Linda," added Polly gaily, "if Matron will give us permission to take her to the show."

Thursday's matinée at the Grand was nearing its end. The stage, now converted into a circus ring, darkened. A spotlight picked out the scarlet-coated ringmaster.

"And now, friends," he boomed, "specially imported from America, a daring, death-defying act on the high wire."

The audience waited, expectant. But Polly was watching Linda in the seat beside her. Matron had readily permitted the two nurses to take Linda among the party. But their hopes that Linda might talk at the circus seemed vain.

"My plan's a flop," thought Polly. Linda didn't even laugh at the trained seal or those funny chimps. And when a girl bareback rider or those tiny Shetland ponies didn't interest her, a high-wire act surely wouldn't.

The stage again blazed into light.

"And now," the ringmaster was saying, "meet those talented artistes, the Baroni brothers. First – Beppo!"

With a spectacular leap, a tall young man in a black-and-silver leotard sprang across the ring and stood bowing.

"Next," called the ringmaster, "meet Bumpsa!"

Bumpsa, much shorter than his brother, seemed just a boy, in spite of his enormous shaggy red wig. He was comically dressed in baggy patched trousers, a ragged coat, several sizes too big, over a gaudily-striped shirt, a huge spotted bow-tie and a long trailing scarf.

Like his brother, he leapt forward – only to land flat on his tummy. There he lay, blowing kisses, till Beppo lifted him by the seat of his trousers and dropped him by the ladder.

Swiftly, Beppo shinned up. "After me, Bumpsa!" he called.

Bumpsa's climb up the ladder, with comic slips every few rungs, made every child in the audience roar with laughter – except Linda.

Beppo had stepped on to the wire. After him, swaggered Bumpsa – and slipped. Gasps of horror changed to laughter as Bumpsa was seen bent double over the wire, till Beppo yanked him up again.

Whatever Beppo did on the wire, Bumpsa imitated. But always, to the delight of his audience, he got into comical difficulties. When their act ended, wild applause and wilder cheering greeted the Baroni brothers. But throughout it all, Linda remained silent.

Polly and Liz escorted their patients back to St. Vincent's and handed Linda over to the staff nurse in the Children's Ward.

"Bye, darling," Polly smiled. "I hope you liked the circus."

Linda drew a deep breath. Polly gripped Liz's arm, as the child's lips moved. "I-I-liked Bumpsa," she faltered. "He was so funny."

Linda could not be persuaded to say more. But Polly and Liz were jubilant as they left the ward.

"Wasn't it fabulous, hearing her speak," said Polly. "Poor pet, she was just too tired and excited to say any more."

Liz smiled. "By tomorrow, she'll have plenty to say. All about Bumpsa!"

But Liz was mistaken. By lunchtime next day, when she met Polly in the staff canteen, Linda had not uttered another word. Moreover, she was feverish. On doctor's orders, she was back in bed.

"Everybody in the ward's tried to get her to talk about Bumpsa. But it's no use." Liz said dolefully. "She's lost her speech completely again."

Polly said nothing. But another plan had flashed into her mind. Bumpsa had helped Linda to speak yesterday. Perhaps he can do the trick again, thought Polly.

Off-duty that afternoon, Polly made an excuse to go into Camberford – alone. She went straight to the Grand's stage door. Luck was with her. The first person she saw, standing chatting near the stage door, was Beppo Baroni. Polly introduced herself, then –

"One of our patients at St. Vincent's needs help, Mr. Baroni." Eagerly, Polly told him everything about Linda. Then added: "I'm sure she'd talk to Bumpsa. She's too ill to come to the circus again. But if only Bumpsa would visit her –"

Beppo's face darkened. "Impossible! My brother's too busy to visit the hospital. Or to talk to you!" He turned to the doorkeeper. "See that this girl leaves the theatre – at once!"

There was only one thing for it now. Outside, Polly bought a ticket, for the performance that evening . . .

Much later, Polly was watching Bumpsa struggling up the ladder. Then, lollipop in hand, he swaggered after Beppo on to the wire . . . and slipped.

Polly stiffened with horror. Something was wrong! This time, Bumpsa did not save himself by folding his body over the wire. He was hanging high above the ring, desperately clutching the wire with one hand.

He fell, but caught the ladder – just in time. He swung round, seeking a foothold on a rung that would mean safety. But again, he slipped. Silent with shock, the audience saw him slide down the ladder, trying to clutch each rung, then lie in a crumpled heap at its foot. But even before Beppo had followed him swiftly down, Bumpsa struggled dazedly to his feet.

The scene darkened. Shortly afterwards, a spotlight picked out the ringmaster. "Due to a slight mishap, ladies and gentlemen, we must change the order of our programme. The next performer will be that lasso-and-gun artiste from the Wildest West . . . Montana Mike."

If Bumpsa's hurt, perhaps I can help, thought Polly. Dashing backstage, she scanned the names on each door till she glimpsed. "The Baroni Brothers." Just as she was about to knock, she heard a voice through the open transom above the door.

It was Beppo's voice. "Listen to me, kid. You're going back on that wire, right after Montana's act. The Baronis *never* miss a show. So pull yourself together – fast."

There was no reply. "You've not broken any bones," Beppo continued harshly. "Just because you're scared, you're not spoiling our big chance here. I'm gonna see the boss right now."

Polly just had time to dart back into the shadows of the passage before Beppo strode out. "I'll tell him," he flung the words back over his shoulder, "that the Baroni brothers will appear at *both* shows tonight – as advertised."

As Beppo hurried off towards the stage. Polly softly approached the door which he had left open. Within the dressing-room, Bumpsa stood, with his back towards her, clinging to a chair.

"Are you ill?" asked Polly. "Can I help you? I'm a nurse."

The boy spun round. He began to sway unsteadily. Polly darted towards him and helped him to a couch.

Suddenly, the boy slumped back on the couch in a dead faint. His shaggy red wig had slipped askew. Gently, Polly eased it off . . . and gasped with astonishment.

But at that moment, someone caught her shoulder and jerked her round. She had been too concerned with Bumpsa to realise that Beppo had returned.

"How dare you come prying in here, girl!" Beppo blazed. "Leave my dressing-room at once!"

Polly angrily flung off his arm. "Certainly not! I'm a nurse and I will not leave my patient," she retorted. "Not till you call a doctor to give Bumpsa a check-up."

Beppo's face darkened. "I'm not calling any doctor, just because my brother got scared and took a tumble."

Polly's temper snapped. "It's you, not Bumpsa who's really scared. Beppo Baroni. And that's why you wouldn't let Bumpsa come to the hospital to visit Linda. That's why you don't want a doctor – or anyone else – to see Bumpsa. You're scared your secret will be discovered."

She turned, pointing to the still figure of Bumpsa lying on the couch, to the mass of silky dark curls, which released from the red wig, framed the quiet delicate little face.

"You've been scared all the time that someone would find out that the Baroni brothers' high-wire act is a phony," Polly went on accusingly, "because Bumpsa is a *girl!*"

Polly saw Beppo's face whiten beneath his make-up. Her discovery that the younger of the Baroni Brothers, highwire acrobats, was a girl seemed to have left him stunned. In stricken silence, he watched Polly, as she bent over her patient.

"Nurse – please!" Beppo said at last, "if the circus boss finds out that Bumpsa's really my kid sister Tina, he'll fire us. Don't give us away," he pleaded.

"I'll keep your secret, Beppo," Polly promised. "But on one condition. Let a doctor see your sister at once!"

Beppo was forced to agree. From a telephone booth in the street outside the theatre. Polly called St. Vincent's Hospital and was lucky enough to catch her friend, Dr. Nick Sloan, just coming off duty. Hurriedly she told him everything about Bumpsa.

"I'll drive down to town now, Polly. See you in a few minutes," said Nick.

Beppo had seen the circus boss, Polly learned on her return to her patient.

"I've arranged to do a solo wire act at the second show tonight," he explained.

For generations, the Baroni family had been circus performers. Beppo told Polly. And there *was* a brother, the real Bumpsa, who partnered Beppo on the wire in small circuses abroad. But just when they got their first engagement in England, Bumpsa fell ill and had to enter a sanatorium. Tina, like her brothers, had grown up in a circus, had learnt to walk the high wire. So Beppo had persuaded her to masquerade as Bumpsa, till their brother recovered.

"She's a grand little trouper, nurse," said Beppo affectionately. "She won't miss the show tomorrow."

But a shock awaited Beppo when, shortly afterwards, Dr. Sloan had examined the patient. "Your sister is suffering acute shock after her fall, Mr. Baroni. She must go into St. Vincent's for complete rest and observation. I will call an ambulance now," said Nick firmly.

So Tina became Polly's patient in the Women's Accident Ward. After two days' rest, as Nick had ordered, Tina seemed to be recovering from shock. But Liz's pet patient in the Children's Ward didn't improve at all.

"I've tried everything – games, stories, toys, to get a word out of Linda." Liz told Polly. "But nothing works. She just gets more pale and quiet every day."

There's still Bumpsa, thought Polly. Seeing the clown the first time made Linda speak. Would it work again? A new plan was already shaping in Polly's mind. She must talk it over with Tina at the first opportunity.

That opportunity came the following afternoon, after Nick had paid his daily visit to Tina. Today, the young doctor decided she could get up. Polly was able to tell her about Linda, the visit to the circus and its result.

"I'm sure Linda would talk to you, if you'd go to see her in the Children's Ward. Will you, Tina?" asked Polly.

"But –" Tina gestured towards her dressing-gown. "She won't recognise me in this."

"She'll recognise your red wig and clown's costume," Polly said eagerly. "I smuggled them from the ambulance to my locker in the nurses' cloakroom. You could change into your circus rig-out there."

"No, no. I can't do it. Don't ask me!" Tina protested.

Suddenly, to Polly's alarm, she sank on to a chair, white-faced and trembling.

"I – I can't wear that costume." A look of fear flashed into Tina's eyes. "I don't even want to see it. It'll bring everything back – that awful moment when I felt myself falling – falling from the wire."

Polly caught the girl's wrist and felt her pulse racing wildly. "I'm sorry I upset you, Tina." She spoke very gently. "I think you'd better go back to bed to rest."

There was no doubt about it, Tina had lost her nerve! Both Polly and Liz were anxious to give extra help to their two special patients. But that became impossible. Some nurses fell ill, especially among the night staff of St. Vincent's. Unexpectedly, the two friends were switched to night duty on their wards.

On Polly's third night on duty, long after the other patients were asleep, she heard Tina tossing restlessly and tiptoed silently to her bedside. "Nurse Martin here, Tina," she whispered. "What's wrong?"

"I can't help thinking about Beppo. This booking in England means so much to him. If only I could face the wire again and not fail him!"

"You must sleep, dear." Polly tried to soothe the unhappy girl. "I'll get you some warm milk. That'll help."

Just as she turned from Tina's bed, Night Sister hurried down the ward, followed, to Polly's surprise, by Liz. They brought bad news.

Linda had disappeared from the Children's Ward while the staff were tending two accident cases sent up from Casualty.

"I must remain on duty," said Night Sister in a worried tone, "but Nurse Blake will search this wing. As you know the missing child, Nurse Martin, I want you to help her."

Tina had overheard. "Sister, I'm allowed up during the day. Let me get up to look for the little girl, too. Please."

For a moment, Sister hesitated, then: "Very well! We need all the help we can get. Go with the nurses, dear."

They left the ward. "Better split up, Polly," Liz said. "I'll search towards the ground floor. You and Tina go the other way."

Polly led Tina in a search that took them to the topmost floor, but there was no sign of Linda. The last corridor they followed ended at a door marked "Exit to Roof". It was unlocked. Evidently workmen were busy up here on repairs, during the day.

Polly gave a sigh of relief as she scanned the roof and the parapet wall that ringed it. "Thank goodness Linda hasn't found her way up here. She must be downstairs somewhere. Let's go, Tina."

As she turned back to the doorway, she glimpsed something moving – *on the roof of the next block.*

A small figure in a billowy nightdress, walking slowly with arms outstretched . . .

Polly raced wildly across the roof, with Tina at her heels.

"It's Linda," cried Polly, "she's sleepwalking! On the parapet wall."

Linda was in terrible danger. One slip, one stumble would send her crashing to the ground far below. "There's only one way to reach her in time," gasped Polly.

With desperate speed, she darted over to the equipment left on the roof by the workmen. It included a builder's long ladder. She began to drag it towards the parapet wall. "I'm going over on to the next roof on this."

Tina gave a sharp cry of fear. "No, no. You mustn't. It's too dangerous," she protested. "You can't balance on a ladder – like – like a circus perfomer."

"No, but I can crawl over – like a fireman," said Polly breathlessly, as she slid the heavy ladder up against the low wall.

Tina herself was crossing the ladder bridge.

"But if you fell, nurse, you'd be killed!"

"So will Linda, if someone doesn't reach her quickly," said Polly.

Without further protest, Tina helped Polly to thrust the long ladder over the space between the two buildings. But by now Linda was much closer to the far edge of the opposite roof.

"Gosh! I haven't much time," Polly gasped in dismay.

"Let me help you, nurse," said Tina, taking a firm grip of Polly's arm.

What happened next took Polly Martin completely by surprise. Suddenly, with all the strength she possessed, Tina pushed Polly and sent her staggering across the roof, away from the ladder. Polly slipped and fell flat. When, dazed and breathless, she scrambled to her feet, she saw. Tina herself was crossing the ladder bridge.

She seemed to have forgotten her fear of falling. Now, balancing herself with arms outspread, she stepped swiftly and confidently from rung to rung of the ladder, across the empty depths of the space below. With a gasp of relief, Polly saw her reach the wall opposite, then run swiftly across the roof towards Linda.

Half an hour later, Polly was tucking Tina into bed.

"You gave a wonderful performance tonight, Tina," she said softly. "You saved Linda. And you proved you needn't be scared of the high-wire any more."

Tina smiled sleepily. "The Baroni Brothers will appear again as advertised," she murmured, "and I shall be Bumpsa again."

And two days later she was.

Polly was able to go ahead with her plan to help Linda to talk. For Tina agreed to visit her now, wearing her clown's costume.

Polly and Liz were there, watching. Linda sat forward in bed, her face beginning to sparkle. Her lips began to move. Then in an eager, excited voice, she called: "It's – Bumpsa! He's the clown I saw at the circus."

Liz and Polly looked at each other joyously. Linda had found her voice again.

VICKY OF SILVERLAKE HOLIDAY CAMP

by Susan Morris

Vicky was a young English girl who worked as a hostess at a holiday camp in Canada. When her friend, Shirley, was falsely suspected of stealing a pearl ring, Vicky had to become a detective.

"There's room for two more in this canoe, Shirley!" called Vicky Fletcher gaily, to the pretty, fair-haired girl. "Jump in!"

Vicky was a young English girl who worked as a junior hostess at the Silverlake Holiday Camp, in Canada, and she was taking a party of young campers to visit a neighbouring Indian village.

Shirley Nevinson smiled at Vicky. Shirley had only recently joined the Camp staff as a dance instructress, but she was already very popular. She had just settled herself in the big, twenty-foot canoe next to Vicky when Mark Lincoln came down to the landing-stage.

"Hello, Mark!" called Cora Browning, one of the girls in the other canoe. "I've kept a place for you."

But Mark didn't seem to hear her. He hurried to Vicky's canoe.

"Got room for another little one?" he asked cheerfully.

Vicky laughed and nodded. "Yes, get in," she smiled. "But surely you don't call yourself little, do you?"

Everyone laughed, for Mark was a big, broad-shouldered boy. There was a lot more teasing, all of which Mark took in good part, as he seated himself behind Shirley.

But Cora's face wore a sulky frown as she looked on from the other canoe. Cora was staying at the Silverlake Camp with her mother, and she had regarded Mark as her special boy-friend until Shirley had arrived at the Camp. Mrs. Browning was a wealthy woman who rather spoiled Cora, and the girl was accustomed to getting her own way. It made her angry and jealous, therefore, when Mark showed that he preferred Shirley to herself. She was still frowning when they pushed off from the landing-stage, heading up the Little Moose lake with Vicky's canoe leading the way.

It was a glorious Summer day, with a clear, blue sky, and the lake was so smooth the pine woods were reflected in it as if in a great mirror. Everybody was in high spirits–except Cora. But as they came to the Indian village, she leapt out of the canoe and grabbed Mark's arm when they landed.

"Oh, Mark," she said, putting on her most winning smile. "You are going to escort me whilst we make the round of the village, aren't you? I shall be so frightened without you. All the Indians in their war paint look so fierce."

Vicky heard this from where she was tying up the boats. But before she could speak, Mark laughed.

"Why, Cora, that's only for show. The Indians won't harm you. And I've already planned to take Shirley round the village."

Cora tossed her head. "Well! I must say she has a nerve bagging you like this," she said furiously. "After all, Shirley *is* only one of the staff."

Mark shook his head at her and looked rather angry.

"She may be one of the staff, Cora," he said quietly. "But I'm only too glad that she was able to come along." And he walked away to join the young dance instructress, while Cora looked after him with tightened lips and angry eyes.

Most of the party had overheard this exchange and were looking rather embarrassed, but Vicky tactfully suggested they should start their tour of the village and buy some souvenirs.

"The Indians do very fine wood carving," she said. "And some of their bead-work is really lovely. They also make unusual ornamental pottery. Let's go and see them."

To her relief, everyone soon forgot about the tiff between Cora and Mark, in the excitement of choosing souvenirs.

As they wandered round the village they came to an old Indian squaw with pointed nose and chin, and cheeks brown and wrinkled.

"Golly! Doesn't she look like a witch?" one of the girls whispered.

"Well, mind she doesn't put a spell on you," said another with a grin.

The party walked on, but Cora stayed behind to examine a beautifully carved little cedar-wood box which the old woman offered for sale. When she rejoined the party, she was carrying it.

"I bought it," she told Vicky airily. "I couldn't understand a word the woman was saying, but it'll do for a souvenir."

Vicky smiled. "She was probably saying the box would bring you good luck," she said. "Was it very expensive?"

"Oh, I've got plenty of money," Cora answered boastfully. "I don't depend on a small salary–like some people."

She glanced across at Shirley as she spoke. Vicky, catching the glint in her eyes, felt vaguely uneasy. For somehow she felt that Cora would make trouble for Shirley, if she could.

Shirley was due to give a dancing lesson that afternoon, and when they returned to the Camp, Vicky could see that she was feeling rather nervous.

"I do hope it proves a success," she confided. "Until now I've only given private tuition, and it scares me to think of taking a whole class–"

"You won't have to worry," Vicky told her cheerfully. "Everyone is very friendly. But I tell you what," she added good-naturedly. "I'll come along to the Recreation Hall this afternoon, if you like."

"Oh, will you?" Shirley cried. "Thank you!"

So after lunch Vicky went along to the big Recreation Hall, and helped Shirley get her pupils paired up for the first dance. Shirley was very nervous at first, and her voice was a little wobbly as she talked to the class, but when Vicky caught her eye from the back of the hall and smiled encouragingly, Shirley looked better.

"Now," she said. "I'll demonstrate what I've been saying. But I shall need a partner–"

"How will I do?" It was Mark Lincoln stepping forward, before she had even finished speaking.

"Fine," Shirley said, with a smile; and they began a demonstration dance in front of the whole class.

Vicky, watching, smiled. She had told Mark how nervous Shirley had been, and she knew he was a good dancer. As she had hoped, Mark had come along to give a hand.

"He's a nice fellow–and Shirley's a nice girl," Vicky thought. "I wonder–"

And then she jumped. From one side of the room came a sharp cry. It was Cora Browning.

"Oh! My pearl ring. It's gone!"

Shirley stopped the hi-fi record player to which she and Mark had been dancing.

"Don't you remember, Cora?" she said. "Your ring was rather loose, so I advised you to take it off your finger while you danced. You put it in that little cedar-wood box you bought at the Indian village this morning."

"Oh, yes," Cora answered, looking suddenly rather foolish. "I forgot for a moment when I saw the ring was missing. It gave me an awful fright, because the pearl is very valuable. I think I'll wear the ring again–I shall feel safer."

Vicky couldn't help wondering whether Cora had staged this little scene just to draw attention to herself and the ring, which really was lovely and valuable. But Shirley smiled patiently.

"Very well, we'll wait while you put it on," she said.

Cora crossed the hut to where a big moose's head hung over the wide fireplace. She fumbled behind the broad-leaved antlers, and brought out the little cedar-wood box.

"Mummy gave the ring to me on my last birthday, and she would never forgive me if I lost it–" she began.

Then she broke off sharply, and gasped as she opened the box.

"What is it?" Vicky asked, hurrying forward.

"The ring! It isn't here! It's gone!" Cora cried.

She held up the box; it was quite empty. Everyone stared blankly.

"Are you sure you put the ring into the box?" Vicky asked.

"Yes! Yes, of course, I am!" Cora cried wildly, "Shirley saw me, didn't you Shirley?"

The young dance instructress nodded. "Yes, you certainly put it in there," she answered.

"Well, what has become of it?" Cora cried, beginning to get quite hysterical. "Someone must have stolen it."

There was a deathly silence in the hall.

"That's a very serious statement," Vicky said at last. "How could anyone have stolen the ring?"

"Perhaps Shirley can explain," Cora said; and suddenly there was a hard, spiteful ring to her voice.

"What do you mean?" the young dance instructress asked, a slight tremor in her voice.

"It was *you* who advised me to take the ring off before I started dancing," Cora said. "And *you* saw me put it in the cedar-wood box, and hide it behind the stuffed moose's head. No one else did."

Shirley was very pale now. "Are you accusing me of stealing your ring?" she asked.

"Yes, I am," Cora snapped.

Everyone seemed to start talking at once then. But Vicky kept her head.

"I think we had better have a good look round before you make any further charges, Cora," she said steadily.

So the search began, but no pearl ring came to light. Meanwhile Cora went off and fetched her mother.

Mrs. Browning was crimson with indignation, and with her was Mr. Munro, the camp warden.

"This is disgraceful!" Mrs. Browning stormed. "I demand this girl be searched."

"Search me if you like, but you won't find the ring," quivered Shirley.

"Because you've hidden it somewhere already!" shrilled Cora.

Poor Shirley blinked to keep back the tears.

"Do you think I took the ring, Mr. Munro?" she asked.

"No, Shirley." The warden looked troubled. "But someone must have done so. I'm sorry such a thing happened during one of your classes, Shirley, and I cannot help feeling you are partly responsible. You should never have told her to put the ring in the box."

Then he dismissed her, and Shirley slipped away to her cabin. Sympathetically, Vicky followed.

"No one believes you took the ring except Cora and her mother," she said comfortingly.

"But I can't *prove* that I'm innocent," Shirley answered miserably. "And I shall always be under suspicion. I shall never be able to face everyone at the dance this evening. I'm going to resign."

"You mustn't do that!" Vicky cried. "Why, that would be almost like confessing you were guilty. No, Shirley, you've got to stay and fight it out. Never fear, we'll find a way of proving you are innocent. I'm sure everything will be all right."

"I do hope so," the young instructress said with a faint smile. "Oh, Vicky, you really are a comfort, believing in me like this."

But Vicky wasn't quite so confident as she had pretended to be.

"Oh dear," she thought, as she made her way back to her cabin, "there must be some way of proving that Shirley didn't take the ring. But how–"

Then a thought suddenly struck her. "I wonder–" she murmured.

It was a big ordeal for Shirley to go to the dance that evening.

Nobody mentioned the mysterious disappearance of the ring, but she had the uncomfortable feeling that it was on everybody's mind.

When Mark arrived, he marched straight up to her. "I want the first dance," he announced.

Shirley smiled at him. Mark, at any rate, didn't doubt her innocence.

"Of course," she replied; and forced herself to sound gay and carefree. "It's a quickstep."

But even as they stepped on to the floor, a voice called to Mark. It was Cora.

"Mind you don't lose your wrist-watch, Mark."

Shirley went deathly pale.

Mark whirled angrily. "What a horrible thing to say! You know full well–"

"I was only warning you," Cora said spitefully. "You never know what might vanish next."

"No, you don't do you?"

And there was Vicky. She was breathless and flushed with hurrying.

"Cora," she said quickly. "Have you got that little cedar-wood box with you?"

Cora nodded. "Yes," she answered.

"Will you take a look inside it, please?" Vicky said mysteriously.

Cora gave Vicky a sharp, suspicious look, but she opened the box.

"You can see it's empty, can't you? Now close it again," Vicky said, "then press your thumb on the moose's head before you open it a second time."

Cora shrugged irritably, then pressed the moose's head which was carved in the lid, before she opened the box once more– then she gasped.

"The ring!" There was the pearl ring winking and gleaming at them! Everyone was amazed, but Vicky laughed.

"I thought this might be the answer," she said. "So I went back to the Indian village and questioned the old squaw who sold Cora the box. She told me that when you put any small object into the box, and close the lid, it slips through a false bottom into a secret compartment. To fetch the object back you have to press on the moose's head before lifting the lid. The old squaw says she tried to tell you this, Cora, but you refused to listen." Cora looked extremely foolish.

"Well, Cora," Mark asked sternly. "Are you going to apologise to Shirley?"

"Oh, no, she doesn't have to do that," Shirley cried at once in a heartfelt voice. "I'm only too glad to be cleared of suspicion."

And her eyes sparkled with happiness as everyone crowded round to congratulate her. Cora did not stay to listen. She hurried out of the hall without saying another word. But Shirley was cleared–that was all that really mattered; and watching her dancing happily with her partner, Mark, Vicky wondered if she had not found a partner for life.

FILM STAR FOR AN AFTERNOON

by Eileen Meadows

Julie Windsor had the most exciting afternoon of her life when she was asked to impersonate a famous film star for an afternoon, but events did not work out exactly as she had planned.

"Thank you, Mr. Carter, for giving me the chance to show what we can do. You know that getting the contract to do all the flower arrangements in the hotel means everything to my sister and I."

Julie Windsor, blue eyes shining, looking spruce and neat in her dainty pink overall, gazed gratefully at the manager of the Seaview Hotel at Sunnicliffe, as they stood just inside the rear door of the hotel. In Julie's arms were two great cardboard boxes full of cut flowers which she had brough with her from the exclusive little flower shop which she and her elder sister, Nanette, called the Bouquet of Flowers, and which they had recently opened in the seaside town of Sunnicliffe.

"I understand, Miss Windsor."

The manager, who had been supervising the checking of the laundry baskets which stood in a row by the door, looked at her with what Julie thought was rather a doubtful expression.

"You are very young," he commented, and sighed. "But your shop is so conveniently close around the corner. Of course, you realise that I shall expect you to go about your work quietly and unobtrusively, and have nothing to do with my guests. Any complaints–and no contract. If my guests are satisfied, then I shall be. Now–start with Angela Dawn's suite today. And remember what I said. Any trouble–no contract!"

"There won't be–not if I can help it!" Julie assured him. "That contract means too much to Nanette and me for that!"

She left the manager then and took her boxes in the service lift to the top floor, the sixth, where Angela Dawn's suite was situated. She was dying to see the young film starlet who was staying at Sunnicliffe during carnival week. For one thing, she was aware that she herself bore a remarkable resemblance to the film star, and she was curious to see if that resemblance was as noticeable off the screen.

To Julie's surprise the young film star herself opened the door to her ring, and Julie saw at once that that likeness was almost startling! The main difference was their different hair styles and the different colour of their eyes.

But Angela Dawn herself was obviously not aware of the resemblance at that moment, for she was looking strangely agitated. She merely nodded briefly to Julie, and allowed her to pass through. Julie put one of her boxes down in the lounge, and took the other into the sumptuous bedroom.

"Whoops!" She almost tripped over the great wicker laundry basket standing in the middle of the room as she gazed around in wonder.

Quickly she set to work, her deft fingers twisting and twining the wire around the flowers, till they stood in glorious sprays in their bowls and vases. In a matter of minutes, the rooms were a riot of blooms. But as she worked, Julie couldn't help noticing the way Angela Dawn was pacing from one room to another, wringing her hands and frequently glancing at the clock. Then, suddenly, to Julie's astonishment, she flung herself down on the bed, and tears streamed down her pretty face.

Julie's tender heart contracted. Angela Dawn looked so unhappy.

"Miss Dawn, what is it?" she whispered impulsively "Can I help?"

Miserably, Angela Dawn shook her head.

"No. No one can," she sobbed. "But–I must tell someone! Can I trust you?" She looked hard at Julie.

Julie pressed her hand. "You can–I promise," she smiled.

Angela Dawn wiped her eyes on a dainty lace handkerchief, and began.

"I–I became engaged last week to a–an airline pilot," she told Julie quiveringly. "It's all absolutely secret. And–he's just phoned from Redwood Airport to say he's just landed and has three hours before he takes off again at five o'clock. He's not allowed to leave the airfield, and he–he wants me to come to him. But"–and the tears flowed again–"Mike–that's Mike Mallory, my publicity agent and manager–has forbidden me to leave the hotel until I go to the Carnival later this afternoon.

"I dare not tell him *why* I want to go. He doesn't know about the engagement either–my studio would be furious. They'd say it is bad for publicity at this stage in my career." Her lip trembled. "But I did so want to see David–I might not have another chance for weeks!"

"Couldn't you manage to sneak out–just for a little while–without this Mike Mallory knowing?" asked Julie.

"No–I have to do everything he says." Angela shook her fair head. "And he's told me to–to just keep making brief appearances on the balcony this morning–to get people's interest," she added. "It probably sounds stupid to you–it does to me sometimes, but it's all part of this build-up they're giving me."

Julie looked at the young film star sympathetically as she heaved a great sigh. She looked so sad. If only there was some way she could help her! Julie hated to see anyone unhappy–especially this girl who resembled her so closely. It seemed to give her an added interest in the film star. If only– And then, suddenly, her face flushed. Her ever-active brain had hit on a daring idea.

"I believe I can help, after all," she breathed softly, and grabbed the startled girl's arm. "It will mean taking an awful risk–" She was silent for a moment, her face serious, thinking of that contract that meant so much to herself and Nanette. Any trouble–no contract, the manager had said. Supposing he found out– But he mustn't, that's all, she told herself. She looked at Angela Dawn, taking in the slim figure, the hair, the heart-shaped face, all so like her own.

"It would take you less than a quarter of an hour to get to Redwood Airport by car, wouldn't it–"

"Yes; but I couldn't take that red and white monstrosity–"

"You don't have to," Julie interrupted. "Listen. Your publicity man said all you'd got to do was just appear now and again on the balcony?"

Angela Dawn nodded.

"Then I could do that," said Julie briskly. "Don't you see how alike we are? If I do my hair in a pony tail, like yours, from a distance no one could tell it wasn't you."

Angela Dawn was staring at her, wide-eyed, for the first time noticing the astonishing likeness.

"We're going to change places for the afternoon," Julie announced, and began unbuttoning her overall. "It's quite simple, really." She pulled the dazed film star to her feet. "Here–put my overall on. Untie your hair and let it hang like mine. That's right. Now" –as Angela Dawn automatically put on the pink overall— "take these empty boxes–hold them in front of your face, and you can walk straight out of the hotel. Take the service lift at the end of the corridor, and you'll find the rear door of the hotel just beside you at the bottom. When you get outside, dash round the corner–you'll see our van there—'Bouquet of Flowers' painted on it. The ignition key is in it–borrow the van and make for the airport. I'll 'phone my sister and let her know I'm lending the van to someone. All right?"

Angela Dawn's eyes were shining now. "I'll–I'll do it!" she breathed. "You–you're a wonder!"

"Hurry, then," urged Julie, then caught her arm, face serious. "But please hurry back, won't you." She explained how she and her sister were hoping to get the contract for flower decoration. "I can hold the fort for a while, but if you're too long and the manager discovers what I've done–I've lost that contract, and let Nanette down!"

"I'll be back–I promise." With a quick pressure of Julie's hand, Angela Dawn grabbed the two empty boxes and rushed from the room.

Left alone, Julie felt a momentary qualm. Had she done right to risk the thing that was most important to her to help Angela Dawn? If Mike Mallory found out–told the manager– Oh, no!

She tried to shake off the feeling, 'phoned Nanette, then tied her hair in a pony tail and put on sunglasses. She walked out on to the balcony overlooking the promenade, stood there for a few moments, then went inside again. Time passed. Three o'clock struck, then four. All seemed well, then suddenly, at a quarter to five, the 'phone in the bedroom shrilled. Julie made a snap decision. Whatever it was, she must answer it. She hurried into the bedroom and picked up the receiver with trembling fingers.

"Hallo?" she said softly.

A voice, vibrant and authoritative, spoke.

"Angela? Mike here. I'm at the Town Hall. Forget what I said about staying in. The Mayor's on his way now to the hotel. You're to go across the road to the beach and judge a sand-picture competition at five o'clock. I doubt if I can get along. Be ready in ten minutes. Wear something suitable, put on your best smile for the photographer–you know what to do. 'Bye for now!"

And the line went dead. Julie replaced the receiver and sank hopelessly on to the wicker laundry basket. The unexpected had happened!

Julie's face was pale. Angela Dawn would not be back for at least half an hour, and if the film star did not turn up on the beach, Mike Mallory would obviously come looking for her; would discover her imposture. Angela Dawn's secret would be out. And as for Julie herself–she bit her lip–the manager would definitely not let her and her sister have that contract if it was known what she had done.

What *could* she do? How could she save the situation? Her heart beat painfully fast. There was only one way out–one way only. She must go down to the beach–pose as the film star, and hope to goodness Mike Mallory did not turn up and discover her. After all, he had implied he might not be able to be there. With any luck she would get away with the impersonation without anyone knowing.

Impulsive as ever, she flew to the great cupboards that held the film star's clothes. A quick search revealed what she wanted–a pair of bright green jeans; a delicate pale pink sweater, pink straw sandals, and a pale pink scarf to wear over her hair.

In a matter of moments the transformation was complete. She put the sunglasses on again and surveyed herself in the mirror.

"Yippee!" she gurgled. "I could be Angela Dawn herself! Now for it!"

With a last quick, satisfied look in the mirror she left the room. Her heart was beating painfully fast now. She took the lift downstairs and stepped out into the reception lounge. And there she almost fell back in dismay. There, by the desk, stood the manager, beaming at a short, stout, grey-haired man, whom she knew, by the chain of office he wore around his neck, must be the Mayor.

They saw her at once, and the Mayor, smiling affably, moved towards her, pushing a small girl before him.

The few guests in the lounge were now watching curiously as Julie, forcing a smile, stepped forward and took the bouquet the little girl handed to her. And then she felt a wild desire to giggle. There was no mistaking Nanette's handiwork. This bouquet had come from their own shop! If Nanette only knew!

The Mayor, after a few words of greeting, led the way across the lounge and out of the hotel, Julie taking great care to avoid meeting the manager's eye.

Outside, a small interested crowd had gathered, and there was a little ripple of applause as she appeared. Julie flushed but, trying to look and behave as she guessed Angela Dawn would, she accompanied the Mayor across the wide promenade on to the beach.

She hesitated only once when a photographer seemed to appear suddenly before her. Quickly, yet with a smile, she partly hid her face in the flowers, then walked on.

The crowd on the beach parted for the Mayor to lead her to a small table on which stood two enormous boxes of chocolates.

"These are the prizes," he told Julie. "Perhaps you would walk along the line of sandpictures and pick the winner?"

"Of course." Despite herself, Julie found herself enjoying it all. No one seemed to have guessed she was an impostor. There appeared to be no sign of Mike Mallory–although she had no idea what he looked like–and she began to breathe more easily.

She walked along the lines of pictures, conscious of the curious stares of the onlookers, and it took only a few minutes to pick the two winners, a small girl with large brown eyes and pigtails, and an older boy who gazed at her aggressively as they accompanied her to the table. Almost forgetting, indeed, that she was playing a part, she presented them with their prizes, exchanging a few words with each. The children moved away, and she turned to speak to the Mayor.

The words died on her lips. For there, in the distance, cruising along the promenade, was a car–an enormous red and white open sports car. It gleamed and shone in the sun. There could be no mistaking it. She

She walked along the line of pictures.

remembered Angela Dawn's words–she had called it a "monstrosity".

"Mike Mallory!" she gasped, then turned frantically to the Mayor, who was eyeing her in surprise. "You–you must excuse me–I–I've just remembered. I–I've got to make an important 'phone call! I–oh dear–excuse me!"

And before he could reply, Julie was racing away. Regardless of the stares of passers by, she hurried across the road, pausing to glance back as she reached the hotel gates. Mike Mallory had obviously not seen her. He was just drawing in to the kerb on the opposite side of the road. He would be looking for her–or, rather, for Angela Dawn! She must get back to the comparative safety of the hotel room!

Breathing fast, she hurried into the hotel and took the lift to the top floor. Once in Angela Dawn's suite again, she rushed into the bedroom, locked the door, and raced out on to the balcony.

A glance towards the gates showed her Mike Mallory striding towards the hotel entrance. Then a movement directly below brought her glance flashing downwards, and she gasped. Angela Dawn was crouched among the rhododendrons six floors below!

Angela was waving frantically. Julie waved back. Thank goodness, she thought, Angela Dawn had returned. Now–to change places.

She stepped back into the bedroom and changed quickly out of the film star's clothes and put her own on again. She was ready. Now–There was a ring at the door of the lounge.

"Hallo, there! Angela! Can I come in?"

"Mike Mallory!" gasped Julie. She went first hot then cold. If Mike Mallory walked in now and saw her it would mean the end of everything. Gone would be all her chances of ever getting that contract! The bell rang again!

Julie's mind was in a whirl. Disaster seemed imminent. To have gone so far and be discovered now–no–she *must* find a way to save both herself and Angela Dawn. She could not give up now. If Mike Mallory became suspicious and sent for the manager–all hopes of gaining that contract would be gone.

There *must* be a way. And then her roving eye rested on the laundry basket still standing in the centre of the room. She caught her breath. A gleam of hope shone in her eyes.

"That's it!" she breathed tensely.

The bell rang again–insistent.

"I've got to hurry," she told herself and, unlocking the bedroom door, she went into the lounge.

"I can't let you in," she called. "I–I'm getting ready for the Carnival. I–I don't want to be disturbed. I'll see you later."

And before Mike Mallory could reply, she flew back into the bedroom. So much depended on her actions now. Feverishly she grabbed a pen and paper; scribbled an urgent note to the waiting film star, then attached it to the coil of wire she had previously been using for the flowers, in order to weight it. Then, going out onto the balcony, she dropped it, and was relieved to see the note land almost at Angela Dawn's feet.

She waited only until she saw the film star read the note, then look up and nod.

Then Julie began to move fast. Her heart was racing madly. She picked up the 'phone and asked for the laundry basket to be taken away, making it clear that the door was unlocked, and the basket was to be removed without her being disturbed. No one else was to be allowed in the room.

That done, she pulled the empty wicker basket into the lounge, shut the bedroom door, then climbed into the basket and closed the lid.

Hardly a minute later she heard the click as the door softly opened; men's voices. And then she felt the jolt as she was lifted: heard the men's expressions of surprise at the weight of the basket. But fortunately they did not lift the lid to see what was inside!

She was being carried, and then, suddenly, so close that she almost gave herself away, a voice spoke–Mike Mallory's.

"O. K. So she doesn't want to be disturbed. Then I'll sit here and wait!"

All Julie hoped was that Mike Mallory would do as he said! She was whisked down to the ground floor in the service lift and felt the bump as the basket was pulled out and pushed against the wall.

And this was the part she dreaded most. Everything depended on what the men did with the laundry basket next.

But, to her relief, she heard receding footsteps; the slam of a door; then silence. Cautiously, holding her breath, she lifted the lid and gazed around. The corridor was deserted!

She was free! But now–to get Angela Dawn back to the room upstairs.

Quickly she climbed out of the basket and pushed open the door through which she had arrived earlier. Angela Dawn was there as Julie had arranged in the note.

"Thank goodness!" she gasped, clutching the film star's arm. "We must be quick. Mike Mallory is waiting for you–outside your room–I hope!"

"Then–then how am I to get in?" gasped Angela in dismay.

"Leave that to me," said Julie. "Now–take off that overall." Angela began to undo the buttons. "Did you see your fiancé, after all?" Julie asked as she did so.

The film star's pretty face glowed.

"Oh, yes. It–it was wonderful. And all thanks to you. I–I got back just as you were dashing into the hotel–I saw Mike outside, and guessed something was wrong. That's why I hid," she explained.

Julie nodded, putting the pink overall on again.

"Now–you must do as I say." Julie began pushing the film star through the door into the hotel. "Quick–get into that basket–" She indicated the laundry basket in which she had escaped. Angela, looking bewildered, did so. "Now," Julie warned, "Don't move; don't breathe, even!" She closed the lid. "I've got to dash now. Every second counts. With any luck you'll be back in your room within five minutes–and no one any the wiser! 'Bye!"

And like a whirlwind she was rushing along the corridor and eventually found herself at the door which led into the great hotel lounge. She slipped through and hurried up to the desk.

"I have a message from Angela Dawn," she said on a note of authority. "A few minutes ago she sent her laundry basket down and has just discovered something of great importance was placed in it by mistake. Will you have the basket returned to her room at once, please?"

"Of course." The young man was already picking up the telephone.

Julie waited only to hear him issue the order, and then slipped out of the hotel.

She was free–but what of Angela Dawn? Would she get back safely? Or would the whole escapade even yet be discovered? A crowd was collecting outside the hotel; she realised with a sense of shock that it was almost time for the Carnival procession to begin. And Angela was taking part in that procession!

Julie found a place near the door, and waited, tense. Had Angela got back safely?

Time passed. Six o'clock struck. And as the minutes dragged by Julie began to feel a cold shiver. The manager of the hotel was standing by the door. She looked at his face. It told her nothing.

The coach, decorated with flowers, in which Angela Dawn was to ride, drew up at the hotel gates.

Still no Angela!

The manager was beginning to look a little restless now. He glanced at his watch, frowned as he peered inside the hotel.

All sorts of disturbing thoughts ran through Julie's mind. Perhaps, even, no one had gone to collect the laundry basket yet. Could Angela still be crouched inside it, despairing of being able to get out of her predicament? Had Julie been *too* clever with her plan and landed the young film star in worse trouble than ever?

For a moment, Julie was tempted to make an excuse to re-enter the hotel in order to find out for herself what was going on, to see whether her fears had any foundation.

And then Julie's heart leapt. There was a stir; movement inside the hotel. The manager opened the big glass door, and Julie gasped, thankfully.

Wearing a dress of pink and white tulle, her fair hair coiled at the back of her head, looking radiant, came Angela Dawn.

"What a transformation!" murmured Julie, and at the same time felt an overwhelming sense of relief. Her plan had worked!

Slowly the film star approached, Mike Mallory on one side of her, the beaming hotel manager on the other.

And then Julie's eyes met those of Angela Dawn, and she saw them soften. The film star, who looked so like herself, paused before Julie, and turned to the manager. "This is the young lady who arranged the flowers in my room so beautifully, isn't it?" she smiled. "I must thank her!"

And as the manager glanced quickly from one to the other, she stepped across to Julie and took her hand.

"Thank you for all you have done," she said softly, and Julie heard the tremble in her voice. Louder, she said: "I shall never forget how beautiful my room looked. You really are an expert florist!" She pressed Julie's hand, then moved on.

Julie was aware that the hotel manager had moved closer. "The job's yours," he hissed. "Be here early–and fill the whole lounge with flowers. From now on the contract's yours!"

And still beaming, he moved off after the young film star and her publicity agent as they pressed through the cheering crowds towards the coach.

Julie stood on the steps as the crowd streamed after them, and her heart was singing now. The contract was theirs! All had ended well! But–how nearly it hadn't–if that laundry basket had not been there! She grinned now as she thought of it–then raced round the corner to the Bouquet of Flowers, to tell Nanette the good news–and all about how she had been a film star for an afternoon!

THE RUNAWAY

by Doris Graham

Carol Meldrum's father owned Meldrum's Mammoth Circus and her special pet was Chérie, the performing monkey. One day, Chérie was found cuddling a marmoset. Where did it come from? The mystery deepened when a valuable necklace was missing.

It was a crisp, cold, sunny December day – very near to Christmas. Smiling happily, pretty Carol Meldrum, daughter of the owner of Meldrum's Mammoth Circus, neat and workmanlike in her blue jeans and warm yellow jersey, hurried down the steps of her smart trailer-caravan.

Around her, in the big field on the outskirts of Parkhampton, spread the rest of the circus – the living-wagons, the tents, the red-and-gold animal wagons. And, dominating them all, the huge Big Top, with its red-and-gold flag fluttering gaily. But like the rest of the circus people, Carol had no time to stand and stare. They were all too busy preparing for what was always the most exciting show of the year – the special children's afternoon matinée.

Even the animals seemed to sense the gaiety in the air and, during rehearsals, seemed to compete with each other for the laughter and applause that was to come.

But the star of this particular show, Carol decided, was to be Chérie, the lovable chimpanzee. It was to Chérie's quarters that Carol was hurrying now, to give the chimp some extra practice in the amusing new tricks she had been learning.

"Cooee!" she called now, knowing that Chérie would start dancing up and down with excitement. "Anybody home?"

With a mischievous laugh Carol stopped in front of the cage and stared up. Then a quick scared pang shot through her. Chérie was neither dancing up and down nor gibbering with excitement. Chérie was crouched in a corner of her cage, arms folded, head bent low, making strange little crooning noises.

Goodness! thought Carol, in sudden consternation. Surely Chérie wasn't ill – not lovable, clever Chérie! Conscious of a little panic, Carol quickly unlocked the door of the cage and stepped in.

As she did so, Chérie advanced into the light. And Carol just stared at her in amazement, and then in delight. For in her arms Chérie clasped a tiny furry creature, squirrel-like with its thick fur and long bushy tail, but with an adorably tiny monkey-like face – now looking very worried and scared.

"A marmoset!" cried Carol. "Oh, you sweet wee thing! Oh, Chérie, please let me hold him for a moment. I won't scare him, I promise you."

Rather reluctantly Chérie relinquished her hold on the tiny creature; but she hovered closely and jealously as Carol nuzzled the marmoset's soft fur and made little crooning noises.

Then, apparently deciding that Carol had taken long enough to get acquainted, Chérie gently but firmly took the marmoset from her, and once again cradled it in her own loving arms, looking down at it with a tender, almost human, expression on her face. Carol smiled. Already Chérie was treating the tiny creature as though it was her very own property, to be guarded, loved and petted.

Yet – where had it come from? It hadn't been here an hour ago, when Carol had last seen Chérie. How had it got here? It would have been easy enough for it to get into the cage, of course. For though the bars were spaced to keep Chérie in, they were wide enough apart for the tiny marmoset to creep through.

But marmosets were such delicate little creatures. This one could not have existed long in this cold weather. That fact suggested that it was somebody's pet, and that the owner could not live far from where the circus was pitched. Perhaps the owner, even now, was worried and distracted at the loss of the little creature. And though Chérie, quite plainly, would be terribly distressed to lose her new-found companion, Carol saw her duty clearly – she must telephone the police.

But when she did telephone the police Carol was again surprised. The police had received no notification of a lost marmoset. They would naturally make enquiries, they said, but meantime, would Carol take charge of it? Carol was delighted to do so. Chérie was even more delighted. And as the days wore on, and still no one claimed the marmoset – now named Kim – Chérie became more and more possessive.

"She won't even part with him during her act," laughed Carol to her father, genial John Meldrum. "She fusses over him like a doting mother. I just – Golly!" She stopped short, her eyes widening and shining. "That gives me an idea! No, Daddy, I'm not going to tell you what it is. Give me a couple of days. I'll know then whether my idea is any good or not."

Carol was almost dancing with excitement as she hurried away. If Chérie would not part with Kim during her act, then Kim must become part of the act. And if Chérie acted like a doting mother with her baby, then that act should be a mother and baby act.

Chérie, always quick to learn new tricks, took to this new idea instantly and enthusiastically. And Kim, willing to put up with anything as long as he was being fussed over by the adoring Chérie, seldom had to be shown how to do anything more than twice.

Carol grew more and more delighted. This new act was wonderful. There was laughter in it; there was also something so warm, so human, and so touching that it occasionally brought a little lump into her throat. If only it should have that effect on the audience, then the act would be a winner, particularly with the children.

"It's perfect," Carol told her father at the end of the third day. "Chérie and Kim work wonderfully together and they adore each other. If the owner turns up now – and I'm beginning to think he won't – then I shall beg him to sell Kim to me. We could never take Kim from Chérie now; it would break her heart. Oh, don't forget my dress rehearsal in the Big Top at ten-thirty to-morrow morning."

Not only John Meldrum, but almost everybody else attached to the circus, was waiting in the Big Top the following morning – waiting with an air of excitement and anticipation. It was a very motherly-looking Chérie that appeared at the ring entrance, attired in a print frock and red coat and hat. She was pushing a doll's pram. In the pram, looking adorable under the satin coverlet and against the frilly white pillow, lay Kim – with a lace bonnet on his head.

Solemnly Chérie wheeled the pram once round the ring, watched by the intrigued audience. Then she pushed the pram and its occupant through a cleverly-designed cardboard opening that represented the front door of a house.

Once inside, Chérie solemnly took off her coat and hat and hung them up, then turned her attention to little Kim. Making loving, fussing noises, she lifted the little marmoset from his pram, took off his bonnet and coat. There was a roar of laughter from the audience as, with a tutting noise and a lovingly reproving look. Chérie took off Kim's little blue pants and replaced them with another pair from an airing rack. Then she seated him in a small high chair at the little table, fussily tying a bib around his neck.

It was uproariously funny to see Kim's naughtiness at the table, and Chérie's attempts to reprove him and teach him manners. Funny too, when tea was finished, to see Chérie undress Kim and pretend to bathe him in a big blue bowl. But the touching moment came when Kim, dressed in a long white nightgown, snuggled up in Chérie's arms as she rocked and crooned to him whilst she fed him from a miniature bottle. With loving devotion, she laid him in his tiny cradle and covered him gently.

There was a moment's silence; then a storm of applause. Laughingly Carol, with Chérie and Kim beside her, took a bow.

"Carol, that act is a top-liner!" said John Meldrum delightedly. "It's got everything! We'll . . . What on earth's the commotion?"

There was a scuffle at the entrance to the Big Top. With an apologetic look at his boss, one the circus hands came forward, clasping by the hand a small and scared-looking little girl.

"I saw her creeping around outside, boss," he said. "Thought I'd . . ."

He stopped as, with a sharp, delighted cry, the little girl snatched her hand from his and darted forward, arms outstretched.

"Mikki!" she cried. "Mikki, darling, I've found you! I thought I'd lost you for ever and ever. Mikki, you must come home with me! You must never, never go away again."

And as Carol and everyone else stared, stunned, the marmoset tore himself from Chérie's arms, and with a delighted squeal leapt at the little girl and clung lovingly around her neck!

"He's my Mikki! He ran away. I cried every night 'cos I thought he'd gone away for ever."

The little girl, Jill Anders, still clutching her beloved marmoset, had been invited to Carol's wagon to await the arrival of her uncle, Charles Anders, her guardian, who kept a jeweller's shop in Parkhampton.

Carol's mind was in a turmoil. Seeing Jill's obvious devotion to her pet and realising the anguished nights and days the little girl must have spent since Mikki's disappearance, she was deeply touched. But she was filled, too, with a very natural disappointment.

She was particularly disappointed that the wonderful act she had worked so hard to perfect was completely finished. For at Carol's gentle hint that Jill might lend Mikki to the circus until after the Christmas matinée, Jill had flatly stated that she could never bring herself to part with Mikki, even for a moment.

But above Carol's disappointment at the abrupt loss of her act was her sympathy and fear for Chérie.

Usually shy and gentle, Chérie could be frightening when roused by pain or grief. And Chérie's grief was enormous at the moment. Even from here, Carol could hear her sharp, anguished cries.

In the short time since he had so mysteriously appeared, Mikki had become the mainspring of Chérie's life. She had lavished on him all her love and devotion. Now, abruptly, she had been parted from him. She didn't understand, and she cried aloud her grief and bewilderment.

There was a knock at the door. The door opened at Carol's invitation, and a man entered. He was a rather stooping, absent-minded-looking man in his late fifties. At the sight of him, Jill leapt to her feet with a glad cry.

"Uncle Charles! Uncle Charles!" she cried excitedly. "I'm sorry I ran away from you, but I came to the circus to see the animals. And look – look! I found my Mikki! Isn't it gorgeous?"

Uncle Charles did not seem all that delighted. He looked, indeed, taken aback and rather vexed. There was certainly no love in the look he bestowed upon the little marmoset.

"H'm! I suppose that means we'll be having him back again," he said rather glumly. "You're sure you wouldn't like to leave him here,

Jill, with Miss Meldrum? Her father tells me they'd be delighted to keep Mikki. And he'd be very happy here with other animal friends."

Jill didn't need to speak. The sudden whitening of her small face, the way she shrank back and clutched Mikki was sufficient answer.

"Oh, well – that's that!" said Charles Anders with a sigh. He smiled – a rather apologetic smile – at Carol. " 'Fraid I don't care much for monkeys," he said. "And this one really has caused trouble for me, as I think you'll agree when I tell you what has happened."

He had, he told Carol, been given a valuable pearl necklace to re-thread by one of his customers. The necklace had vanished, but one of the pearls he had found Mikki's cage.

"Naturally, I blamed Mikki for the loss. I was very anagry . . ."

"And Mikki was so unhappy," piped in Jill, "that he ran away. That's what uncle said. He ran away to your circus."

Jill, who obviously would not be completely free from anxiety until she had Mikki back at home again, was tugging at her uncle's hand. With a word of thanks to Carol for her care of the marmoset, Charles Anders, with Jill still tightly clutching Mikki, hurried across to his car.

As it started up, there came a heart-broken shriek from Chérie's cage. Mikki heard it, and he struggled violently in Jill's arms. Heavy-hearted, Carol watched as Jill restrained him. Then the car sped away. So Mikki, too, was going to be unhappy. Much as he loved his little mistress, he loved dear old Chérie even more. How much better it would have been if Mikki had never come to the circus!

Vaguely, Carol still wondered how the tiny creature had managed to find his way here. But this was no time for vague speculations. Carol had the problem of pacifying the heart-broken and the bewildered Chérie. And that problem, as the day wore on, Carol found increasingly difficult.

At times Chérie crouched forlornly in her cage, giving little cries; now and again looking up at Carol with anguished eyes.

"Why am I being punished?" she seemed to be asking piteously. "What have I done that you should take Mikki away from me?"

Carol couldn't make her understand. She could only swallow back the choking lump in her throat and be extra loving to Chérie.

At other times, Chérie flew into terrible rages, shaking furiously at the bars of her cage. The rages were bad enough – what followed was even worse. Chérie suddenly seemed to give way to utter despair. She crouched listlessly in a corner of her cage. She ignored Carol when she spoke to her; she refused to eat even the choicest morsel.

"She's broken-hearted," solemnly announced Joey, the miniature clown. "If she doesn't soon snap out of it, Miss Carol . . ."

Seeing the anguish on Carol's face, he stopped short. But Carol knew what he meant. A tearing pain filled her. It had been bad enough to lose her delightful Chérie and Mikki act, and to know that, because she was so unhappy, Chérie would probably not even perform her own act at the Christmas matinée. But to lose dear, lovable old Chérie herself!

"Oh, no – no!" thought Carol with a sob.

But what could she do to help? She might plead again with Jill to let her have the marmoset. Jill might relent and part with him for a short while. But she would want him back, and then the trouble would start all over again. There seemed to be no answer to the problem.

Almost sick with worry, Carol cycled into town and bought a bunch of beautiful black grapes. These had never failed to tempt Chérie before. Surely they wouldn't fail now! Once the chimp had started to eat again and to take an interest in something, perhaps she would shake off her listlessness.

Chérie, however, showed no sign of interest when Carol, with the grapes held out temptingly, entered the cage that evening. It was Chérie's immovable hopelessness that made Carol, for the first time, a little careless. She left the cage door open behind her.

"Come along, Chérie!" she said tenderly. "Come along, old girl – have some grapes. You know you love them. They'll make you feel better."

She crept nearer, talking soothingly. Chérie raised her head. Her mournful eyes flickered. Then, with a suddenness that took Carol by complete surprise, Chérie leapt to her feet. With a sweep of her powerful arm she pushed Carol and her grapes aside. With a glad, triumphant cry she leapt to the door of the cage, swung through it and disappeared like a flash into the dusk!

It had all happened so suddenly, so unexpectedly, that Carol had no time even to cry out. But as she scrambled to her feet, and dashed in pursuit of the chimp her heart was pounding wildly.

"Chérie! Chérie! Come back"

Chérie, however, continued on her course and at an even greater rate, drawing away out of Carol's sight.

Carol's legs were aching; she was gasping for breath when finally she reached the outskirts of Parkhampton. Thank goodness, she thought, that this was tea-time, that nobody was about. The shops were closed. Only the lights from the living-quarters above, and from rooms at the rear, showed that they were still occupied.

Carol frantically wondered where Chérie could have gone. She had by now lost sight of the grief-stricken chimp. She glanced around. Then she stared. At a corner of a block of shops was one with heavy shutters. "Charles Anders – Jeweller" was painted above the door.

"Oh, so this is where Jill and her uncle live," Carol thought.

She took a step down the side turning, and saw that a high brick wall with a wooden door in it enclosed the jeweller's garden. Then Carol's eyes opened wide in amazement and relief.

Climbing over the brick wall was Chérie; and in her arms was clasped an excitedly chattering Mikki!

"Chérie!" cried Carol. "Oh, goodness . . ."

At that moment there was a wail from inside the house. A few seconds later the door in the wall was opened. Charles Anders stood there, holding by the hand a sobbing Jill. He stared in alarm at Chérie.

"I shouldn't worry; she's quite gentle now that she's got Mikki back," said Carol, and went on to explain what had happened.

"Naughty little Chérie undid Mikki's chain," said Jill tearfully. "She must have undone it last time, too, 'cos Mikki can't undo it himself. That's what happened, isn't it, uncle?"

As Carol was about to speak, she was interrupted by a shamefaced little laugh from Charles Anders.

"No, that isn't what happened," he said slowly. "I'm in terrible trouble, Miss Meldrum." He looked apologetically at Carol. "Perhaps that will help you to understand and forgive what I have done. I haven't yet found the pearl necklace I lost and the owners are threatening to sue me. Well, I was – I still am – convinced that the marmoset took it. I was scared he would take other things. So, when I knew your circus was near at hand, I took Mikki there and put him into the chimp's cage."

Climbing over the brick wall was Chérie!

"And you told Jill a white lie about her pet running away?" asked Carol dryly. "Well, that clears up the mystery as to how Mikki got into Chérie's cage. But it doesn't clear up the mystery of your missing necklace."

She stood thinking for a moment.

"I've got an idea," said Carol at last. "Mr. Anders, do you mind if we all come inside? I'd like to see that pearl you say Mikki had in his cage."

Mystified, the jeweller ushered them all upstairs into the sitting-room. He took a wash-leather bag from the safe, and produced a gleaming pearl.

"This is it," he said heavily. "It's the only one of the string I have left. If only . . ."

But Carol wasn't listening to him. She was holding the pearl between finger and thumb, revolving it before the eyes of Mikki. For a moment Mikki stared at it as if fascinated, then with a squeal and a chatter he leapt from Chérie's arms on to the high, old-fashioned mantelpiece. For a moment he sat, still chattering, peering at a large crack between mantelshelf and wall. Then, with another squeal, he plunged his tiny hand into the crack. Next moment there came a cry of incredulous delight from the jeweller, for when Mikki withdrew his hand there dangled from it a broken string of pearls.

"Yes, of course!" cried Charles Anders. "Now I've got in! I'm such an absent-minded idiot! I remember now putting the broken pearls on the mantelpiece when I was called to the telephone and this one was loose. The necklace must have slipped into the crack but Mikki found this one and took it to his cage . . ."

"Well, that seems to be the explanation," Carol smiled. "And that's your problem solved. I'm glad." But she sighed heavily.

"You've solved my problem," smiled the jeweller. "I think I can help solve yours. A certain little person hasn't found her pet quite so lovable since he came back from your circus . . ."

"Mikki loves Chérie better than he loves me," said little Jill sorrowfully. "Uncle said he'd be happier at the circus. I – I expect he would," she added with a little choke. "But – but uncle said if I had a little dog to take Mikki's place, he'd never leave me; and he'd play with me and not have to be kept in a cage . . ."

Carol's eyes lit up. Her heart leapt. Charles Anders, who was not very fond of monkeys but who adored dogs, had obviously been having a serious chat with Jill.

"I've got the very thing," she said excitedly. "A darling little cuddly ball of fluff – a pekingese puppy. He'll be all yours, Jill, and he'll never, never love anyone but you. What do you say? Will you change Mikki for the puppy?"

Jill's shining eyes gave her answer. Carol knew that with an adorable puppy around Jill would have no time to regret the departure of Mikki.

THE CASE OF THE KIDNAPPED HEIRESS

by Gladys Mitchell

Candy Maitland, the daughter of a great detective, had to find a six–year old heiress who had been kidnapped. The clues that she and her friend, Pat Duffie, found led them eventually to an eerie old house.

"Good to see you, old girl," said Candy Maitland to her friend Pat Duffie. "We have work to do."

"Another case? Good-oh. What is it this time?"

"It's Dad's case really, but I think we ought to look into it. A little girl of six, heiress to forty thousand pounds, has been kidnapped. Her nurse took her to the park and met someone she knew, and when they had finished gossiping the little girl was gone. The nurse spoke to the park-keeper and they hunted everywhere, but she's still missing. That was two days ago. Her parents suspect kidnapping because of the huge fortune, and Dad has been put on to the case. The trouble is that there's nothing to go on."

"What do you suggest we do, then?"

"Go and have a look round."

"It isn't likely we'd find anything if the police can't, Candy."

"You never know. And Dad's worried. He suspects the relatives may have something to do with it, as no ransom had been demanded. There are an uncle and aunt who would stand to get the money if the child wasn't in their way."

"But surely the police have only to keep them under observation?"

"It sounds easy enough, but they've planned a holiday in South America, and if nothing's proved against them the police can't stop them leaving the country."

Pat whistled. "South America! It sounds pretty suspicious, Candy, doesn't it? I mean, even if they could be proved guilty, once they get over there our police have no power to bring them back."

"Exactly. Of course, Dad's got men on to them, watching their house and all their movements, but if they are guilty it probably means they've got an accomplice, and who that accomplice can be is just anybody's guess. But we're wasting time. Come on."

"The park happened to be rather deserted that day," said Candy, standing with her fists thrust into her blazer pockets as she scanned the scene, "and nobody has come forward to say they saw the little girl being taken away." Suddenly she stiffened. "Pat," she said, "suppose you wanted to hide something in this park, something pretty big, where would you put it?"

"In the house, if I could get in, I suppose."

"Exactly! Pat, I wouldn't mind betting that the little girl is hidden in that old house."

"But, although it's not open to the public, the park-keeper goes into it. I've seen him. You don't mean he could be the accomplice?"

"Oh, heavens, no! I'm perfectly sure of that. Why, he's an ex-policeman!"

"But he'd be certain to find out if the child was there."

"Not necessarily. There are such things as priest holes and secret passages in Tudor houses, Pat. What if she's hidden in one of them? The park-keeper might not know they exist. Let's go and ask him!"

The park-keeper had a great respect for Detective-Inspector Maitland, Candy's father, so he listened sympathetically when Candy put forward her idea. But he shook his head.

"I'll have another search, Miss Candy," he said, "but I think you can take it the little girl is far enough from here by now. Besides, I don't rightly see how anybody could have got her into the house without us knowing. It's all kept locked up, as you know."

Candy and Pat strolled homeward. When they reached Candy's house, Candy said to her friend, "Any objection to a spot of housebreaking, Pat? I'm going to that old Tudor mansion tonight to have a look round. I've a hunch the little girl is in there, whatever the park-keeper says."

"But I don't see how we'd get into the house if it's all locked up," objected Pat. Candy smiled mysteriously.

"There is a way in," she said. "I spotted that. Are you game to come with me or not?"

"What time?"

"Latish. We must be certain the park-keeper's out of the way. He lives in the lodge, and I know a place where it's perfectly easy to get over the wall. Bring a powerful torch and you'd better wear slacks or shorts and rubber shoes. We have some stiffish climbing to do. Meet me here at ten. I'll be waiting for you in the porch."

The girls separated, but as the church clock struck ten Pat was back at Candy's front gate and Candy emerged from the porch. It was not very far to the park, and Candy's statement that there was an easy way over the wall was proved correct.

It was very dark among the trees and the wind whispered eerily. Soon the great house, with its tall, decorated chimneys, loomed against the night sky.

"That's it. See?" said Candy. She indicated one of the tall chimneys which had been struck by lightning. "These Tudor chimneys are terrifically broad except for the actual chimney stack. Well, the stack has gone on that one. All we've got to do is to get on the roof and climb down."

This was more easily said than done, but by dint of scrambling up a stout creeper to the roof of what had been the servant's quarters, and from there up a wide and ornamental drainpipe which gave plenty of foothold, the two girls reached their objective. As Candy had seen from below, lightning had destroyed the tall stack and what remained was as wide as a passage. Moreover, there were bricks sticking out at regular intervals so that, in the old days, the climbing boys could sweep the chimney. Candy shone her torch and then pocketed it and began to climb down. Pat followed her and they soon found themselves in a panelled room.

"The ground floor is more likely. This would have been a bed-rooms," said Candy softly. "Let's find the staircase." They went on to the landing and descended the grand old Tudor stair. Candy led her way to the front door. "Now we'll separate," she said. "There are two main possibilities for a secret room, the chimneys and a hidden door in the panelling. If you think you've discovered anything, for goodness sake be careful, because if the child's here she's probably not alone."

They searched diligently for more than an hour, but without result. Candy began to think that her hunch had misled her. All the downstairs chimneys had been closely inspected by both girls, who, at Candy's suggestion, had changed beats in case one of them missed anything, and Candy, who had brought a tape measure, carefully measured alcoves and spaces while Pat shone a torch, to try to find any depth of wall behind which a small room might have been constructed.

Pat suddenly clutched her arm. "I heard something!" she whispered. Candy had heard it, too.

"Quick!" she said. "In here!" This was a tall cupboard built in at the side of the fireplace. Footsteps came along the stone passage which led from the kitchen. Pat was trembling, but Candy was tense with excitement. The footsteps went past the room they were in, and began to mount the stairs.

"Stay here," whispered Candy. "I'm going to follow that person."

Pat was terrified, but, loyal as ever, obeyed. Candy slipped out, noiseless in her rubber shoes. As she reached the foot of the stairs she could see the flickering flame of a candle casting huge, distorted shadows on the ceiling of the long gallery, off which opened the principal bedrooms. She increased her pace and was in time to see a woman's figure go through one of the doorways. Candy followed, then flattened herself against the door and watched. The woman went to a huge cupboard and opened it. Then she disappeared. Candy crept up to the entrance. There was no sign of the woman but the back of the cupboard had opened, disclosing a dark hole. Candy was more excited than she had ever been in her life. Her detective instinct had been right. The child was in the house. She peeped into the cupboard opening but could see nothing, for the woman's body blocked the way. There was not a sound to be heard. Candy took a pair of dividers and wedged the secret door. Then, rather worried about Pat, who would be wondering what had happened, Candy returned to Pat's hiding place.

"There must be a secret entrance through the kitchen, Pat," she whispered. "The woman may be ages yet. Let's find out how she got in."

This proved very simple, for the woman had left distinctly muddy marks on the floor.

"Underground passage to somewhere near the lake or the river," muttered Pat. "It's dry underfoot in the park."

The woman's footprints led to a small, dark cellar, and in the floor one of the flagstones was up, disclosing some damp, stone steps. Gleefully Candy led the way, and at the foot of the steps was a passage, as she had expected. They crept along it, for it was narrow and very slippery, and to their great excitement they soon felt cold air blowing in their faces. The passage led to a sunken garden near the lake. A part of the garden wall had been swung out on a pivot.

"Now, Pat, this is where the fun begins," said Candy. "One of us must get out of the park and telephone my father. The other will close the end of this passage and await results."

"Suppose the woman just walks out of the front door or climbs out of a window, Candy, if she can't get back this way?"

"Of course there's that. Oh, well, we'll just have to grab her when she comes. She expects to return this way, or she wouldn't have left everything open. I suppose she's the nurse, and has been in the plot all the time. At a safe moment she was to hand the child over to the relatives, and that would be the end of the child." Pat shuddered. Candy continued, "But that's all right now. Listen, Pat, when she comes, grip her firmly and yell your head off to bring the park-keeper here. I'll do the same. He's an ex-policeman, so we'll hand her over to him while we dash back to rescue the kiddie."

She had scarcely finished speaking when they heard the woman returning. They were able to take her completely by surprise, and the park-keeper, brought out by their shrieks and yells, did all the rest. The girls left him marching the woman away, for Candy was right: it was the nurse, and the park-keeper recognised her. She had been tempted by the relatives to conceal the child until it seemed safe to hand her over. The uncle had found a plan of the house in an old book, and had taught the nurse how to use the secret way.

Now that Candy had wedged the door the girls had no difficulty in finding the secret room in which the child was hidden. Late though it was, they thought it best to take her straight to the police station, where their brains and courage earned them a warm tribute and, later, from the child's parents, a very considerable reward.